MELVILLE STUDIES IN CHURCH HISTORY
VOLUME IV

AMERICAN CATHOLICS AND THE FORMATION OF THE UNITED NATIONS

Joseph S. Rossi, S.J.

UNIVERSITY PRESS OF AMERICA

Lanham • New York • London

The Department of
Church History

The Catholic University
of America

Library of Congress Cataloging-in-Publication Data
Rossi, Joseph S. (Joseph Samuel), 1947–
American Catholics and the formation of the United Nations / by
Joseph S. Rossi.
p. cm. — (Melville studies in church history ; v. 4)
"Co-published by arrangement with the Department of Church History,
the Catholic University of America"—T.p. verso.
Includes bibliographical references.
1. Catholic Church—United States—History—20th century.
2. United Nations—History—20th century. I. Title. II. Series.
BX1407.U55R67   1993
341.23'08'822—dc20   92-37604 CIP

ISBN 0–8191–8548–5 (cloth : alk. paper)
ISBN 0–8191–8980–4 (pbk. : alk. paper)

 The paper used in this publication meets the minimum requirements of
American National Standard for Information Sciences—Permanence
of Paper for Printed Library Materials, ANSI Z39.48–1984.

"Those who want peace, it is said, prepare for war. Those who are already at war prepare for peace."
EVAN LUARD

Table of Contents

Preface

At the end of World War II, the once-isolationist American Catholic Church appointed "consultants" to the US delegation at the 1945 United Nations Conference on International Organization at San Francisco (UNCIO). The parley was mandated by the Big Three to draft a charter for a projected world organization. This analysis, based primarily on archival sources from the US State Department, the National Catholic Welfare Conference (NCWC), and the Catholic Association for International Peace (CAIP), focuses on the bid by these international affairs specialists from the NCWC and the CAIP to modify the Dumbarton Oaks and Yalta proposals along lines suggested by Pius XII's "Five Point Peace Program" and the American hierarchy's statements, *On International Order* and *On Organizing World Peace*.

The first section of the present study presents Pius XII's major pronouncements on the structure of the postwar world and the American hierarchy's reaction to them; it also details the State Department's secret "consultant debate" that resulted in its selection of the NCWC and the CAIP, as well as Catholic plans and arrangements for the UNCIO. Chapters IV through VIII survey Catholic achievements at the UNCIO in the matters of the continuance of pre-conference ecumenical cooperation, western hemispheric solidarity, Big Power cooperation, the codification of international law, the Economic and Social Council, an International Bill of Rights, and worldwide labor cooperation. The bases for bitter defeats on the pivotal matters of criteria for UN membership, the Security Council veto, a "peaceful change" amendment for the General Assembly, the International Court of Justice, and "strategic trusteeships" also are investigated. Chapter IX concentrates on American Catholicism's post-conference attempts to define the nature of its future relations with the United Nations and on the deliberations leading to the establishment in October 1946 of the NCWC's United Nations Office in New York. This study proposes that the American Catholic Church realized only partial success in its crusade to "liberalize" the Dumbarton Oaks and Yalta proposals. This limited accomplishment was, nevertheless, sufficient impetus for its progression from public hostility to cautious promotion of the new world organization. The present study also sheds light on contemporary processes and on debates within the NCWC and its relation to ancillary groups such as the CAIP, on the functions of lay and non-episcopal personnel at the Catholic Conference, on American Catholic foreign-policy disputes with the Roosevelt and Truman Administrations, and on the US Church's anti-Soviet stance in the face of the collapse of the Big Three wartime coalition and the onset of the Cold War.

The most pleasant task in writing such a survey must be the expression of appreciation to persons and institutions that have helped the author. In drafting this manuscript, I have benefited from the insights and criticism of three professors at the Catholic University of America. I am exceedingly grateful to my director, the Reverend Robert Trisco, Professor of American Church History. His patience, encouragement, and good judgement were invaluable aids to my research and writing. To Dr. Harold Langley and Monsignor William Kerr, the other members of my board, I am likewise profoundly indebted. While I endeavored to integrate all the recommendations of these scholars into this investigation, I alone am liable for what is either incomplete or inexact.

In the course of my research, I used several key archives in the United States. First and foremost, I was given priceless guidance and assistance by Warren Willis, the archivist of the United States Catholic Conference. Not only did he encourage me to use that extraordinary collection and help me to gain access to its riches, but even after I had completed my investigations there, he went out of his way to keep in contact with me when overlooked data were subsequently uncovered. At the archives of the Archdiocese of Chicago, Mr. John J. Treanor, Archivist, and Mr. Timothy A. Slavin, Assistant Archivist, welcomed me cordially to their facilities. My week's research there was most productive and I even shared the archdiocesan school lunches. This author also owes a special debt of thanks to Mr. Philip Runkel, Assistant Archivist and Curator of the CAIP Collection at the Marquette University Memorial Library. Phil slogged through the biggest blizzard that ever hit Milwaukee in December so that I could use the documents in this unique deposit.

I would like to express my appreciation also to the staffs of the United Nations Library in New York City, the Law Library of the Library of Congress, and the Department of State Collections of the National Archives in Washington, D.C. At these splendid repositories I was extended every conceivable courtesy and assistance during my many research visits.

Finally, my gratitude for the brotherhood, companionship, and community of my fellow Jesuits at Carroll House cannot be adequately expressed. Their love and concern for me was always apparent in their encouragement and praise. The saddest part of the completion of my studies came when I had to leave their company.

CHAPTER I
Prelude to Peace
The Pope's Plan

On Christmas eve 1939 "His Holiness, Pope Pius XII, Bishop of Rome, Vicar of Jesus Christ, Successor of St. Peter, the Prince of the Apostles, Supreme Pontiff, Patriarch of the West, Primate of Italy, Archbishop and Metropolitan of the Roman province, Sovereign of the State of Vatican City" and Servant of the Servants of God,[1] processed into the Sistine Chapel, the heart of the Vatican palace, to deliver his traditional Christmas message to an assembly of twenty members of the Sacred College of Cardinals together with many bishops and other prelates.[2] Once seated on his throne, Pius faced Michelangelo's harrowing fresco of the Last Judgement, commissioned in 1508 by the warrior pope Julius II. This twentieth-century pope was about to give his pivotal address of the war years: a discourse that came to be called the "Five Point Peace Program."

In stark contrast to the ambience and to the florid court language that prefaced the statement:

> Amidst the clash and tumult of earthly events true joy is found only in the repose of the spirit. Here is a fortress which no earthly storm can assail. . . .[3]

the pope presented a straightforward plan to "win the peace" and prevent future wars. Written in relatively down-to-earth prose—at least for a formal papal document—it advanced a quinary approach toward a peace that he hoped was imminent.

In this, his first Christmas message, Pius affirmed that there were five moral principles to be followed by prospective peace-makers if they hoped for a just and honorable solution to ensure that the world would not be plunged into military catas-

1

trophe for a third time in the century. All nations, he wrote, had equal rights to exist and to be independent; when either right was destroyed by outside force, it was to be reestablished with justice and impartiality. Secondly, any international arrangement that would emerge after the conflict had to forgo the arms race; thus an effective way to implement general disarmament had to be included in the peace talks.[4]

In his third point, the pope, clearly alluding to the League of Nations, recounted that attempts in the past to fashion such an international order has failed because they refused to consider with any honesty the verity of human weakness. The League, which was inaugurated after World War I and now lay in ruins, had been simply ill-equipped to deal with international situations as they arose because it lacked the executive and judicial powers to faithfully and equitably fulfill its charter and to revise it whenever necessary. An international body, whether one to be created or reshaped, had to have these powers in order to prevent the arbitrary breaking of agreements.[5]

The pope's fourth point developed this statement. The just demands of nations as well as of national and racial minorities had not been met by "settlements" of the past. This had brought about the new war that was raging even as Pius spoke. The League of Nations, moreover, had been unable to effect the revision of certain unnamed treaties that exacerbated the international situation between the wars. Pius intimated that if the Treaty of Versailles had this flexibility, Germany might not have been driven into the hands of political extremism.

In conclusion the pope had recourse to the foundations underpinning all the principles he had cited. Divine morality and the beatitudes from the Sermon on the Mount were essential for all international agreements. He was most careful to stress, however, that his five points had a substructure that existed within the natural order as well; "justice" and "universal love" were common grounds for all and the only ways to avoid hatred and distrust among nations.[6]

In later pronouncements, Pius would expand on this thesis, remarking that no peace-loving state could conceivably expect the prevention or cessation of hostilities unless it subscribed to the precepts of human equality, free will, liberty of persons, and independence of political entities.[7]

The pope frankly allowed that these five points were not novelties but they were principles that had plainly been ignored in the recent past and consequently not incorporated into the international structure. On both these points, he was undeniably correct. Many of his themes had been articulated by his predecessors, chiefly Benedict XV (1914–1922), who had faced a comparably ominous situation during World War I. That earlier pope had likewise answered the challenge of warfare with a systematic program for peace but it had been summarily dismissed by many.[8]

Like Pius XII, Benedict had pleaded for moral right to be substituted for material force, an international institution to keep the peace, and even penalties for the refusal to submit to binding arbitration. In 1918 Cardinal Gasparri, Benedict's Secretary of State, conceded that the pontiff would support an International Court of Justice within a world organization only if it would put teeth into its decrees by mandating a moral, economic, and financial boycott of any nation manifesting a militaristic spirit. If Pius XII was not quite that insistent, he nonetheless favored this approach to a strong international security system and, like Benedict, he stressed that suspicion among nations was the prime irritant that bred wars.[9]

It is manifest that neither pope extracted all his propositions from Catholic sources. As early as 1898, Jean de Bloch wrote in his famous book, *La Guerre,* that war was bound to become an impossible burden because of the overwhelming moral and financial price that it would impose on a modern nation. In addition, Norman Angell had asserted in *The Great Illusion,* published in 1901, that war had ceased to be a practical method of international policy and, accordingly, could no longer be regarded as one of the foreign policy options of a civilized nation-state.[10]

Documenting these hypotheses, the Carnegie Endowment for International Peace, in its exhaustive *Economic and Social History of the War,* alleged that, for the reasons mentioned above, war was an intolerable calamity for everyone and should accordingly be renounced.[11] Such a sentiment was never more succinctly put than by Pius XII himself in the late summer of 1939 as the awful shadows of war approached; implicitly excluding many traditional Catholic grounds for just wars, he observed that "Nothing is lost with peace; all may be lost with war."[12]

Pius XII could draw, therefore, on a plethora of sources to back up his "Five Point Peace Program." However, neither this weight of evidence nor common sense tempered the war's expansion. By late 1941, even America, which, like the pope, had publicly proclaimed the value of peace, was drawn into the fray. Yet within that country's Catholic population, few people would have had more than a passing familiarity with the pope's five points. This was, to some extent, the fault of the National Catholic Welfare Conference (NCWC), the organization of the hierarchy of the Roman Catholic Church in the United States.

The American Catholic Scene

Within the United States there had always been acute sensitivity among internationalists to the accusation that the country, due to its conspicuous absence, was at least partially responsible for the failure of the League of Nations. Led by Senator Henry Cabot Lodge, the forces of isolationism defeated Woodrow Wilson's bid to obtain Senate ratification of that international organization after World War I. Many Catholic bishops, with Cardinal Gibbons a notable exception, fervently endorsed this isolationism chiefly because the peace conference in Paris, at the bidding of British Prime Minister Lloyd George, had ignored the issue of independence for Ireland.[13]

Groups such as the Catholic Association for International Peace had been established between the wars to further the cause of world understanding. In 1939, however, the Catholic Church in the United States, shepherded by a predominantly

Irish-American hierarchy, had yet to become a hotbed of internationalist thought or sympathies.[14]

An example of this can be seen in the bishops' deliberations on the issue of American neutrality, the most momentous topic of the day. In the minutes of the Administrative Board of the NCWC of April 18, 1939, we see that the presumptive leadership of the Catholic Church in the United States was requested to tackle this issue. But when guidance and counsel on the six neutrality bills then before Congress were requested by Monsignor Michael J. Ready, then NCWC General Secretary, the only response he could elicit from the bishops was a statement that they had no "definite position on neutrality legislation. . . ."[15]

As if this bewilderment was not sufficiently troubling, on the following day Ready suggested that the Board go on record in support of President Roosevelt's recent statement calling upon all aggressors to terminate hostilities and resolve their disputes at the conference table, a statement which, up to that time, had drawn little more than polite yawns from American Catholics. After debating the point, the bishops approved a motion that commended the government's efforts, but earnestly hoped that "the nation in offering its friendly assistance to this end will not be thought to have yielded to those who would embroil us in alien conflicts and dissensions."[16]

Most bishops of Irish lineage customarily interpreted the New Deal's internationalism as little more than a Masonic plot for an "entangling alliance" with the much-hated British. Prominent bishops looked on with horror as FDR shifted American foreign policy toward an all-but-official coalition with the United Kingdom; though the bishops never voiced support for the Nazis, policy decisions such as the Lend-Lease Act of 1941, which directly aided England, were not well received within their ranks.[17]

It would, however, be grossly unfair to say that in this position they misrepresented their flocks. Many descendants of Catholic immigrants who had fled European religious and economic intolerance vividly recalled recent European history. Irish Americans, whether clerical or lay, were not eager to help an embattled England that had for centuries persecuted their ancestors. On the other hand, many German and Italian Americans looked on with considerable pride at the accomplishments of Hitler and Mussolini and felt no ties whatsoever with the British.[18]

In addition, even though the bishops had always been staunch opponents of the ideology emanating from the USSR, there was never a call on their part for direct American intervention to offset world Communism.[19] Naturally, in the matter of the Spanish Civil War, a divisive issue in the United States during the late 1930s, the bishops used their vigorous defense of the Spanish Nationalists to prevent the Roosevelt Administration from succumbing to internal pressures to advance the cause of the Communist-backed Loyalist regime, which was often depicted in the American press as the last bastion of Iberian democracy.[20]

Although the press equated opposition to the leftist-oriented Spanish Republic as evident support of clerical Fascism, many Catholic groups waged a holy war against the American Friends of the Spanish Republic and others, including many Protestant ministers, who lobbied for the modification of the Neutrality Act of 1936 so as to enable the United States to sell arms and munitions to the Loyalists. In 1938 Monsignor Ready went so far as to reproach the Justice Department over alleged instances of recruitment of "American boys" for the Abraham Lincoln Battalion, which was fighting for the Spanish leftists, in alleged violation of the United States Code. By such means, the bishops used their general policy of isolationism to further a "Catholic" cause they held dear.[21]

In June of 1941, the diplomatic scene became even more complicated when Germany invaded its former ally Russia. Only one bishop, Joseph Hurley of St. Augustine, was heard to defend Roosevelt's new initiative to extend Lend-Lease to the Soviets, and he was roundly castigated by his peers.[22] At first, the NCWC warned that America could not be deceived into believing that the Soviet Union had somehow magically been transformed into an ally and compatriot simply because one despot had assaulted another. Under pressure from the Holy See and the US State Department, however, Archbishop John T. McNicholas of Cincinnati, a key figure in the American hierarchy, wrote a pastoral letter in October reinterpreting Pius XI's 1937 encyclical *Divini Redemptoris.* In this pastoral McNicholas differentiated between aid to communism and assistance to the Russian people, a point of view for which Hurley had earlier been denounced. Although this principle was dutifully echoed by the bishops in their November statement, it was obvious that their hearts were not in it. Archbishop Edward Mooney, the chairman of the Administrative Board, for example, was still pondering at this time whether Hitler's defeat would be in the national interest.[23]

In the early 1940s, therefore, only Catholics of Polish descent, alarmed by the Nazi invasion of their native land, were clamoring as a bloc for American assistance to stem the Axis tide, and not even they were demanding direct intervention. All such potential enthusiasm was tempered by the realization that once before in the century, a great war had come out of Europe and America had paid a weighty price in blood. At all costs, most Catholics in the United States wanted to see their country remain at peace. For this reason, America First Committees were often eagerly endorsed by Roman Catholics as well as their clergy.[24]

Before America's entry into the war, some members of the hierarchy had taken a keen interest in Pius XII's "Five Point Peace Program," but only because it kept peace in the forefront at a time when these bishops were fearful that public opinion was shifting in favor of intervention on behalf of Britain. But once the United States entered the war on the side of the United Kingdom—Nazi Germany and Fascist Italy having declared war on America following the Japanese attack on Pearl Harbor—Catholic leaders used the peace plan "to make an American victory a benediction to the world." Only in this way, they reasoned, could all Christian forces be marshalled so that an Allied military success could produce the united nations of "peace-loving" peoples that Pius XII had envisioned.[25]

The bishops, however, had come late to the realization of the importance of the pope's message; on November 12, 1941, less than one month before America's entry into the conflict, the NCWC set up a committee under Archbishop Samuel Stritch of Chicago to "Promote the Pope's Peace Program," and even then, did so only at the urgent request of Cardinal Hinsley, archbishop of Westminster. Admitting that "more could be done to promote the Pope's Peace Plan," the committee was directed by the hierarchy to try to secure a wide understanding and acceptance of Pius XII's peace statements by using the "main avenues of publicity."[26]

Such a broad commitment now made dissemination of the pope's plan more than a mere perfunctory exercise, something it had remained for two years following the publication of the "Five Points" plea. The Administrative Board of the NCWC now earnestly threw itself into the chore of marketing a peace plan, based on the natural law and moral theology, for the barely attentive, much less comprehending, American Catholic public.

Before America's entry into the war, the Catholic Conference had attempted to use the pope's five points to influence the foreign policy of the Roosevelt Administration. Myron C. Taylor, FDR's personal representative to Pius XII, was likewise interested in mutual communication; for his part, however, he hoped to reassure the Vatican that the Allied cause was the Christian one.[27] Nevertheless, statements by "Ambassador" Taylor such as:

> To be the instrument of contact between the Pope as a great spiritual leader and the President of the greatest of the liberty-loving nations not engaged in war necessitates a reserve of expression which is no great innovation to me. 'In the final unfolding of the mysteries which the present-day questions contain, there can be no fair or permanent justice in the world unless these two symbols of civilization at its best operate in harmony.'[28]

caused a national row with the proponents of separation of Church and State such as the "Emergency Committee in Behalf of Religious Liberty." These groups made successful communication, much less concerted activity, between the "two symbols," difficult at best.[29]

Throughout the war years, the NCWC had emphasized several themes in its annual statements, public utterances and letters to the Administration: freedom of worship, of speech, and of education, the need for general disarmament, and the rights of small nations, national minorities, and developing countries eventually to be free. With these, concomitantly, went the assumption that no state could belong to a new international organization unless it subscribed to the tenet that freedom for its people and the populations of its possessions was as important as international peace, and was, in fact, intrinsic to it. All this was, of course, in perfect harmony with Pius XII's pronouncements.[30]

Ironically, the Pope's "Five Point Peace Program," also committed the once isolationist American Catholic Church to the notion of participation in world organization with the United States as an undoubted principal. Unfortunately, the two other prime players in that peace would most likely be "atheistic" Russia, the erstwhile collaborator in Nazi aggression, and "imperialist" Britain. With this distasteful eventuality staring them in the face, the bishops had three choices. They could advise that the United States decline to take part in the new United Nations or bar "imperialist" powers from it; these first two options followed logically from their past statements but would guarantee that there would not be a world organization. The third option, the one they eventually embraced, albeit without enthusiasm, called for American membership in the UN, trusting that the United States would work for its revision from within.[31]

The Atlantic Charter, which had been solemnized by Winston Churchill and Franklin D. Roosevelt on August 14, 1941, had somewhat reassured the hierarchy and other prominent Catholic peace advocates about the Allied war effort and postwar intentions. Presented as altruistic endeavors that would free the world from territorial aggrandizement, respect the rights of all peoples to choose their own form of government, foster worldwide economic interaction, and allow for the abdication of the use of force, they were offered as the means to bring about the fullest international collaboration for fiscal, social, and political reconstruction. As such, the Charter was seen by Catholics and others as the first common program of purposes and principles of the United Nations.[32]

As the war stretched into the middle years of the decade, however, and especially after the "Big Power meetings" at Moscow and Teheran in 1943 and 1944, the bishops began to sense that dust was settling on the good intentions of the Atlantic Charter. Big Power politics, they feared, would once again carve up the world after the bloodshed and, to their chagrin, America was doing little to prevent this. If they needed further confirmation of this, it was provided by the "disappointment" of the Dumbarton Oaks proposals drawn up toward the end of 1944, in which the United States, the Soviet Union, China, and the United Kingdom guaranteed that they would dominate the new global order.[33]

The Dumbarton Oaks Conversations were conducted in a vast, ornate mansion in the Georgetown section of Washington from August 21 through October 9. Although the discussions held in this majestic setting were regarded by the participants as "informal and exploratory," their imperious recommendations would subsequently be presented to the United Nations Conference at San Francisco as the incorporated judgment of the Big Four on matters of international organization. The assumption had been that, "if the Four could reach substantial agreement among themselves, the objections of other powers would not count for very much."[34]

The general response to this point of view, nevertheless, had been instantaneous and hostile. At the Big Three summit at Yalta (the Crimea Conference), Churchill, Stalin, and Roosevelt, aware of the criticism leveled against the Big Power *hubris* of Dumbarton Oaks, made some modifications. With regard to the voting procedure in the projected UN Security Council, for example, a distinction was now drawn between the quasi-official function of the Council in promoting the settlement of disputes, and its political function in taking action for the maintenance of peace. What this meant was that no nation, large or small, could prevent the Security Council from discussing a question that seven members of the Council had determined to review. No Great Power veto could be used at this stage. However, the five permanent members of the Council had to concur in the determination of the existence of a breach of the peace, enforcement action, and matters concerning admission of new members or expulsion of current members.[35]

The NCWC, while aware that Yalta was an advancement over the original Dumbarton Oaks proposals, still opposed the provision that each great power not only had a veto on forceful settlement of disputes to which it was a party, but also had a veto on peaceful settlement of conflicts to which it was not a party. Archbishop Stritch accused the American deputation at the Crimea Conference of making just such compromises with Russia but he would have been livid if he had known that the State Department was keeping secret the fact that the voting procedure accepted at Yalta was an American recommendation.[36]

In the early months of 1945, accordingly, the leaders of the hierarchy in the United States were filled with extraordinary apprehension; few would have quarreled with Archbishop Stritch's terse assessment that "the probability of a good lasting peace is very slight."[37] While still dubious as to how they might alter this predicament, they were handed a singular opportunity by the US Department of State, which invited them to appoint "consultants" to the United Nations Conference on International Organization, which was to begin on April 25 in San Francisco.

This is a history of the events that occurred from February of 1945 until October of 1946, a span in which the Catholic Church in America went from opposition to a "united nations" as proposed by the Dumbarton Oaks Conference to the determination to establish a National Catholic Welfare Conference office to monitor the new United Nations Organization, which, in its view, "was not basically sound," but which merited their support as well as their careful scrutiny.[38]

Notes

1. Robert C. Broderick, ed., *The Catholic Encyclopedia* (Nashville: Nelson, 1976), s.v. "Pope."

2. NCWC News Service Microfilm Reproductions, Roll 20, 39-3720, 12/25/39, "Pope Lists Preliminary Conditions for Peaceful Settlement of Disputes," December 24, 1939, pp. 1–4.

3. Pope Pius XII, *The Pope Speaks: The Words of Pius XII,* ed. Edwin O'Hara (New York: Harcourt, Brace, 1940), *Christmas Message, 1939,* p. 225.

4. The pope was clearly referring to the Russian invasion of Finland on November 30, 1939. He also labeled this incursion a "premeditated aggression" made through the "pretext of a non-existing threat" (Ibid., p. 231).

5. Ibid., p. 232.

6. Ibid.

7. Pope Pius XII, *Pius XII and Peace: 1939–1944,* ed. Catherine Schaefer, *Christmas Message, 1940* (Washington: National Catholic Welfare Conference, 1944), p. 20.

8. "While Benedict's name was not mentioned expressly in the Treaty of Versailles, his influence was felt. It is now generally recognized that Wilson's famous 'Fourteen Points' speech, delivered before a January 8, 1918 joint session of Congress, was built on Benedict's suggestions" (Walter H. Peters, *The Life of Benedict XV* [Milwaukee: Bruce, 1959], p. 172).

9. Ibid., p. 146; *Pope Pius XII, Pius XII and Peace: 1939–1940* (Washington: National Catholic Welfare Conference, 1940), *To Those in Power and to Their Peoples,* p. 17.

10. John A. O'Brien, *The Pope's Way to Peace* (Huntington, Indiana: Our Sunday Visitor Press, 1944), p. 11; Ralph Norman Angell, *The Great Illusion: A Study of the Relation of Military Power to National Advantage,* 4th ed. (London: G.P. Putnam's Sons, 1913), p. 353.

11. James T. Shotwell, gen. ed., *The Economics and History of the World War,* 150 vols. (Washington, D.C.: Carnegie Endowment for International Peace, 1924), vol. 3, American Series: *The Effects of War Upon America* by John Maurice Clark (New Haven: Yale University Press, 1931), p. 289.

12. *To Thus in Power and To Their Peoples,* p. 7; amplifying this point, Pius XII would declare in his Christmas message of 1944 that the use of force was no longer a moral means for even the redress of

transgressed legal rights. According to John Courtney Murray, the pope left only the right of self-defense standing as a just cause for war (Paul Ramsey, *The Just War: Force and Political Responsibility* [New York: Charles Scribner's Sons, 1968], p. 308).

13. John Tracy Ellis, *The Life of James Cardinal Gibbons,* 2 vols. (Milwaukee: Bruce, 1952), 2:285–89; Of the approximately 180 bishops in the American hierarchy in 1941, at least 110 were either Irish-born or of Irish extraction (*The Official Catholic Directory, Anno Domini 1941* [New York: P.J. Kenedy & Sons, 1941], pp. 835–37).

14. The Catholic Association for International Peace was organized in a series of meetings during 1926 and 1927. The first of these was held following the Eucharistic Congress of 1926 in Chicago, the second in Cleveland that fall to form an organizing committee, and the third during Easter Week, 1927, in Washington, D.C., when the permanent organization was established. Its object was "to further in accord with the teachings of the Church, the 'Peace of Christ in the Kingdom of Christ,'" through the preparation, publication, and distribution of studies (committee reports) applying Christian teaching to international life. The Association solicited primarily the membership and cooperation of those whose academic background was such that they could take part in the preparation of such essays (Thomas H. Mahony, *The United Nations Conference* [Washington: The Catholic Association for International Peace, 1945], p. 25).

15. ANCWC 21, MAB 394, April 18, 1939.

16. ANCWC 21, MAB 404, April 19, 1939.

17. James Hennesey, S.J., *American Catholics* (Oxford: Oxford University Press, 1981), pp. 275–79.

18. George Q. Flynn, *Roosevelt and Romanism: Catholics and American Diplomacy, 1937–1945* (Westport, Conn.: Greenwood Press, 1976), p. 72.

19. Ibid., p. 145. Michael J. Curley, Archbishop of Baltimore, was an exception.

20. ANCWC 7b, Ready to Bishop Thomas A. Welch, [D.C.], Jan. 18, 1937, copy.

21. ANCWC 7d, Francis J. Talbot, S.J. to Ready, [New York], February 4, 1938; William F. Montovan to Ready, [D.C.], February 10, 1938, copy.

22. In a radio talk on July 6, 1941, Hurley had defended the loan of arms to the Soviets as not counter to papal teachings on collaboration with communists, and designated National Socialism as a more pressing danger than Stalinist Russia. Hurley had been aided in his preparations for this speech by government intelligence graciously supplied by Sumner Welles, US Assistant Secretary of State (Gerald P. Fogarty, S.J., *The Vatican and the American Hierarchy from 1870 to 1965* [Wilmington: Michael Glazier, 1985], p. 272).

23. Ibid., pp. 232–76. In his pastoral, McNicholas had recourse to Pius XI's *mit brennender Sorge,* which had drawn a distinction between Nazism and the German people; ANCWC 27, Ready to Sumner Welles, [D.C.], August 23, 1941.

24. Flynn, *1937–1945,* pp. 220, 82–83, 84.

25. NCWC News Service Microfilm Reproductions, Roll 26, 41-3296, 12/17/41, "Bishops Urge Pope's Peace Plan Be Followed To Make American Victory Benediction to World," December 17, 1941, p. 1.

26. ANCWC 21, MAB 249, Bishops' Peace Committee, November 12, 1941; NCWC News Service Microfilm Reproductions, Roll 26, 41-3296, 12/17/41, "Prelates' Committee Acts to Spread Knowledge of Principles Enunciated by Pontiff Through Issuance of Further Statements, Fostering of Research, Distribution of Literature, Sponsoring of Forums," December 17, 1941, p. 2.

27. In his Christmas greetings to Pius XII dated Dec. 23, 1945, FDR had declared that it would give him "great satisfaction" to send Myron C. Taylor, a prominent non-Catholic, to be his personal representative at the Vatican with the rank of Ambassador in order that their "parallel endeavors for peace . . . may be assisted. It is well that we encourage a closer association between . . . those in religion and those in government who have a common purpose."

Taylor, an Episcopalian, was born in Lyons, N.Y., on January 18, 1874. He received a Bachelor of Laws degree from Cornell University in 1894. After this he launched a successful business career, which included directorships with the United States Steel Corporation and the American Telephone and Telegraph Company. His life in public service included membership in the executive committee of the President's National Business Survey Conference in 1929 and in the Business Advisory and Planning Council, US Department of Commerce, 1934–1937.

Taylor, no stranger to Italy, was a trustee of the American Academy in Rome, and he maintained a residence, the Villa Schifanoia, in Florence (NCWC News Service Microfilm Reproductions, Roll 20, 39-3716, 12/25/39, "President Names Representative at Vatican," December 23, 1939, pp. 1–4).

28. NCWC News Service Microfilm Reproductions, Roll 25, 41-2252, 9/8/41, "Myron Taylor Calls Pope, President Two Symbols of Civilization at its Best," September 5, 1941, p. 2. Taylor is quoting from an address by Pius XII.

29. "Guard Principles of Free Worship, Farley Urges Conference on Religious Liberty," *Washington Post,* June 12, 1940, p. 1.

30. *The Pastoral Letters of the United States Bishops,* 3 vols., ed. Hugh J. Nolan (Washington: United States Catholic Conference, 1984), vol. 2, *1941–1961, The Essentials of a Good Peace,* November 11, 1943, p. 46.

31. ANCWC 4, "Catholics and the Dumbarton Oaks Proposals," Edward A. Conway, [D.C.], December 1, 1944, p. 5.

32. *The Pastoral Letters. . . ,* vol. 2, *A Statement on International Order,* November 16, 1944, p. 57.

33. ANCWC 21, MAB 31, November 16, 1944; *The Pastoral Letters. . . ,* vol. 2, *Between War and Peace,* November 18, 1945, p. 62.

34. David Evan T. Luard, *A History of the United Nations,* 2 vols. (New York: St. Martin's Press, 1982–1989), vol. 1: *The Years of Western Domination,* p. 27. The chief participants at Dumbarton Oaks were Edward Stettinius, then Under Secretary of State, Lord Cadogan, British ambassador in Washington, and Andrei Gromyko, the Soviet ambassador. Because of the poor state of Sino-Soviet relations— Russia was still officially in alliance with Japan at this time—the two nations' delegates never met at the Conversations. The Soviet Union took part in the first phase of the meetings, which lasted five weeks, but the Chinese conferred with Stettinius and Cadogan for only one week at the end of the sessions (Ibid., p. 25).

35. ANCWC 15, Department of State Press Release 202, March 5, 1945, pp. 1–2.

36. ANCWC 21, MAB 29–30, November 15, 1945; US Department of State, *Foreign Relations of the United States: Diplomatic Papers, 1945* (Washington, D.C.: U.S. Government Printing Office, 1967), vol. 1, *General: The United Nations,* Joseph C. Grew to Stettinius, February 12, 1945, p. 70.

37. ANCWC 21, MAB 31, November 16, 1944.

38. ANCWC 21, MAB 30, November 15, 1945.

CHAPTER II

Invitation to the Conference

On January 20, 1945, the regular monthly meeting of the Notre Dame Branch of the Holy Name Society in New York City drafted a unanimous resolution. Taking its cue from the annual meeting of the Catholic bishops held the previous November, the membership pledged itself to censure of "power politics," support for the Atlantic Charter, advocacy of an international organization to embrace all nations, defense of the independence of every state, pressure for a strong World Court, and maintenance of "Christian Democratic principles."[1]

The bishops at their assembly had harshly criticized the Dumbarton Oaks proposals and the United Nations Conference on International Organization (UNCIO) envisaged there, and said that these agreements offered nothing but "verbiage" in defense of a Moscow-directed armistice that would guarantee only a peace without justice. The USSR was up to its old tricks again, the bishops believed, in attempting to recreate the old Czarist policy for Eastern Europe and the Balkans. The Soviet Union would annex some states and attempt to dominate others in order to forge a postwar "pan-Russianism."

Samuel Stritch, archbishop of Chicago and chairman of the Bishops' Committee on Pius XII's "Five Point Peace Program," recounted to the hierarchy in his annual report that apparently Big Three Powers: Britain, the Soviet Union, and the United States, were planning to partition the world. These three had failed, however, to create a system for settling disputes among themselves. Each of these nations would have a veto in the Security Council and there was a rumor that even the discussion of an issue could be blocked by such a veto. This, Stritch complained, was a recipe for world cataclysm.[2]

In this presentiment the Catholic bishops were joined by other religious leaders who discerned in Dumbarton Oaks a greater desire for the establishment of a world organization than for the avoidance of World War III. Raymond L. Buell, an executive at Time Incorporated and a member of the Federal Council of Churches of Christ in America, was extremely dissatisfied with these agreements. If one studied the transcript, he averred, it was evident that it imposed no commitments on America to guarantee the security of a state against unwarranted aggression by any power that had a veto in the Security Council. On this point he specifically indicted the Soviet Union with regard to the Polish and Greek questions. It did not, furthermore, protect any country from aggression from the United States, which possessed the right of Security Council veto. Finally, Dumbarton Oaks created within America the illusion that when the Senate ratified the charter of the new world organization, World War III would be averted.[3]

Buell, in a letter dated December 26, 1944, to Dr. Walter Van Kirk, Secretary of the Federal Council of Churches, maintained that in the annual statement of the Catholic bishops and in the pope's Christmas message for 1944 he found "some tough thinking in both, which I hope the Protestant churches will emulate and surpass." He contended, moreover, that religious bodies were judging more sensibly on these matters than many of the "so-called peace societies."[4]

The CAIP

With many other American "peace fellowships," the Catholic Association for International Peace (CAIP) had supported the Dumbarton agreements from the start, but the State Department would initially find scant official encouragement from this foremost Roman Catholic peace organization. An affiliate agency of the National Catholic Welfare Conference, with which it shared its Washington headquarters, the CAIP was founded in 1927 by Bishop Thomas J. Shahan, rector of the Catholic University of America, who envisioned a society capable of issuing statements on peace as well as studies on related global problems. By the outbreak of World War II it was composed mainly of Catholic scholars and academics who were concerned with "furthering Christian principles of justice and charity in international life."[5]

The Peace Association provided for the bishops scholarly research with which they could do as they pleased. It was not, however, an independent organization. The Administrative Board of the NCWC had resolved that the association would not be its own master. Therefore, the National Catholic Welfare Conference did not tolerate CAIP deviations from positions that the bishops had publicly taken. When the issue of the relationship between the Bishops' Committee to Implement the Pope's Five Point Peace Plan—popularly labeled the Bishops' Peace Committee—and the CAIP was broached at the Administrative Board meeting on November 14, 1941, it was determined that all materials of the CAIP intended for publication must therefore receive prior clearance by the committee, "so that one group may not be making statements at variance with those of the other."[6]

Toward the end of the war, however, an incident impelled Archbishop Stritch, as chairman of the Peace Committee, to insist that the NCWC enforce the above mentioned policy. In February of 1945 the association had issued a daring pamphlet entitled "Judging the Dumbarton Oaks Proposals." While pointing out flaws in the accords, such as the Yalta concession on voting in the Security Council, the CAIP drew the conclusion that America should accept Dumbarton Oaks but qualify its acceptance by indicating deficiencies in the proposals. This was not well received by the Archbishop, who strongly criticized such a "weak position." The compromises at Dumbarton Oaks and Yalta were nothing less than "radical and ruinous" and Stritch could not imagine that Catholics could do anything but oppose such a world organization forcefully.[7]

In response to Stritch's determined protest, Monsignor Howard J. Carroll, General Secretary of the NCWC, insisted that little could be done with this pamphlet in the way of damage control except to "freeze" it. He had learned, however, from the Reverend Raymond A. McGowan, associate director of the NCWC Social Action Department and CAIP Executive Secretary, that "Judging the Dumbarton Oaks Proposals" was only a "preliminary statement" and had been approved by Bishop Karl J. Alter, honorary president of the Peace Association and chairman of the Social Action Department.[8]

In a terse memorandum, McGowan reminded Carroll that he was not sure "whether Bishop Alter would like the idea of the Bishops' Peace Committee checking on him." He also was at pains to point out that for years "nobody was doing anything about Catholic social teaching on peace" except the Social Action Department and the CAIP. Now that more interest was aroused, constructive criticisms from the Peace Committee were welcome, but Father McGowan did not think that it should have a veto on the association's publications.[9]

Aside from the bureaucratic struggle, this Dumbarton Oaks dichotomy indicates that philosophical and methodological discord existed in the American Catholic Church over issues of peace and world organization. These differences were highlighted in the writings and activities of the Reverend Edward A. Conway, S.J.

In a memorandum of December 1, 1944, this expert on international affairs for the NCWC Social Action Department claimed he was only imparting "the reaction of many outstanding Catholic scholars" when he took a minimalist approach in order to validate Dumbarton Oaks and the United Nations. The important question for Conway was whether Catholics could support the proposals. He argued, "This is asking whether Catholics are determined to have some form of international cooperation to prevent war, or none at all." The least that could be said was that the proposals did not go counter to God's law and did not offend the Christian conscience. This was the minimum that Catholics could accept and Dumbarton Oaks measured up to this. It was therefore the duty of Catholics and all persons of good will "to lose no time in urging that the ten percent of uncertainty with regard to the proposals should be cleared up as rapidly as possible and cleared to the best advantage."[10]

Considering the fact that the bishops had only recently heard from Archbishop Stritch at their November 1944 annual meeting that the Dumbarton Oaks Conversations had contributed "nothing" to peace but a wealth of Great Power sophistry, this estimation is quite remarkable.[11] It is all the more so when one realizes that Conway worked for the NCWC; but like other Catholics professionally committed to international issues, Conway wore two hats: he was also an officer in the CAIP. For that matter, there are indications that he wore a paradoxical third hat as well, but this will be discussed in a later chapter.

Father Conway did not limit himself in his support for the Dumbarton Oaks proposals to confidential memoranda addressed to the NCWC. In February of 1945 he was prominently associated with a telegram sent to all forty-eight American governors asking them to proclaim the week of April 16–22 as "Dumbarton Oaks Week." This celebration of "permanent peace" combined discussions and devotional services meant to awaken citizens to the importance of the San Francisco Conference, which would open a few days later. Neither the NCWC nor the CAIP was listed among organizations associating themselves with the telegram, but in the list of sponsoring persons, "Edward A. Conway, S.J." was listed as belonging to the Catholic Association for International Peace.[12]

If nothing else, Conway's activities confirm that there was a spirited discussion, not unhealthy in the least, within the Catholic community regarding the merits of Dumbarton Oaks. It is clear also that in spite of the Peace Committee's admonition, Catholic groups were publicly at variance with one another! This interchange would eventually lead to an essential reversal of the NCWC position on the United Nations—an abrogation that would come about through CAIP efforts.

A New Broom At State

The State Department was fully aware that religious organizations such as the NCWC, as well as other national groups, were major sources of opposition to the Roosevelt Administration's desire to secure American support for the Dumbarton Oaks proposals and for the upcoming UNCIO slated to begin on April 25, 1945. It was also aware that these organizations accurately reflected a general uneasiness within the American public. Accordingly, soon after the instillation of Secretary of State Edward R. Stettinius in December of 1944, the Department created a new Division of Public and Cultural Relations under the supervision of Assistant Secretary of State Archibald MacLeish, to influence public opinion favorably toward these events. It was to do so, however, in a way that was less heavy-handed than some of the Department's previous efforts.[13]

Archibald MacLeish was born in 1892 of well-to-do parents, who later sent him to Yale and Harvard. Although he became a lawyer, he soon turned his hand to poetry and playwrighting. In 1923 he fled to Paris, the mecca for American expatriate artists of the postwar era. Returning to the United States in 1929, he became editor of *Fortune* and subsequently Librarian of Congress from 1939 to 1944. While in this position he was also on the board of the Office of War Information, a hub of American propaganda activities. In late December of 1944 MacLeish was appointed by FDR to a new post at the State Department.[14]

Being a man of "arts and letters," he claimed to be dismayed at that Department's obvious and often failed attempts to propagandize the American public and special interest groups, and indeed there was abundant evidence of recent instances of Department indoctrination, some of it aimed at the Catholic Church.[15]

Such condescending procedures had not always been the practice of the Department of State. During the first three war years in the term of Secretary of State Cordell Hull, Sumner Welles, serving as his Undersecretary, developed an exceptionally warm working relationship with the General Secretary of the NCWC, Monsignor Michael J. Ready. Throughout this period the two men discussed, through innumerable, relatively informal letters and telephone calls, a wide variety of sensitive issues affecting their organizations. From March 25, 1941 to

June 24, 1943, moreover, Welles had asked to meet formally with Ready on no fewer than fourteen separate occasions—approximately once every two months. After Welles's retirement from the Department on August 23, 1943, the NCWC Archives records no instance of such a meeting between the new Undersecretary, Edward Stettinius, and the NCWC General Secretary. Even more remarkable is the fact that the only direct communication between these two officials came in December of 1944, when Ready sent a brief congratulatory note to Stettinius on the occasion of his Senate confirmation as Secretary of State.[16]

On several occasions during this era of "correct" relations, high officials of the National Catholic Welfare Conference were invited to evening-long dinners at the State Department to discuss sensitive subjects. One of these get-togethers occurred on January 5, 1944, when James Clement Dunn, Special Adviser to Secretary of State Hull, invited Monsignor Ready to discuss "attitudes" on Soviet Russia and on the "Polish-Soviet boundary dispute."[17]

After prefacing his remarks with a disarmingly fascinating insider's look at the Moscow Conference of September–October in 1943, Dunn confided to Ready that, although the Russians were difficult to deal with, he believed in their "absolute sincerity" toward international cooperation for peace, because, if nothing else, of the desperate state of their economy. With regard to the "grave" Polish question Dunn believed that the two sides would make compromises but, since agitation would only make matters worse, he asked if Catholic Church leaders would counsel the Polish people to be calm until President Roosevelt and British Prime Minister Churchill could speak to Joseph Stalin and the Polish Premier.

Ready said he was glad to hear of "future representations" with Stalin, but could not think of any Catholic leader who would counsel the Poles to keep quiet in the face of the "rapacious forces of the Soviets." "Who, after all," he went on, "would exhort the Soviet leaders to be honest in their dealings with Poland." Ready finished his report of the meeting by saying that, although it was worth while to have heard Dunn's views on the subject, "As is the case in such conversations, there were no definite conclusions."[18]

Another such incident occurred in early December of 1944, immediately before MacLeish took up his new position. At the behest of the State Department, the Chicago-based Americans United for World Organization, a ready tool of Administration bidding, sponsored an "important closed conference" to discuss the proposals for establishment of the general international organization drawn up at Dumbarton Oaks. Archbishop Stritch received an enticing invitation to this meeting, which was to be addressed by Acting Secretary of State Joseph T. Grew, who had been the United States delegate to Dumbarton Oaks. Stritch was informed that this was to be an "off-the-record discussion" for a "limited number of key people" in the Chicago area. Although the archbishop attended, his views on Dumbarton Oaks did not mellow and he seems to have recognized this "discussion" for what it obviously was, a ploy to win support for the Department's policy. This type of heavy-handed propagandizing had, therefore, little impact, at least on the NCWC.[19]

Having forsworn the above procedures, MacLeish, robed in all the solemnity of the Assistant Secretariat for Public Relations and Cultural Affairs, would now help plan and publicize the Dumbarton Oaks proposals and the UNCIO by sending out speakers, producing radio broadcasts, and even sponsoring a short documentary film. These "educational" endeavors and the rest of his publicity campaign would climax at the time of the San Francisco Conference.

On February 13, 1945, MacLeish inaugurated this new era, which he hoped would be a critical "departure from the tradition in the policy of American foreign relations."[20] On that date he issued a satement to all officials that the State Department no longer

has the inclination to attempt to 'sell' the Dumbarton Oaks Proposals to the country. In informing the country of the terms of the proposals, the Department will indicate not only their possibilities but their limitations. The people are entitled to know how far, and within what limits, the proposals, if adopted, would prevent war.[21]

It is difficult, nevertheless, to take this declaration at face value, since it was under McLeish's sponsorship that media events such as "Main Street and Dumbarton Oaks" took place. In this, the second of seven radio broadcasts aired on NBC, Acting Secretary of State Grew, Alger Hiss of the State Department's Office of Special Political Affairs, and MacLeish attempted to convince their no doubt enthralled listening audience that, whatever plan might eventually emerge from the Dumbarton Oaks proposals, "We can't afford to turn it down because it isn't perfect. We can be sure the plan will be a good one, entirely adequate to our purpose."[22]

For all his high-sounding prose, it is evident that "Archie" MacLeish only substituted one medium for another; the message seems to have stayed the same. In his defense, however, it must be said that there were many in the State Department who did not greet this interloper with open arms; it is more than likely that he was not allowed the latitude he craved in matters of public-relations policy. Even when he succeeded, it was often not without a struggle.

An Internal Debate

During the month of February in 1945, officials at the Department of State were engaged in a heated debate as to whether private associations such as the National Catholic Welfare Conference should in any capacity be invited to participate in the San Francisco Conference, in conjunction with or as a part of the American delegation. On February 23 a memorandum entitled "Public Participation in the San Francisco Conference" was placed on the desk of Alger Hiss, director of the Office of Special Political Affairs, an adviser to President Roosevelt at the Crimea Conference.[23]

The memorandum, originating from MacLeish's office and apparently reflecting his views, confirmed that public pressures were being exerted on the Department by "all kinds of interest groups" for representation at San Francisco. Because of the hugh influx of mail on this issue—one group, the Christian Peace Committee, had sent 1600 letters in the month of January—it was essential that the Department "define its policy in this matter." It was proposed that a special category of "observers"—not official advisers—be invited to the UNCIO. They would be sanctioned to attend its public functions and to take part in specific meetings with members of the American delegation. All this would fall under the supervision of Mr. MacLeish as Assistant for Public and Cultural Relations.[24]

Two other recommendations were disparaged in the same memorandum: the first suggested an extremely selective list of interest groups that would be empowered to nominate official advisers to the American delegation; the second proposed a larger unofficial "Advisory Council." The former was not favored because it would allocate too few appointments and therefore cause discontent among those excluded. The latter option, it was believed, would create an unwieldy group that might be a "disturbing influence" at the Conference.[25]

By March 10, however, an intense bloc of opposition developed within the Department of State to this memorandum and to the mounting pressure for public representation at the United Nations Conference. It appears to have been centered in the Office of Special Political Affairs (SPA) and if not led by its director, Alger Hiss, it was at least given his tacit patronage. This clique believed that representatives of private organizations should not be appointed as either advisers or consultants "attached to our Delegation in an official or direct manner." Delegates and advisors at San Francisco should be selected solely because of their "technical and expert competence" and not because they represented a particular interest group, however *"bonefide"* [sic].[26]

This opinion held that the Department should nonetheless recognize representatives of all interested organizations and welcome their active concern; it should provide special liaison facilities, occasional meetings with American delegates, information regarding Conference progress, and, naturally, tickets for public sessions. This, however, would be the limit of the Department's consideration of these agents.

The basis for this judgment was that the UNCIO was of such general interest that there were few organizations that did not think they had a claim to be represented on the delegation. To appease all such groups would produce an unmanageable deputation and would probably be seen as a transparent bid to please major pressure groups and therefore would make enemies in the process. In a concise coda to this series of discussions, one member of the SPA team began his March 15 memorandum by declaring, "I do not believe we should *invite* organizations to be represented at San Francisco."[27]

Consequently, on that day, a patronizing letter to all concerned organizations was drafted for Secretary of State Stettinius. Venturing to influence travel plans regarding San Francisco, the prospective communiqué professed that most private national organizations would doubtless find their requirements met by the exhaustive coverage that the press and radio proposed to give the deliberations. If, however, this was not satisfactory, the State Department's Office of Public Liaison would be more than happy to disburse official information *in* Washington. Finally, after pointing out the grave difficulties of finding transportation and accommodations that confronted the organizers of the parley, and appealing to American patriotism in emphasizing that attendance at the Conference had to be kept to a minimum, the letter acknowledged that some groups might still wish to name a representative to follow the UNCIO on the spot. Although this would present untold complications, the Department would oblige.[28]

This announcement and a companion White House release, obligingly drafted by Hiss's office, were never distributed because, when the Secretary of State presented the draft to FDR on March 16, the president rejected it.[29]

As early as March 21, Alger Hiss reported that "via John Dickey," director of Public Affairs under Archibald MacLeish, he learned that the Staff Committee of the Secretary of State had determined that the original MacLeish proposal was to be implemented. In this plan, no representatives of any organizations were to be designated as advisers to the Conference, but it was contemplated that an undetermined number of private organizations would be invited to send one or two representatives to the UNCIO. The MacLeish plan stipulated also that something in the nature of office space would have to be provided; although these "consultants" would have to pay all their own expenses, the Department would assist them in arranging transportation and hotel accommodations.[30]

The only point to which Hiss still had objections was designating these spokespersons as "consultants." He hoped that the Department would not have to interpret the Staff Committee's decision literally; these representatives would be available for consultation as might seem feasible but the delegates and advisors should not have to consult them on every matter. "I feel very strongly . . . that we should not designate these people as 'Consultants.' "[31]

Alger Hiss notwithstanding, on March 30 Stettinius announced to the assembled American delegates that although the president had been made aware of the difficulties of the MacLeish plan, he felt that it would do considerable harm if no formal recognition were given to the leading national organizations. The Department was directed to draw up a restricted list of the "must" group that would be invited to send two consultants each to San Francisco. Two of those organizations were the National Catholic Welfare Conference and the Catholic Association for International Peace.

Protestants And Jews

Although the president seriously considered the advice given by Hiss and his staff at the Office of Special Political Affairs, FDR could not ignore the decisive pressures exerted upon the White House by many powerful national groups, including representative organizations from the most important religious bodies, which insisted upon formal recognition at San Francisco and which up to that time had expressed substantial reservations, if not open hostility, toward his beloved United Nations.[32]

The first sectarian salvo to be felt at the Department of State was fired by an otherwise unknown soldier of the Lord, the Reverend Marion Nollen of the First Presbyterian Church of Cambria, Wisconsin. In a letter to his local congressman, Nollen declared that there ought to be a representative of the "religious forces of our country" at San Francisco. Presuming that Roman Catholics would have an envoy from the Vatican to speak for them, the minister suggested that the "Hebrew people" and the Protestants also should appoint delegates. Other Protestants, many more prominent than Nollen, also were lobbying at this time for a chance to articulate the Christian message at San Francisco.[33]

The Protestant politician's point of view was expressed directly to the State Department by Louis Ludlow, a member of Congress from Indiana. In a speech delivered from the floor of the House of Representatives, the congressman proposed the formation of a "Religious Advisory Council" representing the principal religious organizations in the country, Protestant, Catholic, and Jewish, to confer with the State Department on the matter "of the peace." Dean Acheson, Assistant Secretary of State for Congressional Relations, replied that if the appropriate religious organizations did set up such a council, the Department would welcome the opportunity to discuss peace issues with it.[34]

The Jews were spoken for by several Zionist groups: one national and two international associations. The first, the American Zionist Emergency Council, pleaded that the Jewish people should have an opportunity to present their case, "bound up as it is with the measureless suffering and losses" they had sustained. An agent for this group, Dr. Stephen S. Wise, recommended the Jewish Agency for Palestine, an "internationally recognized organ of the Jewish people in all matters affecting Palestine."[35]

The Jewish Agency, in any event, had dispatched its own advocate, Dr. Nahum Goldmann. Dr. Goldmann was troubled that the League of Nations' Mandate for Palestine, which protected the Jewish population in that part of the world, could be revised at San Francisco without the Conference hearing from the Agency's leaders, Dr. Chaim Weizmann and David Ben-Gurion. Although he realized that there was no question of his group's being granted formal membership in the Conference, even though various Arab states would be represented, Goldmann did petition the State Department to request that someone be allowed to present his agency's views on the Palestinian question.[36]

The worldwide Zionist organization, the International Jewish Committee of Action, headquartered in Rome, also contacted the American State Department. It was alarmed over the "beginning of the end of the Jewish Nation," a fear that had been aroused by the recent Roman Catholic conversion and baptism of the Chief Rabbi of Rome. Advising the Department that it had been informed that an unofficial Jewish delegation was to be dispatched to San Francisco, the Jewish Committee insisted, among other things, that a new Jewish "Mother Country"—the Northwest part of Germany—be given all the Jewish property confiscated by the Nazis and be declared *de jure* an Allied nation able to participate in the upcoming peace conferences and to form a Confederation with Palestine.[37]

To these assertions the State Department had no reply but it did notify Drs. Wise and Goldmann that the UNCIO was not designed to be a peace conference in any way. Questions of boundaries, the future disposition of any specific territories, and like questions were not within its domain. For this reason, it did not seem appropriate for the Palestine question to be raised at San Francisco.[38]

The Dulles Controversy

Catholics too expressed more than a passing interest in the part they were to play in the UNCIO, but their ardor was apparently cooled by cautious officials at the NCWC.

On January 24, 1945, Congressman Gordon L. McDonough, a newly elected Democrat and a Roman Catholic, introduced a joint resolution, which was referred to the House Committee on Foreign Affairs. His resolution expressed the sense of Congress that "members of the clergy of the religious faiths," including a "Catholic priest" should be appointed as members of the American delegation at San Francisco. Monsignor Howard J. Carroll, a Washington veteran unimpressed with this burst of freshman enthusiasm, directed the NCWC legal department to look into the topic and then discuss it with McDonough. On March 1, Eugene J. Butler, assistant director of that department, reported that after a lengthy discussion with the congressman they had decided that the subject should not be "pressed at this time." McDonough was made to see the impracticability of his campaign.[39]

Another Catholic who objected to the absence of his coreligionists in the delegation was Michael Francis Doyle, an eminent Philadelphia jurist and authority in the field of international law, who had been appointed a member of the permanent court of arbitration at the Hague by Roosevelt in 1938.[40] On March 20, 1945, Doyle had a conversation in Washington with Alger Hiss. Although Doyle discussed other issues, Hiss informed Secretary of State Stettinius that he had the distinct impression that the issue of a Catholic delegate was the primary purpose of the lawyer's visit.[41]

Hiss pointed out to Doyle that officials of the United States Government were by their oaths required to represent all segments of American citizenry, but the sixty-eight-year-old Doyle would hear none of this. The Catholic community was disturbed, he insisted, over recent world developments, over Poland in particular, and many of its prominent members believed that the omission of Catholics from "the representatives at conferences relating to world organization was deliberate." This was a serious and delicate situation that the Department should not disregard.[42]

Hiss reported to Stettinius, however, that the conversation was extremely cordial throughout and that Doyle had spoken as an ally of the Administration. The official's surprise at Doyle's uncharacteristically passive acceptance of the *status quo* is clear from his final comments. "He apparently felt that he had completed satisfactorily the purpose of his calling . . . and gave no indication that he would pursue the matter further."[43] It is more than likely that Doyle, a key figure in the American

Catholic Church, was aware of the NCWC's non-aggressive policy with regard to Catholic representation at San Francisco.

Therefore, while other denominations publicly lobbied the Roosevelt Administration for a say at the UNCIO, Catholics were officially advised "not to press the issue." This artificial lull, however, came to an abrupt end on the front page of *The New York Times*. Paradoxically, the person at the center of this "scoop" was not even a Catholic.

In a signed article dated March 20, 1945, the same day that Michael Francis Doyle was meeting with Alger Hiss, *New York Times* reporter James B. Reston disclosed that there was a possibility that John Foster Dulles might be selected by the Department of State as an advisor at the United Nations Security Conference. The newspaper further contended that Mr. Dulles was being sought "not because of his connections with the Republican Party but because of his position as head of the Federal Council of Churches' Commission" on a Just and Durable Peace.[44]

The first reaction to this announcement came from the office of Donald L. O'Toole, a Catholic member of Congress from the state of New York, who wrote a personal letter to Secretary of State Stettinius inquiring whether the Reston article was factual. If it was, then the congressman wondered at the justice of a verdict that would forbid the Catholic and Jewish faiths from having emissaries at the Conference. He closed with a maxim of political survival: "It is but democratic that if one faith is to be represented, that [sic] the others should also have a voice."[45]

The National Catholic Welfare Conference was not kept in the dark with respect to O'Toole's annoyance at this affair; he immediately sent a copy of his letter across town to the NCWC headquarters on Massachusetts Avenue.[46] There is no record of a reply to the congressman from the NCWC, but nothing they could have said or done would have lessened the pressure on the Administration to mollify feelings over religious representation at the UN Conference.

The alleged scoundrel in this villainy, John Foster Dulles, was a unique figure in the American political landscape of the day. Born in Washington, D.C., on February 25, 1888, Dulles could count among his ancestors innumerable ministers as well as two secretaries of state. He acquired his first significant diplomatic experience as a participant in the Reparations Commission of the Versailles Conference of 1919.[47]

In the 1920s and 1930s, Dulles was involved in various international conventions dealing with commerce and with global reconciliation. A sincerely devout man, he advanced the doctrine that Western civilization must rediscover its lost sense of spiritual intent. During the war years he was a prestigious international attorney and monetary counselor with a business address on Wall Street. These careers, however, did not encompass the full extent of his concerns. He was also chairman of the Commission on a Just and Durable Peace established by the Federal Council of Churches of Christ in America. In this capacity he supervised the commission's famous political statement based on Christian principles, *The Six Pillars of Peace*.[48]

The Reverend Marion Nollen, who had first protested to the State Department the need for American religious participation at the UNCIO, also volunteered that a person such as John Foster Dulles, with a profound knowledge of global affairs, would be an asset to the Conference. And indeed Dulles was far from inactive with regard to the San Francisco Conference. As late as March 14, 1945, in two letters to the Secretary of State, he made a request for Bishop G. Bromley Oxnam, an official of the FCC, and himself, as chairman of the Commission on a Just and Durable Peace, to present their attitudes on Dumbarton Oaks and the upcoming UN Conference. Their perspective on the agreements was generally more favorable than that of the National Catholic Welfare Conference or even of several prestigious members of the Federal Council.[49]

In the second letter, Dulles congratulated Stettinius, as he had done publicly in a recent *New York Times* article, on his "very real achievements" at Yalta and at the Pan-American Conference at Mexico City. He added that he was writing concurrently to ask for another appointment so that he could talk to Stettinius alone either before or after the meeting with Bishop Oxnam, most likely to discuss his personal plans with regard to the San Francisco Conference. Under separate cover Dulles sent a copy of an address that he was to deliver later that week to the Foreign Policy Association.[50] From all this activity, one could conclude that Dulles was angling for a position of some sort with regard to the UNCIO. In all fairness, however, it must be mentioned that Dulles was being encouraged in this by some of the most eminent political personages in America. He had been approached, for example, by Senator Arthur H. Vandenberg of Michigan, the senior Republican on the Senate Foreign Relations Committee and his party's congressional expert on international concerns.[51]

Ultimately, Dulles would receive the last official appointment to the American delegation. Ironically, the controversy surrounding his selection as an advisor to the US deputation to the UNCIO probably led the State Department to select the broadest range of religious representatives possible.

Delegates, Advisors, And Consultants

When the United Nations Conference on International Organization was first contemplated, it was assumed that the United States, as the only major power that had not endured the catastrophic destruction of the war, would bear the brunt of arrangements and organization for the Conference. It was presumed also that former Secretary of State Cordell Hull, who had retired because of poor health, would preside over the parley and serve as chairman of the US delegation. Whereas the United States did orchestrate most conference preparations, Hull's health did not permit his functioning in any on-scene capacity at San Francisco. It fell, therefore, to Secretary of State Stettinius to lead his country's deputation.[52]

Participants in the preliminary discussions at the State Department were understandably apprehensive over the make-up of the American delegation. It was assumed that it would include two senators, two members of the House of Representatives, a prominent Republican, a prominent Democrat, and an outstanding woman leader. This pragmatic approach was not based on political expediency alone but also on a genuine yearning to represent as much of the country's points of view as was feasible. However, considerations such as sectarian affiliation were considered improper criteria and beside the point.

President Roosevelt, while at the Yalta Conference, approved on February 11 the Department's recommended list of eight delegates. Renowned persons who were evaluated by the State Department but who either were not appointed or who declined such appointments included Governor Thomas E. Dewey, former Chief Justice Charles Evans Hughes, and several members of the Supreme Court.[53]

The final list was nevertheless an excellent portrait of the political landscape of the day. Out of respect for his lengthy experience, Hull was kept on the delegation even though he never set foot in San Francisco during the Conference. The former Secretary of State was, however, in close touch with the work of the American delegation and frequently offered his advice by telephone and telegraph. He was given the title of "Senior Advisor" and his name appeared directly under Stettinius's whenever a list of the delegates was furnished.[54]

From Capitol Hill, Senator Vandenberg was to be accompanied by his Democratic colleague from the Senate Foreign Relations Committee, Tom Connally of Texas, and the senior members of the House Committee on Foreign Affairs: its chairman, Sol Bloom of New York and Charles Aubrey Eaton, Republican of New Jersey.[55] The "prominent Republican" turned out to be former Governor Harold Stassen of Minnesota, who would double as the representative of the "fighting man," since he had seen service during the war as Flag Secretary to Fleet Admiral William "Bull" Halsey. The "outstanding woman's" position went to Dean Virginia Gildersleeve of Hunter College.[56]

In spite of the NCWC's reticence, at least one important Catholic figure took public exception to the fact that no minorities were included in the delegation. Monsignor Donald A. MacLean, a professor at the Catholic University of America, urged the State Department to appoint additional delegates representing, among others, "Catholics and colored people."

According to MacLean, all these groups had played significant roles during the war in the cause of democracy. "America should not at this stage of its democratic development tolerate in its major national activities the development or creation of unrepresented minority groups."[57]

When it came to the selection of advisers, it was initially determined that there would be a need for fifteen or twenty "other prominent persons," including high officials of the State Department (in particular some of the participants in the Dumbarton Oaks Conversations), representatives of other government departments and agencies, such as Labor, Justice, and Commerce, ranking Army and Navy officers, and business, farm, labor, and church leaders.[58] The final list of advisors would include eighteen representatives from all the above categories except the business, farm, labor, and church leaders, who would now be consolidated under a new classification.[59]

There would, of course, be one exception to this rule. On March 31, 1945, the Secretary of State finally coaxed John Foster Dulles to come to Washington to discuss the matter of his service at the UN Conference. At that meeting Stettinius informed Dulles that FDR himself had requested that he accept the post of "general advisor" to the American delegation at San Francisco. After several days of "reflection," Dulles announced in a letter to Stettinius that, since it was the will of the President as well as of the State Department that he act in an official capacity at UNCIO, he would accept.[60]

At an April 5 press interview, Dulles averred, no doubt correctly, "that there was no question of religious representation involved" in connection with his recent appointment as a general advisor to the delegation. To be sure that this point was made, Dulles resigned from the chairmanship of the Federal Council of Churches' Commission on a Just and Durable Peace.[61]

On April 10 the State Department announced that invitations had been sent to forty-two national organizations to designate representatives to serve as consultants to the American delegation. The Department professed to have attempted to select organizations that, taken as a whole, constituted a "fair cross section of citizen groups." Not all interested groups could possibly be invited, but if some still preferred to send representatives to the Conference, the Department would provide liaison facilities.[62]

The designated affiliations included two legal groups, three labor federations, three education congresses, four farm bureaus, four fraternal internationals, four business associations, five women's leagues, five peace councils, and the National Association for the Advancement of Colored People. Six religious groups were selected: the American Jewish Conference and the American Jewish Committee, the Protestant Church Peace Union and the Federal Council of Churches of Christ in America, and the National Catholic Welfare Conference and the Catholic Association for International Peace.[63]

A strong case can be made that the Administration did try its level-headed best to encompass the broadest cross section of civic organizations in the country. It was in its own political interest to do so. Even so, many groups, from the American War Dads to the Camp Fire Girls, clamored for recognition, only to be turned down by State Department officials pleading "physical limitations of travel and living accommodations." Such rejections were seldom well received and charges of favoritism and partially filled the air.[64]

Among the Catholic groups most offended by failure to receive one of the coveted invitations were the National Councils of Catholic Men and Women, the Catholic War Veterans, and many Slavic and Eastern European associations. The ethnic organizations were particularly alarmed about potential communist domination in that region of the world.

One of the most persistent Catholic supplicants was the Reverend A. Lekarczyk, president of the Polish Roman Catholic Clergy. His organization desperately yearned to have its own observer at San Francisco so as to present the case for Catholic Poland. He bemoaned the fact that no Polish Catholic organization had received a bid to the Conference "whereas the Krzycki mob of Communistic CIO will have their representation." Lekarczyk begged, therefore, to have a Polish Catholic observer join the NCWC delegation.[65]

Pleading that the Conference had a great number of similar requests, Monsignor Carroll told Lekarczyk that the NCWC consultant and his two associates had already received accreditation from the State Department, which now informed him that it was henceforth impossible to accredit any further organizations. If, however, the Polish Roman Catholic Clergy decided to send an observer to San Francisco, the NCWC deputation would be glad to exchange information and consult with him.[66]

With regard to the National Councils, the State Department explained that men's and women's organizations with a religious affiliation were deemed to be represented through their parent organizations—in this case, the NCWC. The Department recommended that such groups petition their parent organization to select a person as associate consultant. The Councils took this advice and the NCWC adopted the State Department's recommendation.[67]

This policy decision of the State Department was due in large measure to Mrs. Eleanor Roosevelt, who made a point of discussing the topic of women consultants with Archibald MacLeish. She said that the National Councils of Jewish, Negro, and Catholic women should be covered by having among the representatives of other organizations observers from these groups.[68]

Richard Pattee And The Other Consultants

In his telegram to the chosen organizations, Secretary of State Stettinius said "if you desire to appoint a consultant please wire the name of the person."[69] No prospective organization turned down this ticket-of-the-year. On April 19, 1945, both Catholic organizations notified the Department of State that they would accept the invitation.

The NCWC named Dr. Richard Pattee as its consultant.

Pattee was born in Prescott, Arizona, on April 17, 1906. After earning his M.A. at the Catholic University of America (CUA) in 1927, he opted for the life of a confirmed traveler. He later put his love of roaming to practical use, earned a Ph.D in International Affairs from CUA and joined the State Department's Division of the American Republics in 1938. Subsequently he was attached to its Division of Cultural Relations. He served for a time as a lecturer at the Catholic University of America in Washington, D.C. He joined the NCWC in 1943 as a specialist in Latin American affairs. Through his travels as an observer and writer for the NC News Service, he became thoroughly familiar with the procedures of international conferences. The NCWC hoped that because of this background, he would be acquainted with many of the delegates at San Francisco. He had, in fact, already been recalled from Latin America expressly to cover the UN Conference for the News Service.[70]

As Pattee's NCWC associates the Catholic Conference chose Henry F. Grady of the National Council of Catholic Men and Elinor Falvey of the National Council of Catholic Women, both active members of their organizations in the San Francisco area. Grady had been an Assistant Secretary of State from 1939 to 1941. He lectured at Georgetown University's School of Foreign Service and had been Dean of the College of Commerce at the University of California at Berkeley. In 1945 he was president of both the San Francisco Chamber of Commerce and American President Lines. Miss Falvey, a lawyer, had served since 1939 as a deputy district attorney for San Mateo County and was active in charity work. These associates of Dr. Pattee were to play only minuscule roles in the Catholic effort at San Francisco; their appointments were made primarily to appease the two powerful organizations which they represented.[71]

The consultant for the Catholic Association for International Peace was Thomas H. Mahony, a lawyer from Boston and a vice-president of the CAIP, who was well versed in international law. His associate, Miss Catherine Schaefer, was assistant to the Reverend Raymond McGowan, the Association's

Executive Secretary. Schaefer was also employed by the Social Action Department of the NCWC, where McGowan was associate director. McGowan himself was listed by the Peace Association as an "associate consultant," but the press of work at the NCWC prevented him from attending the Conference.[72]

As we shall see in the next chapter, however, the Catholic Church in the United States did not prepare for the UNCIO merely by purchasing train tickets for these experts. It launched a passionate crusade to win both the Conference and American public opinion to its views on world peace and security.

Notes

1. AAC 2967H, Resolution of the Notre Dame Branch of the Holy Name Society, New York City, January 20, 1945.

2. ANCWC 21, MAB 29–31, November 16, 1945.

3. RG 59a 1977, Folder 1, Raymond Buell to Dr. Walter W. Van Kirk, Dec. 26, 1944, p. 1.

4. Ibid.

5. ANCWC 30, "The Catholic Association for International Peace." This is a one-page history of the Peace Association.

6. ANCWC 21, MAB 480, Nov. 14, 1941.

7. In the matter of voting, the Dumbarton Oaks Proposals were expanded by the Yalta conferees through the following provisions: 1. Each member of the Security Council should have one vote; 2. Decisions of the Security Council on procedural matters should be made by an affirmative vote of seven members; 3. Decisions of the Security Council on all other matters should be made by an affirmative vote of seven members, including the concurring votes of the permanent members (ANCWC 15, Department of State Press Release 202; AAC 2964C, Stritch to Carroll: March 10, 1945).

8. AAC 2967S, Carroll to Stritch, March 21, 1945; ANCWC 4, Raymond A. McGowan to Carroll, March 23, 1945.

9. Ibid.

10. ANCWC 4, "The Dumbarton Oaks Proposals 28" by Edward Conway, December, 1944; "Catholics and the Dumbarton Oaks Proposals."

11. ANCWC 21, MAB 28–32, November 16, 1944.

12. ANCWC 4, Telegram sent to forty-eight US Governors, February 20, 1945, copy.

13. RG 59i, The theme of the correspondence in the early months

of MacLeish's tenure is that a new order has come to the State Department.

14. John E. Findling, ed. *The Dictionary of American Diplomatic History* (Westport, Conn.: Greenwood Press, 1980), s.v. "Archibald MacLeish."

15. There can be little doubt that Secretary of State Stettinius was the force behind this appointment, which would dictate the direction of a large public information program. On December 15, 1944, he commented on the importance of having the American public discuss and understand that the peace to come had to rest on "the firm foundations of popular support and participation—"truly a people's peace" (Robert H. Ferrell, gen. ed., *The American Secretaries of State and Their Diplomacy*, 17 vols. [New York: Cooper Square, 1965], vol. 14, *E.R. Stettinius, Jr.,* by Richard L. Walker, p. 65).

16. ANCWC 27, This NCWC file contains innumerable correspondence between Ready and Welles, which illustrates the cordial but businesslike relationship that they shared during these years.

17. ANCWC 20, January 5, 1944, 6 pages. This is Ready's memorandum on a meeting at the State Department with Dunn.

18. Ibid., pp. 5–6.

19. AAC 2975S, Arlin Elmendorf to Stritch, [Chicago], December 2, 1944.

20. RG 59i, Box 2, Folder June–Sept. 1945, Carlton Sprague Smith to MacLeish, [Sao Paulo, Brazil,] August 22, 1945.

21. *Foreign Relations of the United States . . . ,* "Policy of the Department of State on the Department's Presentation to the Country on the Dumbarton Oaks Proposals," Archibald MacLeish, p. 69.

22. ANCWC 4, *What is American Foreign Policy and Main Street and Dumbarton Oaks* (Washington: Government Printing Office, 1945), p. 31. This pamphlet contains the first two radio broadcasts by the Department of State on the subject of "Building the Peace." They were transmitted on February 24 and March 3, 1945. Participants in these broadcasts were Edward R. Stettinius, Jr., Dean Acheson, Joseph C. Grew, and Archibald MacLeish.

23. RG 59h, Kotschnig to Sandifer, February 23, 1945, 4 pages. Memorandum on "Public Participation in the San Francisco Conference."

24. Ibid., p. 1.

25. Ibid., p. 2.

26. RG 59h, J. F. Green to Alger Hiss, March 10, 1945. Memorandum on "Representation of Unofficial Organizations at the San Francisco Conference."

27. RG 59h, Secret memorandum to Hiss, "Representation of Private Organizations in American Delegation at San Francisco Conference," March 15, 1945, pp. 1–2; Mr. Morin to Hiss, Memorandum

on "Unofficial Status at San Francisco for representatives of organized groups," March 15, 1945, p. 1.

28. RG 59h, Attachment to Morin memorandum, March 15, 1945, "Draft letter to organizations," pp. 1–2.

29. RG 59h, Secretary of State to the President of the United States, March 16, 1945, pp. 1–2.

30. RG 59h, Alger Hiss to "Mr. Ross," March 21, 1945, Memorandum on "Representation at the Conference of Private United States Organizations," p. 1.

31. Ibid.

32. The president approved Hiss's designation as Secretary General of the UNCIO under the Conference President. His duties included general supervision of the organization and administration of the Conference Secretariat. The president also designated Stettinius as Temporary President of the Conference and asked Hiss to assist him in connection with any responsibilities as head of the American delegation and of the Conference (RG 59c, Box 2, Stettinius to Hiss, [D.C.], April 7, 1945).

33. RG 59a 1977, Representative Robert K. Henry, to Edward R. Stettinius, [D.C.], February 26, 1945, copy.

34. RG 59a 1980, Ludlow to Stettinius, [D.C.], March 14, 1945; Dean Acheson to Ludlow, [D.C.], April 5, 1945.

35. RG 59a 1996, Stephen S. Wise to Stettinius, [New York], March 21, 1945.

36. RG 59a 1980, Memorandum of Conversation between State Department officials and Dr. Nahum Goldmann of the Jewish Agency, March 15, 1945, pp. 1–2.

37. The Chief Rabbi of Rome, Professor Israel Zolli, became a Roman Catholic on February 13, 1945. He was baptized, together with his wife and daughter, in the Church of Santa Maria degli Angeli (RG 59a 1980, International Jewish Committee of Action to State Department, [Rome], March 15, 1945).

38. Memorandum of Conversation with Goldmann, March 15, 1945.

39. ANCWC 6, House Joint Resolution 83, January 24, 1945. Enclosed with letter of McDonough to Carroll, Washington, D.C., January 31, 1945; Eugene J. Butler to Carroll, March 1, 1945.

40. Doyle was born in Philadelphia on July 12, 1877. He received his law degree at the University of Pennsylvania and was admitted to the Pennsylvania bar in 1897. He became an expert in the field of international law and represented the State Department in Europe during World War I. While there, he defended the Irish patriot Eamon de Valera after the uprising in 1922. Over the years, he had been part of several American delegations to international conferences and had been Chairman of the American committee at the League of Nations

in Geneva in 1929–39. He was a founding member of the National Conference of Catholic Charities and was made a papal chamberlain by Pope John XXIII in 1959. He died in Philadelphia on March 25, 1960 (John J. Delaney, *The Dictionary of American Catholic Biography* [Garden City, New York: Doubleday, 1984], s.v. "Doyle, Michael Francis.")

41. RG 59h, Box 9, Memorandum of Conversation between Doyle and Hiss, March 20, 1945, p. 2.

42. Ibid. There were no Catholics among the American delegates to the Dumbarton Oaks Conversations.

43. Ibid., p. 3.

44. "Dulles as 'Adviser' at Parley In View," *The New York Times,* March 20, 1945, p. 3.

45. ANCWC 15, Representative Donald L. O'Toole to Stettinius, Washington, D.C., March 20, 1945.

46. Ibid.

47. Townsend Hoopes, *The Devil and John Foster Dulles* (Boston: Little, Brown, 1973) p. 28.

48. Mark G. Toulouse, *The Transformation of John Foster Dulles* (Macon, Georgia: Mercer University Press, 1985) p. 54; *The Devil and John Foster Dulles,* pp. 33–39; The Federal Council of Churches of Christ in America was a Protestant ecumenical organization founded in 1908 to facilitate cooperative action among the denominations. It was the forerunner of the National Council of Churches (*Transformation,* pp. 61–86); "The substance of the six pillars called for continuing Allied cooperation after the war, and was to include as soon as possible the neutral and enemy nations, provision for international economic agreements, treaty structures that would be adaptable to changing conditions, assurances of autonomy for subject peoples, control of military establishments, and recognition 'in principle' of the right of religious and intellectual liberty of peoples everywhere" (Ibid., p. 68).

49. RG 59a 1982, *From Yalta to San Francisco,* Digest of Address of John Foster Dulles at the Foreign Policy Association, March 17, 1945. After stating that the Dumbarton Oaks Proposals provided some hope, Mr. Dulles suggested that two changes be made: "1. The international organization should be infused with an ethical spirit, the spirit of justice. It should develop conceptions of justice by which it will be guided. 2. The procedure for amending the international organization's charter should be liberalized. A perpetual right of veto should not be given to each of the 'Big Five' states."

50. Ibid.

51. RG 59a 1977, Memorandum of Conversation between Dean Acheson and Senator Vendenberg, February 19, 1945.

52. RG 59b, "Discussion of Composition of United States Delegation" by Secretary's (of State) Staff Committee, March 20, 1945.

53. Ibid.

54. *Foreign Relations of the United States,* p. 70, Footnotes 16 and 17.

55. While the other selected delegates sent grateful letters to the President thanking him for the great honor, Senator Vandenberg wrote to FDR complaining that he had first read about his nomination in the press. He could not possibly accept the position until he knew "the extent of his responsibilities and the latitude which would be allowed him" (Memorandum of Conversation between Dean Acheson and Arthur Vandenberg, February 19, 1945).

56. Wilfrid Parsons, writing in the Jesuit weekly *America,* presented some general facts about the American delegation from a Catholic perspective. "Judge" Hull would be the U.S.'s "greatest asset." It remained to be seen if the forty-five-year-old Stettinius had the flexibility and intellectual dexterity that would be required at "such a rough-and-tumble affair" as the UNCIO. Both senators were friendly to "Big Business," but Vandenberg, to his credit, had espoused justice and law as the aims of the UN Charter. Bloom and Eaton from the House of Representatives were aged and in rather poor health. Harold E. Stassen, at thirty-eight, was the most intelligent member of the deputation and would perhaps be the next president of the United States. Dean Gildersleeve was the next most intelligent, and through his experiences with her Parsons could attest that she was not unfriendly to Catholic values. Stassen, Connally, Vandenberg, and Bloom were known Masons; Eaton and Stettinius apparently were not. Hull had never publicly or privately declared his religious affiliation.
Parsons hoped that, with regard to the US "team," God would answer President Truman's supplication for divine assistance with which he had ended his radio address to the conference (Wilfrid Parsons, "The American Team at the U.N. Conference," *America,* May 12, 1945, p. 108).

57. ANCWC 14, "Asks Minority Delegates: Msgr. MacLean Tells Truman Catholics, Negroes Should be Represented," *The New York Times,* April 26, 1945.

58. Ibid.

59. RG 59b, Minutes of third meeting of the American Delegation, March 30, 1945.

60. RG 59i, Dulles to Stettinius, [New York], March 31, 1945; RG 59c, Dulles to Stettinius, [New York], April 4, 1945.

61. RG 59a 1982, Stettinius to O'Toole, [D.C.], April 9, 1945, copy.

62. ANCWC 15, April 10, 1945, Press Release #323.

63. Ibid.

64. RG 59a 1994, Dean Acheson to Senator Alexander Wiley, [D.C.], April 18, 1945, copy.

65. ANCWC 15, Lekarczyk to Carroll, [Webster, Mass.], April 14, 1945.

66. ANCWC 15, Carroll to Lekarczyk, [D.C.], April 18, 1945.

67. ANCWC 15, "Miss Craven to Carroll," April 11, 1945. Memorandum on "Conference with Mr. Williams of State Department on N.C.C.W. representation at SFC."

68. RG 59i, Box 1, MacLeish to Dickey, March 22, 1945.

69. ANCWC 15, Stettinius to Ready, [D.C.], April 9, 1945.

70. ANCWC 13c, "Special Coverage at the S.F. Conference," Frank Hall, April 23, 1945; Earl Boyea, "The National Catholic Welfare Conference: An Experience in Episcopal Leadership, 1935–1945" (Ph. D. dissertation, The Catholic University of America, 1987), p. 213.

71. ANCWC 15, Howard J. Carroll to Francis H. Russell, [D.C.], April 19, 1945, copy; AAC 2964S, "The U.N. Charter and Organization," Carroll to Stritch, [D.C.], April 25, 1945.

72. AMU, Series 6, Box 1, Stettinius to Mahony, [D.C.], April 19, 1945, copy.

CHAPTER III

Preparing for San Francisco

On March 9, 1945, John J. Mitty, Archbishop of San Francisco, wrote to Monsignor Howard Carroll, asking what, if anything, the NCWC planned to do about the United Nations Conference on International Organization scheduled to begin on April 25.[1] Mitty thought that the parley would most likely be a "closed affair" like Dumbarton Oaks, but that it would be wise if the NCWC had an observer on the scene. He also thought that its News Service should send "some able layman" to cover the deliberations for the Catholic press.[2]

Monsignor Carroll replied that the Administrative Board of the Catholic Conference was scheduled to meet before the UNCIO and he was sure that the topic would come up. But since the Board was set to convene only two weeks before the deliberations in San Francisco, he had submitted a tentative proposal for coverage of the Conference. Father Conway, who was "watching the developments in the planning for the peace," intended to be at the UN Conference. He had, therefore, been designated the NCWC News Service's man-on-the-scene. Other coverage was possible, but Carroll insisted that Conway was acquainted with many persons who would be close to events. The NCWC would be kept well informed.[3]

Edward A. Conway, S.J.

In this matter the General Secretary was most certainly right. If ever there was a person at the NCWC with "contacts," it was Father Conway. For this reason there was no better liaison in the American Catholic Church on the issue of peace.

Born in Milwaukee in 1902, Edward A. Conway, S.J., graduated from the College of the Holy Cross in 1924 and one year later entered the Missouri Province of the Society of Jesus. After pursuing studies at St. Louis University and the Gregorian University in Rome, he was ordained in 1936.[4] A former member of the faculty of Regis College in Denver, Conway had become a specialist on Pius XII's Peace Points. Since 1944 he had written a weekly column for the Catholic press elucidating the quest for peace in light of the Papal plan. He was also a member of the CAIP.[5]

In 1943 his activities in the field of Christian social teachings on peace and religious cooperation had prompted an improbable joint statement by Catholic, Protestant, and Jewish leaders entitled *Pattern for Peace*. This document, which was eventually signed by 147 religious leaders from all three faiths, committed them to a moral law governing world order, to an organization of international institutions to maintain the peace, to international economic cooperation, to a just social order within each state, and to the protection of the rights of the individual, the oppressed, colonial peoples, and minorities.[6]

Splendid as this was, it was even more remarkable that such a document came about at all. Only the year before, the Administrative Board of the NCWC had determined that such "joint action in outlining world peace terms" was impossible for Catholics because of the theological difficulties involved. Typically, Conway did not circumvent the interdict; instead he went directly to the Board with his seven-point *Pattern* and the Board changed its mind. Karl J. Alter, episcopal director of both the CAIP and the Social Action Department of the NCWC, was instructed to review the text. Finding no difficulties with it, he encouraged an educational campaign to "put over" its ideas. Copies were sent to all the members of the Administrative Board and each was canvassed. The resulting vote endorsed *Pattern* as expressing the minimal requirements for a just and lasting peace. Father Conway was now an official spokesman for the Catholic Church in the United States.[7]

More than twenty years later Senator Hubert H. Humphrey would hail Conway for his groundbreaking efforts toward inter-religious cooperation for peace. "Long before most of us knew the word 'ecumenical,' " Humphrey said, "Father Edward A. Conway developed peace education on an interfaith basis." The senator was not mistaken in his tribute to the Jesuit. Although Conway was not an original thinker, he had the good sense to draw inspiration from John A. Ryan, John Courtney Murray, and Wilfrid Parsons, three of the most illustrious Catholic theorists of the twentieth century. Astutely applying their ideas, he was, more than any other individual, responsible for interdenominational endeavors for peace during the war years.[8]

Goals For San Francisco

By the time of the Dumbarton Oaks Conversations at the end of 1944, the three faiths had resolved to produce another "synthesis," which would improve the 1943 statement. Conway, who was now officially employed by the NCWC's Social Action Department, with the Reverend Richard M. Fagley, Secretary of the Federal Council of Churches' Commission on a Just and Durable Peace, and with Rabbi Ahron Opher, Secretary of the Committee on Peace of the Synagogue Council of America, drafted *Goals for San Francisco,* which was subtitled "A joint study of Catholic, Jewish and Protestant pronouncements on world organization."[9]

Once again Conway had secured the hierarchy's formal authorization, by judiciously approaching the Administrative Board through a deliberate series of steps. Setting out the preliminaries in his regular weekly column for the NCWC News Service, he proposed a "Program for United Action." This was well received by Protestant and Jewish leaders. Fagley and Opher met with him informally to draft a tentative plan. When the ten recommendations were ready, Conway wrote to Edward Mooney, archbishop of Detroit and chairman of the Administrative Board, seeking an opportunity to speak to him on the matter. Conway had conveniently planned to be in Detroit on one of his speaking tours.[10]

He explained to Mooney that the recommendations in *Goals* were based on official commentaries on the Dumbarton Oaks proposals by the Administrative Board, the Synagogue Council, and the Federal Council of Churches. For this reason, the three authors hoped that the heads of these respective organizations would independently consent to send the statement to President Roosevelt. Conway divulged that the plan was for Bishop C. Bromley Oxnam, Rabbi Goldstein, and Mooney to transmit identical declarations to FDR so that a nationwide drive to promote the suggested improvements could be inaugurated.[11]

Father Conway assured Archbishop Mooney that he would welcome any revisions that Mooney or the bishops of the Administrative Board desired. Mentioning that Bishop Oxnam and Rabbi Goldstein had "already indicated general agreement," Conway urged that a decision be reached as quickly as possible. He forwarded copies of the recommendations to Monsignor Carroll at the NCWC so that if a poll of the Board was required, as it had been for *Pattern for Peace,* copies could be sent at the chairman's instruction. Mooney did so direct. On March 13 airmail special-delivery letters were dispatched to the members of the Board, who subsequently approved the joint study.[12]

During the months of March and April, Conway with *Goals* in hand conducted a lightning crusade, christened "Countdown to San Francisco," in which he toured the country, addressed Catholic groups, and wrote voluminously for the NCWC News Service on the importance of the UNCIO. All this was done with the tacit permission of a somwhat-awed NCWC.[13]

Not one to understate a case, Conway lectured his audiences that the UNCIO could well prove to be the most vital "conclave in the history of the human race." He was often inspired to allude to a letter John Adams wrote to his wife, Abigail, on July 3, 1776.

Yesterday the greatest question was decided which ever was debated in America; and a greater perhaps never was, nor will be, decided among men. A resolution was passed without one dissenting colony that these United Colonies are, and of right ought to be, free and independent states.[14]

Not to be outdone by a mere Founding Father, Conway went on to say that a greater question was to be debated at San Francisco than even that which had been argued at Philadelphia.

Such a grave undertaking required careful thought, and in *Goals for San Francisco* its authors hoped to provide the United Nations Conference with sound Judeo-Christian reflection. In the form of ten "constructive" recommendations, they offered "practical" guidelines for peace. A general security organization had to be created, and its charter must acknowledge that moral principles governed states as well as persons. This charter would develop a code of international law and would enforce it. It would provide, furthermore, for the revision of international agreements as well as safeguard the economic and political rights of small nations. Membership would be open only to states willing to abide by such a charter. Smaller states as well as the great powers would play a part in shaping the policies of the organization, including disarmament, human rights, and the rights of dependent peoples. Finally, no member state could veto a judgment in any international dispute.[15]

In its most popular form, *Goals* was a one-page statement that briefly explained the ten recommendations. A one-paragraph foreword announced that these had been culled from individual proclamations of the three religious groups involved. But the full text of the study was much more engrossing. In its six pages it put forward each of the ten suggestions with their concurring Protestant, Jewish, and Catholic sources elucidated underneath.[16]

A revealing example of this can be seen in point eight, which dealt with "voting power," an issue that became urgent in March of 1945, when it was revealed that the Big Three representatives at the Yalta Conference had compromised somewhat on the voting procedure in the Security Council, but had still retained ultimate Big Power veto control in international disputes. After remarking that no nation should be given the right to sit in judgment on itself, the document listed all the applicable statements that the subscribed religious organizations had made. Because *On International Order,* the annual statement of the Catholic bishops for 1944, was in direct reaction to Dumbarton Oaks, it was the most pointed on this subject.

> Before it [the Security Council] every nation must stand on its rights, and not on its power. It must not allow any nation to sit in judgment in its own case.[17]

No Protestant or Jewish document dissented, and this unity on a controversial issue was indicative of the homogeneity within the American religious community on most concerns relating to world organization.[18]

On April 5 *The New York Times* reported that Fagley, Opher, and Conway, representing their respective religious organizations, had announced the results of their joint study. The story characterized the resulting document, *Goals for San Francisco,* as a recapitulation of statements made previously by the three groups.[19] What it did not mention was the attempt that the organizations would make to publicize the ten recommendations.

It came, therefore, as a surprise to the United States delegation that, during its preparations for the UNCIO, it began to receive much mail referring to recommendations made in *Goals.* This swell of public opinion was first recorded by the State Department's confidential *Daily Summary of Opinion Studies,* published about three weeks after the April 5 announcement. This synopsis related that several thousand letters had been received from both individuals and groups. Most was of religious origin, and the bulk was Catholic. The correspondents urged that the American delegation consider the trifaith statement in its deliberations previous to the UN Security Conference.[20]

Although the sheer quantity of mail was remarkable, it should not have come as a complete shock, especially to the State Department. For it was not only the efforts of the Federal Council of Churches, the Synagogue Council of America, and the NCWC that made *Goals for San Francisco* such a resounding popular success. It seems that an Assistant Secretary of State was lending a hand through a Catholic connection.

Conway And The State Department

At the end of the San Francisco Conference, Father Conway mentioned to Archibald MacLeish that he was putting the finishing touches on a document entitled *San Francisco, Goals and Achievements.* Asserting that it would be a follow-up to *Goals for San Francisco,* Conway inquired whether the Assistant secretary "could suggest an 'angel' who would help us scatter these about as we did *Goals for San Francisco.*"[21] Evidently the State Department thought that it would be in its interests to distribute Conway's material. MacLeish believed that it would be to the Administration's advantage to supply Conway with "charts and analyses" on his grand tour of the country, ostensibly in behalf of *Goals.*[22]

There can be no question that Conway was sincere in his efforts to bring about a UN Charter that reflected as much as possible the views of the three American religious bodies and, in particular, of the Catholic Church. His commitment to an American presentation of the pope's peace plan was genuine. However, his involvement with the State Department, whose views were somewhat at odds with those of the NCWC, is and somewhat puzzling.

Both he and the Department were in general agreement that a UN Charter had to come out of San Francisco. They disagreed on some specifics but probably not enough to blind them to the fact that it was to their mutual benefit to cooperate whenever possible. By helping Conway, the Administration increased Catholic support for the San Francisco Conference; by aiding the State Department, Conway was able to utilize a far more efficient communications network than the NCWC could provide. He stated that in his experience with *Patterns for Peace,*

> We tried to get an educational campaign going. You've got to have a tremendous educational organ to put over any ideas at all and we [the NCWC] didn't have the greatest.[23]

When, at the end of the Conference, Conway asked "Archie"

MacLeish to secure for him a letter of commendation from
Secretary of State "Ed" Stettinius, MacLeish was delighted to
do so and Stettinius accordingly wrote the letter. MacLeish
commented:

> I think you have done a superb job. It would certainly be in
> the interest of the Charter if you could continue your work of
> public education about its provisions.[24]

And Conway had done a fine job; at least both the Catholic
Church and the State Department thought so. However, as we
shall see, this balancing act appears all the more extraordinary
when one realizes that at the time of this letter, June 19, 1945,
the NCWC had yet to make up its mind officially whether or
not it would recommend Senate ratification of the UN Charter.

It will be a concern of this study to determine how Father
Conway carried out his activities and responsibilities during
the formation of the United Nations in 1945 and 1946. In order
to do this it will be necessary to investigate Conway's behavior
before, during, and after the San Francisco Conference. Since
he played a significant part in the Catholic Church's role in
these events, such an investigation will not take us away from
the principal topic.

Catholic Interests

There is ample proof that Father Conway's first loyalty was to
the Catholic Church and to the National Catholic Welfare
Conference, which employed him. A testimony to this commitment is a series of memoranda designated "Catholic Interests
Involved in the San Francisco Conference," which the Jesuit
wrote during the week of April 11, 1945.[25]

Divided into two categories, these Catholic interests are
labeled "Ideological Issues" and "Practical Issues." The ideological questions included the World Court, disarmament, regional arrangements, and international law, all of which will
later be discussed in detail. The fifth ideological issue, however,
"The Great Powers and World Security," was intimately bound

up with the preparations for the UNCIO and therefore is appropriately covered in this section. It was furthermore an issue on which the American State Department and the Catholic Church found themselves on opposite sides.[26]

Even after the initial confusion had cleared around the ambiguous point of "unanimous ratification by the Big Five," which had emerged from the Dumbarton Oaks Conversations and from "clarifications" on the veto power contributed by the Yalta Conference, the State Department was forced to admit that a permanent member of the Security Council could still not only veto economic and military sanctions in a case in which it was involved, but also vote down recommendations and decisions as to whether the peace was threatened in a case in which it was not involved.[27]

Conway pointed out that the doctrine of peaceful change, which this procedural rule would inhibit if not destroy, had long been one of the cardinal points of the Papal Peace program. it also occupied a prominent place in *Pattern for Peace* and in *Goals for San Francisco,* which had been officially released only the week before. Point five of *Goals* demanded that the UN Charter, in the form in which it emerged from Dumbarton Oaks and Yalta "should provide more explicitly for the revision of treaties and of other agreements." This was something the Great Powers' veto would most likely prevent.[28]

Allying himself with two of the Department's most outspoken critics, former President Herbert Hoover and Senator Arthur Vandenberg, Conway spoke of the Security Council veto proposal as a bid by the major powers to freeze as far as possible the status quo. World War II had been caused, according to Hoover, by those who aspired to prevent change.[29] And in a famous speech on the Senate floor, Vandenberg claimed that "the art of peace" was not identified with stasis. Hoover, Vandenberg, and Conway were in agreement, therefore, that the Security Council veto aimed to maintain the status quo at the expense of small nations and at the expense of justice.[30]

The "Practical Issues" that Conway addressed in his memorandum on "Catholic Interests" at the UNCIO included education, dependent peoples, membership in the international organization, and human rights. As with some of the "Ideological Issues," the first two points from this category will be covered in following chapters, but membership and human rights will be examined now.

Conway stated quite bluntly that it was "important that the 'Catholic' nations be included [in the United Nations] as soon as possible—before all the decisions of the Organization are taken."[31] He contended that at the meeting in San Francisco, Catholicism would be rather thinly represented. Germany, Italy, Spain, Portugal, Austria, Ireland, Poland, and Switzerland would have no delegations. Some of these countries, such as Spain, Italy, and Portugal, had colonies with Catholic missionaries that had been administered by their nationals and that now would be trust territories of the new world organization. Moreover, practically all the nations mentioned above, that is, those which were not to be represented by delegates, had many missionaries in other territories. Conway estimated that 15,000 priests, brothers, and sisters, or about 25 percent of the Catholic Church's missionary force, would therefore not be represented at the UNCIO.[32]

This memorandum would unfortunately have its consequences. Because of the supposed need for more Catholic participation at the UN Conference, the NCWC would become embroiled in futile attempts to acquire membership for several countries mentioned above and would also be intimately involved in the successful but highly contentions struggle to get Argentina, a Catholic but formerly pro-fascist nation, into the world organization.

This alarm over the absence of Catholic participants in the world body is perplexing. By early April of 1945, the time of the memorandum's composition, all the nations of Central and South America, with the exception of Argentina, had stated their intention of enrolling in the UN. Furthermore, when an unofficial head count of all delegates was taken by the Archdiocese of San Francisco at the beginning of the Conference, it was discovered that a majority were at least nominally Catholic.[33]

There was a distinct possibility, however, that the missionary interests of the Church could suffer because many Catholic missions were in areas that would most likely be trust territories of the new international organization. Since some of these missionaries were nationals of Axis or neutral countries not participating in the UN Conference, Conway could legitimately fret that the Church's interests would not be safeguarded by the new world association.

John Courtney Murray And Human Rights

Another practical matter that Conway assumed would be of interest to the Catholic Church at the San Francisco Conference was human rights, which included "religious freedom." The bishops of the Administrative Board of the NCWC agreed. In their April 10, 1945 meeting, it was revealed that some Protestant leaders were contemplating a demand for creation of a permanent international commission on religious freedom, for which they proposed to solicit Catholic support. The ostensible reason for this maneuver was that Americn Protestant missionaries, who had recently tried to establish a foothold in Latin America, were experiencing, in their words, "discriminatory practices" by the governments of those countries with full knowledge, if not consent, of the long-established Roman Catholic Church.[34]

The bishops intended to deal with this predicament in two ways. First they urged that the General Secretary of the NCWC arrange that appropriate Catholic experts be present in San Francisco if discussions on this subject did take place. Once the NCWC determined to accept the State Department's invitation to the UN Conference, it was almost inevitable that Richard Pattee, the NCWC's expert in Latin American affairs, would be designated as Catholic observer at the Conference.[35]

The bishops' second step was to request the aid of one of the nation's foremost Catholic theologians, the Jesuit John Courtney Murray of Woodstock College in Maryland.[36] Anticipating a discussion on religious freedom, Monsignor Carroll requested from Murray a detailed summary of his latest thoughts on the topic. With some hesitation, the Woodstock professor sent the requested study, which arrived only one day before the Board was scheduled to convene in Washington. The bishops were therefore able to use Murray's reflections on this sensitive subject to guide their discussions.[37]

Murray was teaching theology to Jesuit seminarians in the Maryland countryside when the NCWC called upon him in April 1945 to address the issue of religious freedom. Earlier that year, the American hierarchy was made aware of the theologian's interest in the subject through his series of articles in recent issues of *Theological Studies,* a Jesuit publication of Woodstock College.[38] For the bishops, however, Murray was far less reserved in his musings than he had been for the periodical, and he admitted to a certain nervousness over this "sticky stuff," preferring that it not get around.[39]

Defining "freedom of religion" or "religious liberty," terms that Murray disliked because of their secularist origins, he suggested that the issue should be discussed on three levels: in terms of the ethical, theological, and political problems involved. In order to make his complicated study explicable to the NCWC, he summarized eighteen pages of exacting reflection by recommending an answer to the frequently heard question, "Are we Catholics prepared to demand religious liberty for all men today?"[40]

Murray prefaced his remarks on this "very delicate and difficult matter" by noting that people who made such inquiries seldom delimited what they meant by religious liberty. He then presented the four commonly employed definitions of the term.

If the expression "religious liberty" connoted that each person within a state must be permitted by that state to freely adopt the manner in which he or she personally worshipped God, then the answer was, "Yes, Catholics were for freedom of religion." Murray subsequently noted that although this was the second of the famous Four Freedoms,[41] it was not tantamount to an admission that all denominations were equally valid.[42]

Secondly, if the term freedom of religion signified the inher-

ent liberty of conscience, which he had specified in the previous paragraph, then he could again respond in the affirmative. But if the term denoted that "all kinds of religion are
'equally probable, equally good, equally acceptable to God,'"
then by the ruling of Leo XIII in the encyclical *Immortale Dei*
(1885) the answer was "no."

It should be understood by Protestants that this was a theological consideration, a concern of conscience for Roman Catholics. Murray was aware that many non-Catholics insisted that
unity did not necessarily mean uniformity. On this premise he
offered the rationale that Catholics could be "united" with
others not of their faith in the preservation of freedom of
religion without being "uniform" in the belief that all religions
were objectively true.[43]

Finally, if the term religious liberty would commit Catholics
to the assertion that "no religion in any country of the world
should occupy a position of privilege before the State," then a
Catholic could not concede that the Church ought to advocate
such a right. This Protestant egalitarianism was unreasonable,
indefensible, and even undemocratic, Murray insisted, because
in certain circumstances the common good would demand that
a unity of church and state exist.[44]

Murray concluded that all men and women of faith should
work for a freedom of religion that was based not on specific
theological creeds of whatever variety, but on the basis of the
natural law. In a world divided by religion, this was the hope of
the human race.

> Furthermore, the demands thus formulated would be de-
> signed for insertion into a political charter for humanity in its
> present state of religious division. For this purpose, a for-
> mulation in terms of natural law would be the good thing
> indicated by the exigencies of the common good in today's
> conditions. It would be a minimal formulation, but sufficient
> for its purpose.[45]

Taking their cue from Murray's ground-breaking views (at
least for Catholicism in 1945), the bishops of the Administrative
Board resigned themselves to the probability that they would

have to be content with a statement on religious rights coming out of the San Francisco Conference that would be based on the natural law and not the "truths of revelation." They also used his study to formulate a working definition of religious liberty. Citing Murray's observations, they determined that freedom of religion presupposed the right of citizens to protection from hindrance on the part of the state with regard to their allegiance to conscience in private domestic matters, in the religious training of their children, in unfettered association for purposes of creed, and in proselytizing their belief in God and the decrees of the moral law.[46]

The leaders of the American Catholic hierarchy were apparently grateful to John Courtney Murray for his resourceful insights. They had appealed to him at a time when they believed they were in a predicament due to the United Nations Conference. There their representatives would be in close contact with many American Protestants and Jews, and Murray had provided them with theories they could use in their deliberations with these other consultants.

Murray had also given them material they could employ in their public utterances, one of which was issued immediately after the Board's April meeting. This document, fashioned with the UN Conference in mind, reflected the current judgments of the Catholic Church in the United States on world organization and peace and was as such a shot fired across the bow of the American ship-of-state.

The April Manifesto

At the meeting of the American delegation on April 17, 1945, the participants were greeted by a handout that contained a summary of a communiqué issued only two days before by the NCWC. It was entitled *On Organizing World Peace*.[47]

Along with pressing topics to be debated at San Francisco and revisions of the UN Charter that the delegates were discussing, the bishops' statement was given high priority at that morning session. The leadership of a major American constituency had spoken out on issues that could decide the fate of the UN Charter and even the future of world organization. No one in the room underestimated the seriousness of the bishops' report, least of all the officials from the Department of State whose duty it was to stage-manage a successful UN Conference.[48]

The archbishops and bishops who constituted the Administrative Board had mused over the statement in a spirit of sober reflection. Acknowledging the approaching UN Conference, they had determined to express their views at this strategic moment in the preparations for that conclave. Wishing to supplement their earlier statement of November 16, 1944, the Board's members at first intended only to highlight the difficulties faced by millions of war refuges so that the UN Conference might recognize their plight. When, however, Archbishop Stritch moved that the chairman of the Board, Archbishop Mooney, draft the document, it was a signal that its scope would be widened.[49]

Declaring that a solid international organization was not a quixotic illusion, Mooney ignored accusations of "perfectionism" leveled at the bishops for their criticisms of Dumbarton Oaks.[50] If all nations pledged goodwill in international relations the great victory at hand could result in a genuine peace. But if great power isolationism—the surrounding of a strong nation by its puppet states, for example—was allowed to dictate policy to the new organization then "abstentionist" isolationism would spring up in America once again. In both eventualities, the tragedies associated with the League of Nations would repeat themselves.[51] True peace and world security were theoretically within the reach of San Francisco, Mooney insisted, but certain provisions in the projected UN Charter gave "rise to doubt and fear" that the Conference would not be able to achieve these desired goals.[52]

With regard to the voting procedure in the Security Council, the method agreed to at Yalta was seriously deficient because the delegates to those deliberations had apparently ignored the Dumbarton Oaks profession of equality for all "peace-loving" nations. It seemed unjust and even dangerous to give any nation, however deserving or powerful, a perpetual veto on treatment for all countries, especially since this interdict extended to cases before the World Court. "Powerful aggressors" and their friends seemed to be the only beneficiaries here.[53]

Mooney asked for more power for the General Assembly, where small nations could have a greater say, authority for the UN to make changes in peace treaties and other global settlements, and an International Bill of Rights, which would be a condition for membership in the world body. Poland deserved a "free secret ballot," he declared, and the United States had no right to countenance the subjugation of the Baltic States. Furthermore, former enemies should be handled justly but firmly and liberated states must be allowed to set up free and democratic governments.[54]

In the document's conclusion, the Administrative Board released all its pent-up fury at a supposedly "peace-loving" ally. The Marxist totalitarianism of Soviet Russia was a mockery of God and of democracy. It perpetuated itself by violating the innate human rights that the UN Charter proposed to secure. America had to guard forever against the lies and propaganda of this essentially alien system.[55]

Behind the rhetoric of *On Organizing World Peace,* the American Catholic Church had several goals in mind, which could not yet be discussed in the public forum. It expected that former enemies or Fascist countries, namely Japan, Italy, Germany, and Spain—all, with the exception of the first, sustaining large Catholic populations—would eventually be permitted to join the UN. After all, no nation could be expelled from international society forever. The bishops also hoped for a humanitarian council within the new organization. The Church imagined that in this way its missionary efforts would be protected. Finally, although the NCWC was pushing for an International Bill of Rights, which would, of course, include freedom of religion, it intended to stave off an onslaught in behalf of religious liberty for Protestant missionaries in South America by stressing Protestant "offensive tactics."[56]

But the biggest secret that the NCWC withheld was the fact that the CAIP minimalists, such as Edward Conway, had already won. Although the bishops were stern in their demands and appeared unyielding on many points, they were, by April 15, 1945, ready to yield so that the United Nations could be established. In a subsequent NCWC memorandum, hope for a future peace was enunciated in two phrases: "juridic organization" and "building up international law." In other words, the United States should work within the UN under the principle of legal authority so that a body of world laws would eventually be created and enforced by the organization. In this, the NCWC was in actual agreement with the American State Department, but the Administration did not know it.[57]

Nowhere is this ignorance more evident than in a memorandum written to Secretary of State Stettinius by Archibald Mac-Leish only one week before the San Francisco Conference. MacLeish had just been in communication with Adlai Stevenson, Jr., a Special Assistant Secretary of State, with regard to the April manifesto of the NCWC. This interoffice communication is worthy of unabridged quotation.

I agree with Adlai's memorandum. This is a carefully reasoned, carefully matured, statement of the Catholic Church. They can't be argued out of it by a friendly conversation. Also, we have invited comment and criticism, and it would be risky to seem to object to any. All we can do, I think, is to try to persuade the Bishops that we must all keep our eyes on the main objective—to establish a beginning of international organization—and not to let specific questions, no matter what they may be, defeat our purpose. How this can be done, except by seizing every opportunity which presents itself, I don't know. I will, however, think about it as hard as I can.[58]

The Department of State was understandably apprehensive over the bishops' pronouncement, unaware that unanimity was closer than this published declaration might indicate. The Administration, therefore, went into the UNCIO with a guarded admiration for the American Catholic Church, and accordingly the NCWC and CAIP were able to obtain a more equitable hearing for their positions than even they anticipated.

Catholic Press Coverage

While the NCWC's Administrative Board was issuing *On Organizing World Peace,* Monsignor Howard Carroll was disclosing that the Catholic Conference would take extraordinary steps to provide news coverage of the UNCIO. At that time, before the consultants from the NCWC and the CAIP were chosen, it was determined that Father Conway and Dr. Pattee would be in attendance as accredited news correspondents. Miss Catherine Schaefer would serve as an observer for the publications of the Catholic Association for International Peace.[59]

Selection of consultants for the two Catholic organizations was governed, at least in part, by these journalist assignments. Pattee and Schaefer would now perform dual roles, with their consultants' positions awarding them a finer vantage point than anyone could have foreseen. But Frank A. Hall, director of the NCWC News Service, believed that the UN Conference was a story of "high importance"—one of the crucial events of the postwar era. Especially after the designation of the consultants, who would now be too busy to provide adequate coverage, and an incident involving Father Conway, which will be discussed later in this section, Hall encouraged the choice of another correspondent, a full-time professional.[60]

The person who best fitted this bill was Burke Walsh, assistant director of the NCWC News Service. Walsh was a seasoned newsman who spent many years covering the White House, Congress, and various departments of the federal government. He had recently concluded a tour of duty as a war correspondent in Europe, where he had been quartered in Rome and had specialized in Vatican affairs.[61]

The Catholic News Service also covered the San Francisco

Conference through the syndication of a series of articles, "Catholic Spotlights on San Francisco," written by world-famous Catholic pundits. Although the views of these authors diverged at some points, the News Service hoped that they would "light up facets of the San Francisco meeting from numerous interesting angles and give a vigorous point of departure for Catholic thought."[62]

One of these "interesting angles" was contributed by Professor Guido Gonella, the author of *A World to Reconstruct*, a book prepared under the direction of Archbishop Stritch's Committee on the Pope's Peace Plan. Gonella, who was arrested by Mussolini in 1939 for anti-Fascist activities, had long been a columnist for *Osservatore Romano* when in 1944 he was made editor of *Il Popolo*, the newly-founded daily paper of the Christian Democratic Party in Italy.[63]

Professing to understand the "Holy Father's anxiety" over some "dangers" to the United Nations, Gonella declared that the pope longed for neutral nations to be included in the international organization. Further he reported that the pope was not pleased with the Yalta Conference, where the Big Three had brazenly centralized their power in the Security Council and made the General Assembly of the UN little more than a "formal and academic body."[64]

Other leading Catholic scholars who placed their bylines under "Spotlights" were Dr. Victor Andres Belaunde, a Peruvian diplomat who had recently attended the Pan-American Conference at Chapultepec; Don Luigi Sturzo, the famous Italian priest and statesman; and Bishop Paul Yu-Pin, who was to be one of China's delegates to the UN Conference. Dr. Yves Simon of the Institut Catholique was also to be found there discussing the "nature and functions of authority." Finally, several Eastern European academics interpreted happenings in that part of the world, stressing Soviet motives toward the international body and Poland's right to be represented at the UN Conference. Although these columnists could not possibly live up to the News Service's publicity, which trumpeted "as imposing a collection of scholars and writers as has ever been brought together from the four corners of the world," they collectively serve as a neat and authoritative compendium of international Catholic thought at the end of the war.[65]

On the same day as the "Spotlights" series was being launched by the News Service, its director, Frank A. Hall, wrote a highly confidential memorandum to the General Secretary of the NCWC. Not wishing to sound "alarmist," Hall nonetheless thought that the Catholic Conference was in some jeopardy on a matter pertaining to Father Conway.

Conway was the first to promote himself as the logical representative of the News Service at San Francisco. Without objection, Hall sent a verification of this to the Standing Committee of the Congressional Press Galleries, which served as judge and jury over who might be accredited "a working newspaper man" at the UNCIO. Although the Jesuit had no difficulty in receiving his credentials, Hall was now having serious misgivings.

> I am quite convinced that Father Conway's mind is filled up with other things than doing newspaper work. He has just engineered a Catholic-Protestant-Jewish speaking, [sic] and was bubbling over with another project whereby he would be the Catholic signatory to another sort of conference-of-Christian-Jewish three-way statement on peace matters. In other words, there is the danger that he will be so thoroughly identified as a propagandist that it will be transparent that he is not doing newspaper work.[66]

What directly provoked Hall's memorandum was Conway's entreaty that he is allocated another writer to "help" him or even be his "ghost writer" while in San Francisco. Conway was evidently aware that he would not be doing a straight job of writing, and Hall feared that someone, "*Time* Magazine . . . or a Southern Baptist" would spill the beans that the News Service had planted a "ringer" in the Press Galleries so that a Catholic priest-propagandist could have the choicest credentials.

The News Service director insisted that both the NCWC and the Standing Committee were being "used." The Catholic Conference was one thing, but the congressional correspondents could not be "kidded by amateur devices." Hall strongly urged that a regular newsman such as Burke Walsh be sent to the Conference and be given the NCWC's press credentials. "It would be ridiculous," he argued, "for a working newspaper man to be out there without credentials while a man not devoting his time to newspaper work sat at the press table." Hall insisted that Conway and Pattee would still be able to turn in their weekly columns while fulfilling their other obligations.[67]

Conway took strong exception to Hall's suggestion, and urged that the "confidential character" of some of the work he was supposed to do required an assistant to finish his various articles and columns. The Jesuit even recommended a "Mr. Enzler" for that position. But all this bravado was in vain, because Carroll had already resolved to propose to the Administrative Board that Walsh be selected. On April 15 he informed Conway of the Board's concurrence with his motion. The priest would have to relinquish his elite press credentials and finish off his own columns.[68]

Father Conway was not the kind of man to let such things get him down. With or without his "ghost-writer," he would fight for world peace at the UNCIO. One of many columns in which he waged this battle was in a series entitled "Days of Decision," which employed as one of its "hooks" a "countdown to San Francisco." As "C-Day" approached, Conway called on the spirit of the patron saint of that city and the "holy genius of Pius XII" to descend upon the deliberations there. Exorcising the "devils of discord" from the UN Conference, just as the friar of Assisi had defeated those at Arezzo so many centuries before, this NCWC "priest-propagandist" prayed for the UN, which would be "a shaky thing at best, wobbling on its weak legs like a new-born colt."[69]

Archbishop Mitty's Production

When Archbishop John J. Mitty first wrote to Howard Carroll on March 9, 1945 asking about the Catholic Conference's

UNCIO strategy, very little thought had been given to a concerted Catholic response to the UN Conference. The General Secretary had mentioned only the tentative plan to send Father Conway to San Francisco; as we have seen, even that understanding of the priest's role was later modified. The NCWC had not contemplated a local effort.

Two days after Carroll's response to Mitty, the General Secretary received a proposal from Father McGowan containing some hastily-compiled suggestions for Mitty regarding projects that the Archdiocese of San Francisco could undertake in conjunction with the UN Conference. McGowan's rather elaborate tactics focused on a Mass at the cathedral to pray for God's blessing on the Conference. His blueprint did not overlook such details as the date for that ceremony—the first Sunday after the opening session—and the nature of the sermon, which should avoid controversial details and dwell on "religious principles of international organization and justice." The NCWC could help, if asked, by providing a list of known Catholic delegates, and once Catherine Schaefer arrived in San Francisco she could continue the search at that end. Finally, an eminent cleric should be invited to preach the homily and this fact had to be publicized well in advance.[70]

The second component in McGowan's scheme was a special supplement in the archdiocesan newspaper like one the NCWC masterminded a few years before for the Diocese of Cleveland and an international peace symposium there.

What McGowan did not recommend, however, was a "large Catholic mass meeting," because he feared that such a rally would draw some foes of the United Nations and might leave an impression that only Roman Catholics were in opposition. If a massive gathering were held, it should be under joint sponsorship with Catholic collaboration.[71]

Carroll did not write to Mitty until more than one week after McGowan's memorandum had been sent to him; even then, he only introduced tactfully the latter's ideas, no doubt so as not to overwhelm or rankle the formidable archbishop. The General Secretary prefaced his remarks by mentioning that Catherine Schaefer would attend the Conference. He also re-

lated that Archbishop Mooney "hoped very much" that Mitty
would be able to attend the Administrative Board meeting on
April 10 and 11, since the UN Conference would be a major
item on the agenda and Mitty as San Francisco ordinary could
provide invaluable data on developments there.[72]

Still laying the groundwork for what he believed Mitty would
consider extreme suggestions, the General Secretary mentioned that a "Mr. Charles Thomson" of the State Department's
Cultural Cooperation Division would be departing shortly for
San Francisco. Although not a Catholic, he was well acquainted with NCWC personnel and knew the value of con-
tacting ecclesiastical authorities. Carroll hinted that he might
be of assistance. Only after all these preliminaries did Carroll
allude to McGowan's plan.

Since Miss Schaefer was going to San Francisco anyway, he
had asked her to collect the names of Catholic delegates and
give that information to Mitty in the event that a religious
function was to be planned. Perhaps, even a special supplement
to *The Monitor,* the San Francisco Archdiocesan newspaper,
might be produced, something in which the NCWC's Social
Action Department had collaborated in the past. Carroll ended
the letter by trusting that Mitty would not hesitate to call upon
the Catholic Conference for any unspecified help he might
need.[73]

Mitty was known as one of the most irascible figures within
the American hierarchy, but Carroll need not have feared his
temper this time. For the UN Conference had caught the imagination of the sixty-one-year-old prelate and no Catholic plan
would have been too elaborate or extraordinary for the occasion. In fact, the archbishop would brush aside Mooney's request that he attend the April Administrative Board meeting,
not because he was uninterested in its UN agenda, but because
of involvement in his own preparations for the Conference.[74]

The NCWC soon got wind of Mitty's enthusiasm through a
flutter of telegrams that descended on its headquarters within
days after Carroll's second letter arrived in San Francisco. The
first of these to appear came from the editor of *The (San*

Francisco) Monitor, who had been detailed by his boss to get "all data in reference to proposed supplements." A very relieved Carroll immediately requisitioned from McGowan all necessary information, labeling the project "top priority." He expected the NCWC to be as helpful to Mitty as it could possibly be.[75] Accordingly, the appropriate data went out the next day, but with a question attached: "Is any special religious service anticipated either before or during conference?"[76]

That question was answered the same day by yet another telegram disclosing that a Pontifical High Mass would be celebrated on Sunday, April 29, at Saint Mary's Cathedral, at which Duane D. Hunt, bishop of Salt Lake City and a Mitty protege, would preach. But the biggest surprise was still to come. A "mass meeting" would be held in the San Francisco Civic Auditorium on Wednesday evening, April 18, "sponsored by Archbishop John J. Mitty." No less a figure than Fulton J. Sheen would address this rally on "The Moral Basis of Peace."[77]

All these preparations were made without Mitty apprising the NCWC or Archbishop Mooney beforehand. Mitty had taken full charge, just as the NCWC hoped he would; the local plans of the Catholic Church with regard to the UNCIO were now in his very able hands. If he seemed to be pursuing some stratagems of which it might not approve, there is no indication that the Catholic Conference tried to stop him.

Mitty had accurately gauged the great excitement enveloping anything to do with the UN Conference. He remarked to Carroll that there was "a great deal of interest here on the part of our Catholic people"; but even he could not have imagined the reaction to the disclosure that Fulton J. Sheen was to make an appearance.[78]

Even before television, Monsignor Sheen, "the microphone of God," had captivated a huge national audience with his dynamic and eloquent preaching. Since 1930 he had been a frequent participant on the "Catholic Hour" radio program, which millions of Americans, Catholics and non-Catholics alike, heard regularly.[79] It soon became clear that he had so many fervent admirers in the Bay area that all of them could not possibly fit into one auditorium at the same time. Therefore the archbishop secured two more venues: one across the bay in Oakland and the other down the Peninsula in San Jose. At these three locations Sheen was given the singular opportunity to deliver the Catholic Church's last official pronouncement on the UNCIO before its inauguration. He would do so before overflow crowds and with the rapt attention of the American media.[80]

Sheen was a brilliant popularizer of Catholic philosophy, and far too clever a professional entertainer to waste such a moment. He presented to his mass audience his "five personal amendments to the Dumbarton Oaks proposals." Although he claimed to speak only for himself as an American citizen and not for the Church, his speeches, sponsored by the Archdiocese of San Francisco and presided over by Archbishop Mitty, the official representative of the Catholic Church in San Francisco, paralleled in every way the official statements of the NCWC on world peace and security. They were therefore treated by the press and public as formal ecclesiastical proclamations.

Sheen insisted that a sound moral basis for the peace could be built only on the platform of equal voting power in the UN, the creation of an International Bill of Rights, justice as the foundation of peace, UN membership for "law-abiding States" (i.e., neutrals and former enemies) as well as those that were "peace-loving" (i.e., allies), and a United Nations able to revise unjust treaties. For good Catholic measure he defended the notions of a juridic World Court and a free Poland. In all this he simply reiterated, in his own spellbinding manner, the NCWC's hardline position that the Big Five would have to exhibit purity of motives on each of these points.[81]

Although Sheen was technically correct in saying that his was not a formal Catholic position, for all anyone cared, it might as well have been. The National Catholic Welfare Conference therefore owed Archbishop Mitty and Monsignor Sheen much gratitude because they had underlined to the Administration that the NCWC was apparently not wavering in its unyielding posture expressed in *On Organizing World Peace*. Ironically, the American Catholic Church was now well situated to negotiate for its principles from a position of strength within the American delegation. Sheen's addresses and Mitty's other endeavors dramatically highlighted the Catholic position at the outset of the parley. This was probably their single greatest contribution to the overall Catholic effort at the UN-CIO.

Notes

1. John Joseph Mitty was born in New York City on January 20, 1884. He was educated at Manhattan College and then at St. Joseph's Seminary in Dunwoodie, N.Y. After ordination in 1906, he studied at the Catholic University of America and the Pontifical Seminary in Rome, where he received an S.T.D. He was appointed bishop of Salt Lake City in 1926 and coadjutor archbishop of San Francisco in 1932. He succeeded to that see in 1935. He died in 1961. (*Dictionary of American Catholic Biography,* "Mitty, John Joseph").

2. ANCWC 15, Mitty to Carroll, [San Francisco], March 9, 1945.

3. ANCWC 15, Carroll to Mitty, [D.C.], March 13, 1945, copy. Pattee had not yet been recalled by the News Service.

4. AMU, Series 8, Box 2, Biographical note on Conway.

5. ANCWC 13c, "Special Coverage of the San Francisco Conference," April 23, 1945, p. 1; Edward A. Conway was international affairs editor of the Jesuit weekly *America* from 1948 to 1954. In 1954 Father Conway was appointed Professor of Political Science at Creighton University in Omaha. In 1961 he received a grant from Columbia University to establish a Center for Peace Research at Creighton. In 1962 President John F. Kennedy appointed Conway to the General Advisory Committee of the United States Arms Control and Disarmament Agency. Father Conway died in Omaha on May 24, 1965 (AMU, Series 8, Box 2, Biographical notes and obituary).

6. AMU Series 8, Box 2, Biographical note on Conway; AMU Series 8, Box 2, "Big Man for Peace," *The Catholic Reporter* (Kansas City, Missouri), June 12, 1964.

7. ANCWC 21, MAB 501, November 9, 1942; AMU, Series 8, Box 2, "Peace Movement's Hidden Story," *The Catholic Reporter,* June 26, 1964; AAC 2957C, Conway to Mooney, [D.C.], March 7, 1945, copy.

8. AMU, Series 8, Box 2, "Father Conway Hailed for Peace

Efforts," *The True Voice* (Omaha), June 12, 1964; Ibid., "Peace Movement's Hidden Story."

9. ANCWC 15, Edward A. Conway, S.J. et al., *Goals for San Francisco: A Joint Study of Catholic, Jewish and Protestant Pronouncements on World Organization,* April 5, 1945.

10. AAC 2967C, Conway to Mooney, [D.C.], March 7, 1945, copy.

11. Ibid.

12. AAC 2967C, Carroll to Stritch, [D.C.], March 13, 1945.

13. ANCWC 4, Conway to Carroll, [D.C.], December 1, 1944.

14. ANCWC 15, Text of a broadcast delivered by Conway in Indianapolis on March 11, 1945.

15. *Goals for San Francisco,* p. 2.

16. ANCWC 15, Memorandum from Father Conway: March 27, 1945.

17. Ibid.

18. ANCWC 15, Conway to Carroll, [D.C.], March 27, 1945. At the beginning of 1945, formal pronouncements issued by the Federal Council of Churches and the Synagogue Council of America supported the principle that no nation be allowed to sit in judgement on itself in the UN Security Council:

"All nations needs must accept such limitations of absolute sovereignty [equality within the structure of international organization] as shall make possible the good of all . . ." (Synagogue Council of America, January, 1945).

"A nation, while having the right to discuss its own case, should not be permitted to vote when its case is being judged in accordance with prdetermined international law" (The Cleveland Conference of the Federal Council of Churches, January, 1945).

19. "Three Faiths Map Ideas For Charter: Agree on 10 Recommendations on Moral Foundations for a Just World Order," *The New York Times,* April 5, 1945, p. 12.

20. RG 59e, April 25, 1945, "UNCIO, US Delegation."

21. RG 59a 2016, Folder 1, Conway to MacLeish, [D.C.], June 18, 1945.

22. ANCWC 4, Conway to Carroll, [D.C.], December 1, 1944.

23. "Peace Movement's Hidden Story."

24. RG 59a 2016, MacLeish to Conway, [D.C.], June 19, 1945, copy.

25. ANCWC 15, "Catholic Interests Involved in the San Francisco Conference," Conway to Carroll, [D.C.], April 11, 1945.

26. Ibid.

27. ANCWC 15, Text of speech, "The Great Powers and World Security," Edward A. Conway, April, 1945.

28. Ibid.

29. ANCWC 14, "Hoover Asks Pacts Be Open To Change," *The New York Times,* April 26, 1945.

30. U.S., Congress, Senate, Speech of Senator Arthur Vandenberg, 79th Cong., 1st Sess., March 15, 1945, *Congressional Record* 91:3549.

31. "Catholic Interests. . . ," Section I, Number 4.

32. ANCWC 15, Conway to Carroll, [D.C.], April 11, 1945.

33. ANCWC 15, Schaefer to Carroll, [D.C.], April 30, 1945.

34. ANCWC 21, MAB 616, April 10, 1945.

35. Ibid.

36. John Courtney Murray was born into the family of a New York City lawyer in 1904. Entering the Jesuits in 1920, he studied at Woodstock College, Maryland, and at the Gregorian University in Rome. He was sent to the Philippine Missions while still a scholastic and was ordained there in 1932. Four years later he joined the faculty at Woodstock, where he taught dogmatic theology to Jesuit seminarians. In the 1950s, Murray became famous as an authority on church-state relations, attempting to harmonize the heritage of the Catholic Church with the realities of pluralistic society in the United States. In 1954, this undertaking created an international theological furor which resulted in an order from John Baptist Janssens, the General of the Jesuits, restraining him from writing and lecturing on the subject. Murray was exonerated, however, at Vatican II, where he was the principal author of the Declaration on Religious Freedom approved in 1965. He died in New York City on August 16, 1967 (*Dictionary of American Catholic Biography,* p. 413, "Murray, John Courtney").

37. ANCWC 21, MAB 616, April 10, 1945.

38. *Theological Studies* is a quarterly journal published by Theological Studies, Inc., "for the Theological Faculties of the Society of Jesus in the United States." It was founded in 1940. John Courtney Murray (1904–1967) had been editor of the journal since 1941.

39. ANCWC 15, Murray to Carroll, [Woodstock, Maryland], April 6, 1945.

40. ANCWC 15, *Notes on the Theory of Religious Liberty,* John Courney Murray, April 6, 1945, p. 18.

41. President Franklin D. Roosevelt in his Annual Message to Congress on January 6, 1941 had enunciated the principle of the "Four Freedoms." They were freedom of speech and expression, freedom of religion, freedom from want, and freedom from fear, i.e., a worldwide reduction in armaments. These freedoms were God-given rights extended to all peoples and all nations, and the president pledged that the United States would "seek to make secure . . . a world founded upon" these principles (Thomas H. Greer, *What Roosevelt Thought: The*

Political and Social Ideas of Franklin D. Roosevelt [East Lansing, Michigan: Michigan State University Press, 1965], pp. 11–13).

42. *Notes on the Theory of Religious Liberty,* p. 18.

43. Ibid.

44. Ibid., p. 17.

45. Ibid.

46. ANCWC 21, MAB 616, April 10, 1945.

47. At this time, the Administrative Board of the National Catholic Welfare Conference consisted of Archbishops Edward Mooney of Detroit, Chairman, Samuel A. Stritch of Chicago, Vice-Chairman, Francis J. Spellman of New York, John T. McNicholas of Cincinnati, John Gregory Murray of St. Paul, John J. Mitty of San Francisco, and Joseph F. Rummel of New Orleans, as well as Bishops John F. Noll of Fort Wayne, Karl J. Alter of Toledo, and James H. Ryan of Omaha. The Board's November 16, 1944 statement had been approved by this same group.

48. RG 59b, Folder 6, Minutes of the 9:00 A.M. American Delegation Meeting, April 17, 1945.

49. AMCWC 21, MAB 614, April 10, 1945.

50. ANCWC 4, Conway to Carroll, [D.C.], December 1, 1944.

51. ANCWC 15, *The Bishops Speak Out on World Peace: Two Statements by Catholic Bishops of the United States* (Washington, D.C.: National Catholic Welfare Conference, 1945), *On Organizing World Peace,* April 15, 1945, p. 1.

52. RG 59f, Box 22, Dumbarton Oaks Proposals, Current Developments and Comment Report #20, week ending April 17, 1945, p. 2.

53. "On Organizing World Peace," p. 1.

54. Ibid., p. 2.

55. Ibid.

56. ANCWC 15, "Ideological Notes," Memorandum by Father Paul Tanner, *On Organizing World Peace.* This document is undated but was written soon after the April Statement.

57. Ibid.

58. RG 59i, Box 1, Folder 1, MacLeish to Stettinius, [D.C.], April 20, 1945, copy.

59. ANCWC 21, MAB 614, April 10, 1945.

60. ANCWC 13c, Hall to (Catholic) Editors, [D.C.], April 23, 1945.

61. Ibid.

62. ANCWC 13b, "On Catholic Spotlights," Hall to (Catholic) Editors, [D.C.], April 9, 1945.

63. Ibid.

64. ANCWC 13b "Rights of Small Nations Must be Considered," Guido Gonella, April 9, 1945.

65. ANCWC 13b, "A Galaxy of By-Lines," Hall to (Catholic) Editors, [D.C.], 1945, p. 2.

66. ANCWC 15, Hall to Carroll, [D.C.] April 4, 1945.

67. Ibid.

68. ANCWC 15, Conway to Carroll, [D.C.], April 3, 1945; Carroll to Conway, [D.C.], April 15, 1945, copy.

69. ANCWC 13a, "The Spirit of San Francisco," E. A. Conway, S.J., April 16, 1945.

70. AMU, Series 6, Box 1, McGowan to Carroll, [D.C.], March 15, 1945.

71. Ibid.

72. ANCWC 15, Carroll to Mitty, [D.C.], March 21, 1945, copy.

73. Ibid.

74. ANCWC 15, Mitty to Carroll, [San Francisco], March 21, 1945.

75. ANCWC 15, D.A. Bazzanella to Carroll, [San Francisco], March 27, 1945.

76. ANCWC 15, James A. Lawler to D.A. Bazzanella, [D.C.], March 28, 1945, copy.

77. ANCWC 15, Bazzanella to Lawler, [San Francisco], March 28, 1945; Mitty to Carroll, [San Francisco], March 27, 1945.

78. ANCWC 15, Mitty to Carroll, [San Francisco], March 27, 1945.

79. Fulton J. Sheen, *Treasure in Clay* (Garden City, New York: Doubleday, 1980), 336 pp.

80. "Thirty More U.S. Aides at San Francisco," *The New York Times,* April 18, 1945, p. 7.

81. "The Moral Basis of Peace," *The (San Francisco) Monitor,* April 21, 1945, p. 1.

CHAPTER IV

The United Nations Membership Debate

A Mass for the United Nations

While a number of Californians had visualized a religious ceremony for the success of the UN conference among the natural wonders of Muir Woods,[1] Catholics of the Archdiocese of San Francisco were envisioning a less bucolic observance. On the advice of Father Raymond McGowan, Archbishop John J. Mitty had planned a Solemn Pontifical Mass at Saint Mary's Cathedral for April 29, the first Sunday after the opening of the United Nations Conference. In honor of the Holy Spirit, the rite was envisioned as a plea for divine guidance and aid for the delegates.[2]

In organizing the three UN rallies at which 40,000 people heard Fulton Sheen, Mitty's strategists discovered that the Catholic public in San Francisco yearned to be a part of world history. Now, in the arrangements for the United Nations Mass, it became apparent that no cathedral would be able to accommodate the faithful who were planning to attend. Mitty was delighted. He proudly announced that the city's Civic Auditorium, the site of Sheen's largest triumph, would be transformed into a temporary cathedral, episcopal throne included, from which he would preside over his flock.[3]

The ceremony would surpass the wildest expectations of even the most devout. More than fifteen thousand persons, including many delegates and advisers, along with civic officials and members of the press, packed the hall. A choir of 1,000 school children led the congregation in hymns and *The Star-Spangled Banner,* which for some inexplicable reason served as the finale for this UN rite. From a giant raised platform, Archbishop Mitty, flanked by three other bishops, declared that by the providence of God the Conference was being held "in the city of St. Francis . . . the saint of universal love." He prayed that this would augur success.[4]

The sermon was preached by Duane D. Hunt, bishop of Salt Lake City, who pleaded with the rulers of the earth to strive not for power but for unselfishness so that peace could once again be a possibility. Hunt claimed that, after the sufferings of a bitter and terrible war, the world was waiting for just such demonstrations. If forthright leaders did not speak up at the UNCIO, the civilization they embodied would perish and so would the fruits of their deliberations. Risks had to be taken in the name of peace; "nothing could more quickly clarify and electrify the atmosphere around the Conference."[5]

To accent the global nature of the event, the ceremony's planners appropriately arranged the flags of all the forty-six nations participating in the UNCIO (up to that point) behind the high altar.[6] But this was not the only indication of the worldwide flavor of the gathering. Invitations had been extended to members of all national delegations and a sizable number were present. Burke Walsh, who was reporting the event for the NCWC News Service, declared that no less than thirty deputations had representatives in attendance. Ambassador Victor Andres Belaunde of Peru, the Minister of Foreign Affairs from the Netherlands, and T. V. Soong, head of the Chinese delegation, were among the distinguished personages in the reserved section of the congregation. Walsh reported that, as a matter of course, the flag of the Soviet Union stood in the sanctuary, but no member of that delegation was sighted at the mass.[7]

The Roman Catholic Church could not have improved on this ingenious demonstration of its manifest presence at the Conference and, incidentally, its desire for universal UN membership. It seemed that Father Conway's initial fear that the church would be "thinly represented" at the Conference was not borne out by the genuinely awe-inspiring response that both the public and the delegates gave to Archbishop Mitty's

Mass. In fact, if one were impiously taking a head-count, this Pontifical Mass was a timely inventory of at least the nominal Catholic participation at the UNCIO.

First Impressions

Once the Catholic consultants and correspondents settled into their hotel rooms and had a chance to look around the Conference, they reported to the NCWC that Conway's consternation over a shortage of Catholic diplomats had been rash and, indeed, missed the point. First of all, it was discovered that while almost every ethic group and segment of the human race was to be found at the meeting, twenty-four invited nations were predominantly Catholic. Twenty-two countries were catalogued as "non-Catholic." In this category were to be found the four sponsoring powers—the Soviet Union, China, the United Kingdom, and the United States. No Catholics were listed among the thirty-eight delegates from these four states but a few of their advisors were prominent laymen, and one was a cleric. This gentleman, Bishop Paul Yu-Pin, Vicar-Apostolic of Nanking, had no official capacity, but Generalissimo Chiang Kai-Shek had anointed him the representative of all non-governmental agencies in China.[8]

In spite of their absence from the four major delegations, Walsh announced that almost half of all representatives to the parley were Roman Catholic. Although most of these could be found in the deputations from the seventeen Latin American countries, there were also several prominent Catholic leaders from other areas of the world. Walsh reported to the NCWC that Georges Bidault, Minister of Foreign Affairs of France, and Francis Michael Forde, Deputy Prime Minister of Australia, had already become influential figures during the Conference preliminaries.[9]

After perusing this somewhat surprising tally, Richard Pattee was not quite as sanguine as Walsh. Watching Catherine Schaefer compiling lists of the Catholic delegates to the UN Conference in order to hand them over to Archbishop Mitty, he was struck by the futility of it all. Although these rolls were a good source for the archbishop's invitation lists for his various receptions, Pattee wondered aloud at their substantive value.[10]

From his first report, he insisted that it would be a miscalculation to count Catholics in the hope that all of them would exhibit "vigorous and conscious Catholic thinking." This group—if it could be called that—would not be able to speak as one, since it was made up of persons from different countries and disparate parts of the world. More to the point, they probably had no desire to do so. Pattee had detected no Catholic coordination at the UN Conference, and an "absence of anything religious in the atmosphere" precluded its development. There was little probability, therefore, that Catholics would speak their minds in explicit religious terms. It would be foolhardy for the NCWC to anticipate UNCIO decisions that resembled Pius XII's "Five Point Peace Program." Drawing up great lists of Catholic delegates was, in Pattee's opinion, a rather meaningless exercise.[11]

Pattee, however, was far from pessimistic. Like Burke Walsh, he mentioned Forde, Bidault, and Belaunde as outstanding Catholic laymen. Many others could be included in this inventory. It was not dishonest to say that exceptional Catholic leadership was present at the Conference, but it was not very important either. The NCWC should not be discouraged if these good Catholics did not fight for the Church's specific stances on all occasions. Much that might ensue from the Conference would be tolerably Catholic, even though it would not be labelled as such. Pattee concluded his analysis with this sensible advice: "Perhaps this is a far more important way of obtaining the incorporation of sound principles than to stand for specific Catholic ideas."[12]

Other Catholic agents also were realistic about the chances for Catholic ideals in the secular environment of San Francisco. Even Walsh agreed with Pattee that an arbitrary sectarian division of the delegates by no means offered a true appraisal of how Catholic standards might sway votes on points of world organization.[13]

The initial reaction of the Catholic consultants to the San

Francisco Conference was therefore generally favorable and this was true also of their estimation of the American delegation. Secretary of State Stettinius met with all the unofficial observers on April 26, the second day of the Conference. At that time he assured them that they would be kept well informed on UNCIO proceedings and that their views would be sought by the US representatives. John S. Dickey of the State Department's Office of Public Affairs, as liaison officer for the American delegation, would be the consultants' chief tie to this group. Since Dickey was directly under Archibald MacLeish, Assistant Secretary for Cultural and Public Relations, a division known for its propaganda efforts, there had been some apprehension, no doubt fed by much speculation in the press, that the whole "consultant phenomenon" was little more than a publicity "gimmick."[14]

Such ruminations were naturally uppermost in the minds of the Catholic representatives as the UNCIO began. Elinor Falvey, associate consultant for the NCWC, had presumed that she would be allowed only to wear an officious badge, listen to a few speeches, and have very little responsibility. She was surprised that the American delegation and its advisors planned to meet two or three times a week with the consultants to assess points be placed on the agenda of the Conference. Large meetings were also to be held each week, at which explanatory talks would be delivered by members of the delegation, with question-and-answer sessions to follow.[15]

Pattee also had assumed that the consultants were to be little more than window-dressing. He too was pleased at the discovery that they were receiving more attention and thought than he had anticipated. After a few days, the NCWC representative began to think of himself as "more than a purely decorative" fixture. He compared Dickey to a "stage manager and general attendant," who organized meetings, got the consultants good seats, and tried to keep them informed on what was happening at any given time. Pattee confessed to Monsignor Carroll that, thanks in part to Dickey's efforts, there was an ironic twist to all this. Because he had not expected to have much to do as a consultant, he was soon "at loose ends in view of the necessity of handling the News Service angle, keeping up contacts with foreign delegates, sitting at consultants' meetings and exchanging general impressions all over the lot."[16]

All was not perfect, however. In this same letter, Pattee irritably remarked in passing that the forty-two consultants did not really function as a group, since persons with similar points of view tended to bunch together in order to advance their programs. This preliminary comment by Pattee is significant as the earliest indication that the consultant from the NCWC did not feel altogether comfortable at the State Department's meetings.[17]

As we shall see, this was not the case with Thomas Mahony or Catherine Schaefer, the CAIP consultants. Such feelings would determine the nature and scope of each consultant's activities in San Francisco. It also goes far to explain why some Catholics developed their own Conference methods and routine.

If some Catholic agents found hard going within the consultant structure, they learned to tread delicately through the other universe they inhabited, the world of journalism. Quarrels here often developed over the great dichotomy between Russia and America that quickly became the overarching conflict in San Francisco.

Burke Walsh was confronted with this difficulty before he had his first meal in the city. As his train was pulling into town, he spied an old friend he had known in Italy. This friend introduced him to his companion, "Izzy Stone" (I.F. Stone), who was, at the time, a writer for *PM,* a news and opinion magazine.[18] Later that day, as he and Pattee were having their lunch at a press hangout, "Izzy" yelled at him from across the restaurant: "Hey Walsh, what's the matter with the Hierarchy? What are they trying to do to Russia?" Walsh informed the NCWC that Stone later apologized, saying that he had been drinking too much at the time—which Walsh doubted—but Stone still wanted to argue with him later about the bishops' statement.[19]

Conway too encountered vocal opposition to the Administrative Board's April statement. One reporter asked him: "What do they want us to do, fight Russia?" For this reason Conway always spoke darkly of radical "pressure groups." Walsh was not sure of this, but he did remark to Carroll that there were a lot of "leftwingers" to be seen around the fringes of the UN Conference, including many movie stars and journalists.[20]

In spite of these scattered negative reactions, the first few days of the Conference were positive ones for the Catholic representatives. But questions of UN membership debated in the Conference's plenary sessions were to exacerbate the differences that these outbursts revealed.[21]

Membership Selection

At Yalta the United States was formally licensed by the Soviet Union and the United Kingdom to persuade the affronted nations, China and France—which suffered the international indignity of exclusion from that meeting—to join in sponsoring invitations to a United Nations organizational Conference. China would eventually acquiesce, but France, citing its absence from Dumbarton Oaks and deeply offended at the failure to invite DeGaulle to the Crimea, agreed only to participate in the UNCIO.[22] Accordingly, on March 5, 1945, the United States, on behalf of only four sponsoring powers, presented to the governments of thirty-nine other nations invitations to the parley to be held in San Francisco. In this summons the sponsoring powers limited the scope of the meeting to the preparation of "a charter for a general international organization for the maintenance of peace and security."[23]

The invitation was distributed only to those "peace-loving" countries that had declared a state of war with one or more of the Axis powers and adhered to the Declaration of the United Nations of January 1, 1942.[24] This agreement, signed by twenty-six nations in Washington, committed its signatories to continued cooperation after the cessation of hostilities. These requirements automatically excluded a significant number of nations that did not conform to this paradoxical portrait of a "peace-loving" state.[25]

Excluded from this select caste were such Axis powers as Germany, Japan, Austria, Hungary, and a former Axis nation, Italy. Although there were some demands by Italian-Americans for the latter's inclusion in the UN, the United States refused to take up this cause.[26] Also excluded were Germany's "fascist" friends, nations that, while remaining officially neutral, scarcely disguised their preference for an Axis victory. Into this classification were lumped the Iberian nations of Portugal and Spain as well as Argentina.[27]

Since all neutrals had by definition failed to declare war on the Axis, they too were ostracized. Ireland, Sweden, and Switzerland fell into this unlucky grouping. Finally, several nations whose status was controversial were initially barred from the Conference pending an investigation of their cases at the plenary sessions scheduled for late April. Poland, Denmark, and the Byelorussian (White Russian) and Ukrainian Soviet Republics were the outstanding nations in this division.[28]

Consequently, after their discreet consultations at the Black Sea, the Great Powers invited only those states on their circumscribed list of "united nations."[29] This roster was not, however, to be the final word on the matter of membership at the UNCIO As soon as the announcement was published, international bickering on the subject of United Nations participation began in earnest.[30]

The Polish Dilemma

The Conference was inaugurated with eight plenary sessions in the San Francisco Opera House. During these public assemblies the chairmen of the delegations of the sponsoring powers, and then the chairmen of various other delegations, addressed the Conference.[31] Each chairman expressed the views of his government on the general nature and objectives of the UNCIO and many rendered homage to the late President Franklin D.

Roosevelt, from whose leadership and inspiration the United Nations had evolved.[32] This ceremonial aspect of the Conference took four days but was much more than a mere preliminary exercise. For instance, during these sessions, the chairmen of the delegations were permitted to discuss their contemplated amendments to the Dumbarton Oaks proposals.[33]

While these introductory meetings were proceeding, the four sponsoring powers were engaged in intense private discussions on the organizational facets of the Conference. The most apparent necessity was the setting up of four commissions to which the delegations would have to submit their amendments to the Charter.[34] Father Conway remarked that no one could have foreseen before the Conference that the majority of the membership, dissatisfied with the Big Four's proposals, would submit over 800 pages of amendments. Even greater delays would ensue, however, due to the protracted Big Three discussions on Polish representation at San Francisco.[35]

This predicament originated presumably in San Francisco when Vyacheslav M. Molotov, Soviet Foreign Minister and chairman of his country's delegation, insisted that a ready-made, Moscow-spawned Polish Government—the Polish Committee of National Liberation—be recognized by the United Nations, and a government of exiled Poles in London, headed by Stanislaus Mikolajczyk, be repudiated.[36] In fact, however, the quarrel had begun in earnest immediately after Yalta. At that conference Stalin had apparently agreed with Great Britain and the United States that neither the provisional government then functioning in Poland, nor the London cabinet represented the people of Poland as a whole. Accordingly it had been acknowledged by all three delegations that a more broadly based government should be formed: one with an extensive democratic base. This new government would be called the "Polish Provisional Government of National Unity."

Within one week, however, the American Ambassador in Moscow, W. Averell Harriman, received from the Soviets an *aide-memoire* on the Crimea Conference, which stated that a

National Unity Government would be admitted to the UNCIO only if the reorganization was completed before the opening date of the parley. Otherwise the Soviet Government would insist that the Polish regime in Warsaw, called the Lublin Committee, be accredited.[37] Indignant over what it understood to be a Russian about-face on this issue, the State Department directed Harriman to inform Molotov that the United States could not consent to extend even a tentative UN invitation to the Warsaw government, since that act would undermine the establishment of a regime of National Unity. Furthermore, if no such government were set up before the convening of the UNCIO, then the United States was of the view that "Poland could not be represented at the Conference."[38]

On the evening of April 24, 1945, the day before the opening session of the San Francisco Conference, a last-minute discussion was called, at which high foreign-service officials of the United States and the Soviet Union, meeting in Stettinius's luxurious penthouse suite atop the Fairmont Hotel, futilely attempted to remove their differences so that this dispute would not interfere with the progress of the UNCIO.[39]

The Secretary of State began the session by saying that the failure of the three powers to reach agreement on the Polish question cast doubt on the solidarity and collaboration between these states, which was the very keystone of the Dumbarton Oaks proposals. Although the US was firmly committed to the creation of a United Nations, it saw this question as a "test case" for the three powers. He then offered Molotov distinct assurances that if Russia were to abide by the compromise at Yalta—assimilating both Polish factions into a single government—the United States would do all in its power to see that the Conference would sanction two Soviet Republics as full members in the world organization—a major objective of the Soviet's UN diplomacy.[40]

At this point the discussion became heated. Molotov accused the United States and Great Britain of treating the Soviet Union as a second-rate power by dictating terms that would result in a hostile regime in Warsaw, namely the unity coalition. If the USSR were compelled to accept anything but a favorable settlement in Poland, "after all the Russian blood that had been shed for Polish liberation," any other solution would mean that this blood had been shed in vain and the Soviets had lost the war. He concluded by saying that aggression had come through Poland twice in a generation. On this basis, the Soviet Union would never again forsake the interests and safety of its people.[41]

Molotov insisted on knowing why the United States and Great Britain were now placing obstacles, such as the Polish question, in the way of Big Power unity. Why, he persisted, had there been such a deterioration in the goodwill that was so evident at the Crimea Conference? Stettinius flatly denied that there was any change in attitude on the part of the United States and said the problem resulted from Russia's refusal to abide by its Yalta commitments. On that note, the pointless discussion ended.[42]

The American State Department had always contended that it favored only a Polish Provisional Government of National Unity. It had done so in the expectation that the two sides—the Polish governments in London and Warsaw—would, if unconstrained, negotiate a coalition in good faith before the start of the San Francisco Conference.[43] The Catholic Church in the United States, however, maintained no such impartiality.

The NCWC's inclination in this matter was illustrated when the London-based government, dominated by Catholic Poles, issued a diplomatic memorandum emphasizing "justice, calmness and thorough consideration" of international problems at the UNCIO. Through its Ambassador in Washington, Jan Ciechanowski, it dispatched a copy of this document to the NCWC with a cordial cover letter expressing confidence that the Church would ensure the statement wide distribution in the Catholic press.[44]

The NCWC News Service readily obliged by prominently mentioning in its coverage of the release that even though the London Poles had not been invited to participate in the world organization, they nonetheless believed it their primary duty, as the only legal representatives of the Polish nation, to submit constructive suggestions to the UNCIO on behalf of Poland.

Moreover, the News Service did not excise a bellicose assertion in the text, untimely as it was, coming on the eve of the UN
Conference, which contended that the Big Powers could not
"escape responsibility for the maintenance and defense of a
just peace settlement, even by force, if the necessity should
arise."[45] Lastly, Monsignor Howard Carroll cordially responded to Ambassador Ciechanowski's letter that he was
edified by the document and was hopeful that it would receive
the welcome in the Catholic press that it richly merited.[46]

Carroll was not the only Catholic leader to champion the
non-Communist Polish government. During his speeches in
San Francisco at the three United Nations rallies, Monsignor
Sheen had called the Polish question a "cameo of the world
situation." No great power, he proclaimed, should unilaterally,
and by force, impose itself on a smaller nation without the
world organization's stopping it.[47] On May 6, 1945, Archbishop
John J. Mitty added his voice to the appeal by pleading for a
democratic Poland at a Mass specifically dedicated to that
cause. Catholics who attended the service were asked to re-
member in prayer sixteen democratic Polish leaders arrested
by the Soviets in March of 1945.[48]

These prelates were in complete harmony with the American hierarchy's statements on the subject. In April the NCWC
Administrative Board expressed disappointment at the Yalta
compromise on the Polish question. The bishops stressed the
necessity of guaranteeing to the Poles the right of a free secret
ballot not dominated by any foreign power. At that time, Senator Arthur Vandenberg, the most prominent Republican member of the American delegation, had without delay come to the
Board's defense on this point. Upholding the bishops' procla-
mation, he stated that a free Poland was an "acid test" of
whether the Allies had won a true peace.[49]

Finally Oscar Halecki, a former Polish diplomat and one of
the Catholic scholars writing for the NCWC's "Spotlights on
San Francisco," demanded democratic representation for Poland at the UN Conference and complete rejection of the Yalta
Pact.[50]

Pattee and Mahony worked in tandem to bring these Catholic views to the attention of the members of the American delegation and their colleagues among the consultants, but to little effect. The United States and Great Britain had already committed themselves to a Polish Government of National Unity, which, of course, barred exclusive recognition to either the Lublin Committee or the government-in-exile in London. So all entreaties by the Catholic consultants in defense of the London Poles were politely received but not endorsed.

The immediate result of the Polish stalemate was an overwhelming vote in the UNCIO on April 27, that barred the Soviet-supported Lublin Poles from the world organization. Molotov was thereafter forced to agree to a Belgian compromise, which expressed the hope that if a new and representative Polish government were formed before the Conference adjourned, it should be encouraged to send delegates to San Francisco. As Conway reported, both Polish factions were left to hold highly emotional press conferences at which their emissaries hurled recriminations to no effect. In his opinion, neither side handled its case "any too well."[51]

The final chapter of this episode was a disaster for the Catholic Poles and their supporters. On June 21, 1945, Stalin succeeded in establishing a new Communist-controlled state in Poland. The final settlement, made in Moscow, was completed only after Russian troops arrested all moderate politicians in the country. Although it called itself a "national unity government," the Big Four at Postdam would admit it into the United Nations only after Mikolajczyk, who had headed the London cabinet, accepted the position of Vice Premier.[52]

The Soviet Republics And Argentina

With the Polish crisis still hanging like the sword of Damocles over the opening days of UNCIO, a related controversy came to the fore. Naturally it too had its origins in the Crimea Conference.

At Yalta the United States and Britain accepted a Russian

proposal whereby two Soviet republics, White Russia and the Ukraine, would be accorded what was described as "initial membership" in the United Nations.[53] Almost as soon as the conferees parted, however, disagreements arose between the American State Department and the Soviet Foreign Ministry over the definition of that phrase. The State Department's interpretation held that the United States had committed itself to support a Soviet proposal at the UNCIO whereby a vote would be taken on whether to admit the two Republics to the eventual world organization. The Russians were convinced that Roosevelt had pledged that his country would uphold the seating of the republics at the UN Conference itself. The United States was not ready, however, to embrace this Russian interpretation of events, particularly since the State Department considered that the Soviets had reneged on their Yalta commitment to promote a Polish Government of National Unity.[54]

To further complicate the situation, discontent broke out within the Roosevelt Administration over even the concession to the Soviets of three seats in the projected Assembly. The President was, therefore, persuaded to ask for US parity in seats with the Soviets: in other words, that America be allotted three votes in the UN General Assembly to duplicate the three ballots Russia and its two autonomous republics would have. This was seen as equalizing the voting power of the Big Three, since the United Kingdom and its dominions had six votes in the assembly. In any event, the US never really pressed this claim at the UNCIO.[55]

The Latin Americans, who were closely allied with the United States, at first opposed the admission of the two Soviet Republics, either at the Conference or in the General Assembly. But with American insistence that the final resolution of this question lay with the UNCIO, these nations announced to Nelson Rockefeller, Assistant Secretary of State for Latin American Affairs, that they now saw a way to barter successfully with Russia on a South American matter, the admission of Argentina to the Conference.[56]

On February 21, 1945 representatives of the United States and the nations of Latin America had gathered at Chapultepec, a suburb of Mexico City, for the Inter-American Conference on Problems of War and Peace. At this meeting the countries present vowed Pan-American solidarity, even in the eventuality of world organization. A regional security pact, such as the one that was signed at this parley, was seen by the conferees as a necessity in order to manage a type of local crisis it was believed the United Nations would be ill-equipped to handle. At the signing of the Chapultepec Declaration, the states of the Americas congratulated themselves for solving just such a problem.[57]

The difficulty stemmed from the Republic of Argentina's wartime sympathy with the Axis Powers and its consequent failure to join in the allied effort against Germany. Under the influence of Colonel Juan Peron (1895–1976), the government in Buenos Aires had been in close contact with the German Embassy, had aided Nazi espionage efforts in South America, and had allowed a growing number of German immigrants into the country on "humanitarian grounds." Twice during the war the regime had sent a secret envoy to Spain to pursue an arms deal with the Germans.[58]

As if this were not bad enough, Peron professed heartfelt admiration for Benito Mussolini and thought that *Il Duce* was a millennial figure. Politically he was guided by the fundamental premise that Fascist Italy and Nazi Germany were merely alternatives to capitalism and communism. World War II was therefore, in his view, no more than a mutual effort by these dominant systems, led by the United States and the Soviet Union, to crush their aspiring competitors. He did identify, however, even more closely with Francisco Franco in Spain and Antonio Salazar in Portugal. Needless to say, all this did not endear Argentina to the triumphant Allies, who were in absolute command of the UNCIO.[59]

Although most US Catholic spokespersons were hesitant to criticize Argentina publicly in the face of extensive governmental and non-Catholic condemnation, *Commonweal,* a "progressive" Catholic magazine under lay editorship, censured the so-called Argentine "nationalists" who hoped for an Axis victory. The periodical went on to relate that the "Anglo-Saxon, Protestant, and liberal-democratic culture," i.e., the United States, which had produced the Pan-American Union, was despised in Buenos Aires by reason of its hindrance of a *sacrum imperium* that would rule the postwar world in the form of three or four Holy Roman Empires—Argentina being the Latin American variant. Finally, *Commonweal* castigated the vast majority of lay leaders in Argentina who lent their weight to forces "destructive of characteristically Christian values."[60]

The nineteen nations that gathered at Mexico City thought that they dealt adequately with the "Peron problem." Carefully examining the situation in Argentina, which many critics labelled "fascist," they required that nation to concur with the Chapultepec agreement, which obligated her to accept the democratic principles enunciated in the Atlantic Charter as well as to declare war on Germany. She was also required to resume diplomatic relations with the United States. Argentina fulfilled these requirements by April 9, 1945, and the conferees accordingly invited her to participate in the UNCIO.

Arriving at San Francisco, the Chapultepec conferees were proud of what they thought had been an extensive and even-handed scrutiny of the affair. They fully expected the other nations of the world to respect their deliberations, but they soon discovered that some states were not as gratified by Inter-American understanding as were its beneficiaries. Leading the charge against this hemispheric solidarity was a covetous Soviet Union, which had yet to develop a sizable UN bloc of its own. The first public opportunity that the Russian delegation had to express this sentiment came with the United States' petition for admission of Argentina into the security organization.[61]

Refusing to bargain publicly for admittance of the two Soviet Republics in exchange for membership of a "fascist" regime, Molotov took a roundabout approach: he attempted to revive the Polish issue, which was thought to have been resolved. In the Executive Committee of the Conference, he eulogized the sacrifices and heroism of the Polish people and agonized over the iniquity of those who would prevent their just representation at the Conference. When this committee, which had been charged with all matters concerning admissions, still resolved to admit Argentina and refused to reconsider the Polish compromise, Molotov persisted in taking the issue to the floor of a plenary session, where he denounced the allegedly "fascist" state. Although the Latin Americans were quite sympathetic to the plight of Poland, they were in no mood to have their efforts at Chapultepec ignored. Infuriated by this perceived insult to their integrity, one Latin American delegate after another climbed to the speaker's platform to take issue with the Soviets.[62]

Predictably, Catholic sympathies in this affair were virtually unanimous in support of the United States and of the Chapultepec signatories. Regarding the Argentine question as "an essentially American problem," the Catholic agents at San Francisco praised the unity of the nations of the western hemisphere in behalf of Argentina and criticized the Soviets for grandstanding on the matter.[63] *Commonweal* alone dared offer criticism of the US position and therefore indirectly of the Catholic consultants. The periodical "devoutly wished that our delegates had taken the opposite alternative of seeking to persuade the other Americas to oppose the dispatch of an invitation to Buenos Aires."[64]

In judging US Catholic consultants on the issue of Argentina, one must in hindsight consider that the majority were at the same time regionalists, universalists, and anti-communists. Through their regionalism they strove to foster the principle of a world organization that would welcome all nations of the earth—including pro-Fascist Argentina—into a union for postwar peace. This Catholic brand of universalism, on the other hand, went against the grain of the United Nations allies who were not prepared to admit former enemies, their allies, or even non-combatants into the UN. Finally, Catholic anti-communism was fueled at this time by fears of a Russia that was simultaneously suppressing religious freedom and other liberties in the Balkans, the Baltic, and other borderlands, while championing the same in San Francisco—a fact that was not permitted to clutter the policies of other allied nations. Although *Commonweal* challenged Catholics to "a more highly principled line of action," one can in retrospect envision a limited regionalism, under the aegis of a potent UN universalism, with coequal status for all, preventing the kind of solid-bloc internationalism that would taint the Cold War era.[65]

After a lengthy debate, a vote of the delegations was taken and, with the solid support of the American republics, Argentina's UN membership was decreed. Molotov was able, however, to salvage something from this apparent setback. He did secure US backing for admittance of the two Soviet republics into the UNCIO, a move generally seen as an American peace-offering after the Soviet defeat on Argentina. The Lublin Poles nevertheless received no invitation. Although both sides appeared to have reached a satisfactory compromise, the United States and the Catholic Church would come to realize that they would have to pay a huge price for their first great victory of the Conference. *America,* the Jesuit weekly magazine, however, speaking for most Catholics, was gratified by the entry of Argentina into the world body, since that country could now serve as a standard for the "later admission of other states that had been cool to the war program of the United Nations."[66] This realization was, of course, precisely what unnerved a majority of UNCIO delegates.

Suddenly many delegates, even some from countries that had supported the Argentine bid for UN membership, were disturbed by the recognition that they had allowed a "fascist" regime to be admitted into the "peace-loving" United Nations. Non-Catholic opinion in the United States was likewise disapproving. The State Department was quickly alerted to the international disposition by its delegates at the UNCIO, but it was even more concerned over the attitude within the country. Only an extremely small number of American editorial writers supported the Administration's promotion of Argentina, and a substantial amount of mail was received which violently criticized the decision. Public opinion tended to go on two parallel tracks: shock and anxiety over the acceptance of a fascist government into the "family of democratic nations," and the perception that a Western hemispheric bloc was bound to have adverse effects on US relations with the Russians and with European allies.[67]

The Catholic observers at San Francisco, like the American government itself, had been slow to appreciate the intensity of this national mood. In fact, neither the Catholic Church nor the State Department exhibited any knowledge of these feelings until after the Soviet Union had reaped a great propaganda advantage—even within the United States—as a defender of the United Nations against a fascist threat to future peace. Burke Walsh, for example, was quite surprised by the journalistic reaction.

> I was amazed at the tendency of a considerable number of American newsmen to harshly criticize Stettinius after his speech that brought the Argentine matter to a vote. There seem to be a lot of them with Leftist leanings.[68]

American Catholic judgments on Russia were formed by prewar encounters with atheistic Communism at home and abroad. These preconceived and somewhat fixed notions may explain the myopia of its UN representatives who were caught off guard during the Argentine membership debate. Once that issue was resolved and its ramifications understood, Catholic consultants and correspondents entered into an extensive appraisal of the Soviet presence at San Francisco and determined that it would be a problem, but one that could be dealt with.[69]

It was at this point that the Conference was to undergo a momentous debate on the topic of United Nations membership: a deliberation on the theoretical nature of UN affiliation and of the disposition for participation in the world organization. In the UNCIO discussions that ensued, the Catholic

Church in the United States found itself solidly on one side of the issue.

The Nature Of UN Membership

Chapter III of the Dumbarton Oaks proposals stipulated that membership in the United Nations should be limited to all "peace-loving" states, without defining that term. Once the initial problems of affiliation were settled at the plenary sessions, the fourteen-member Executive Committee was to discuss requirments for participation in the proposed world organization. Many delegations argued their amendments before this committee, but it soon became apparent that there were two major schools of thought on the subject: one favored restricted membership and another advocated universal entry. Thomas Mahony would take an active part in this debate, eloquently championing the "universalist" school at consultant meetings.[70]

Chile advanced a proposal that the United Nations should admit only "peace-loving" states with democratic systems. Although this looked impressive on paper, Mahony was quick to note one glaring inconsistency: Russia and China, two of the "inviting members" of the UNCIO, did not fit into everyone's definition of a democratic state. The Netherlands then submitted that the world body be composed of only "peace loving states which may be expected on account of their institutions and by their international behavior faithfully to observe and carry out international commitments." Mahony felt compelled to remind the American consultants of the weakness of this definition. The United States, in a fit of international misbehavior only a short time before December 7, 1941, had sold Japan materials that that country had used in its invasion of China.[71] Furthermore, Mahony contended, the phrase "international behavior" was being defined by some members to exclude all neutrals and former friends of Axis nations. If this became the accepted interpretation, then Sweden, Ireland, Portugal, Switzerland, and Spain would be excluded.

Mahony then ventured to clarify the vague expression

"peace-loving," but not before he suggested that some nations preferred its ambiguity. The five permanent members of the Security Council had conspicuously made no attempt to amend this part of the Dumbarton proposals. Since the General Assembly could elect new members only "upon recommendation of the Security Council," the Great Powers understood only too well the enormous flexibility they possessed in this respect.[72] Even if the other members of the United Nations sincerely endorsed the term, Mahony went on, it was totally inadequate. Axis Germany and Japan had asserted that their wars were defensive and therefore could theoretically have qualified for membership within the confines of this definition. Most preposterously, he concluded, neutral countries that had not engaged in the war but remained at peace were being indicted by some as "non-peace-loving," since they had not battled to overthrow the Axis.

Although the Philippines tried to refine the argument by substituting "law-abiding" for "peace-loving," Mahony pointed out that the former was only a slight improvement, since this term was almost as indefinite as the latter. With what law was a nation to comply? The natural law? International law? By what definition of international law?[73]

A second school of thought on UN membership was led by Mexico and Brazil, and was composed mainly but not entirely of Latin Americans. It suggested "universal and obligatory" UN association, while skirting the controversy over former enemy participation by placing a temporary restriction on the UN prerogatives of the vanquished states. Mahony championed this interpretation but with a qualification. He recommended to the American delegates and consultants that they support an Australian proposal that stipulated membership for any state "which accepts the obligations of this charter." This was, however, somewhat removed from the traditional Catholic position promoted by Pattee, who wanted no adulteration of the Latin American plan.

In his argument Pattee cited the statement of the Catholic bishops of November 16, 1944. That document maintained that the United Nations should be a universal body, embracing all states, "large and small, strong and weak." All the countries of the world were to be automatically accepted and therefore subject to international law as defined by an organization powerful enough to enforce its will. No state could withdraw from this global community nor could it be expelled.[74]

Outside the Conference, *America* lobbied for this "open-door policy." It stood to reason, its editors proclaimed, that if the new league remained strictly a "United Nations organization," (i.e., a meeting of the conquering belligerents) then the job of bringing about "One World" would be only half completed. If barriers to admission were to linger, then neutral and former-enemy nations would be offended and the world community demoralized. The postwar climate would require a genuinely universal organization, not merely a "long-term coalition of the victorious Powers."[75]

Father Conway and the other authors of *Goals for San Francisco,* the ecumenical study of world organization, had also promoted universal UN membership. They contended that the United Nations Charter should stipulate that the world association had to be open to all states "willing and able to fulfill the obligations" it imposed. Without this, a just and enduring peace was not possible.[76]

In this matter the American Church had taken its cue from twentieth-century papal pronouncements that strongly endorsed a universal approach to membership in any world organization. After World War I Benedict XV urged that all countries be granted membership in the League of Nations, which was to be a "family of peoples, calculated both to maintain their own independence and safeguard the order of human society."[77] Guido Gonella, in an article for the NCWC News Service series, "Catholic Spotlights," claimed that another pope, Pius XII, was dissatisfied with the limitations imposed on the international body by the definitions given to the phrase "peace-loving nations." Pius was concerned that these interpretations pertained only to the allied states. Were not those who had maintained a "dignified neutrality" also able to contribute to world order? And what of those peoples who had been forced to side with the Axis cause? The new plans for the reconstruction of the world demanded the cooperation of all persons of good will.[78]

Mahony and Pattee worked dilgently to put over their moderately different notions of universal UN membership, and in the end the US delegation would vote to admit some neutral nations into the world organization. Catholic neutrals, however, did not fare well at all. For various reasons the Conference finally refused to admit Ireland, Portugal, Spain, and the now-nonaligned Italy into the world body. As for the principle of universal UN membership, none of the Big Three was as yet willing to sanction admittance of certain governments that had in any way been on the "wrong side" during the war.

As the membership debate progressed, it became evident that there was growing sentiment for the exclusion of governments that had participated in any way in the fascist war effort or were closely allied to the Axis powers. This feeling was only intensified in the aftermath of the Argentine imbroglio, as more and more delegates came to regret their support for the admission of a fascist state into the UN. Under the pressure of liberal public opinion, many delegates were anxious to safeguard the United Nations as an association of "peace-loving" states.

This absolute dichotomy between "peace-loving" nations and "fascist" states was brought to the fore when Franco's Spain sought admission as a charter member of the security organization. Accordingly, the NCWC's efforts in favor of universal membership were now directed toward the dispute over application of the most controversial Catholic nation on earth.

Franco And The United Nations

On April 20, 1945, *The New York Times* recounted the circuitous journey of an exile group calling itself the Spanish Committee of Liberation. Traveling to the UN Conference by way of Mexico and various American cities, the panel was armed with a declaration attacking the government of Francisco Franco. The authors of the document urged the UNCIO to withdraw recognition of the Franco regime—which, in their opinion, had unadvisedly had been granted neutral status by the Allies. They said that this was the only way to expedite the re-establishment of democracy in Spain.

The delegation, which had no formal standing at the Conference, consisted of four former Cabinet members in the Loyalist government. Hoping to acquaint the citizens of North America with the situation in Spain, the republican politicians held press conferences at which they recited evidence of the collaboration of the Franco Government with the Axis powers, together with a plea for the repudiation of the Falangists, who they claimed were rejected by fully 90 percent of the Spanish people. "It would be too terrible to believe," the delegates proclaimed, "that the United Nations . . . would deny to the Spanish people the moral and political support to which they are entitled in their efforts to achieve their freedom on the basis of democracy and brotherhood."[79]

The disclosure that the UNCIO had the ability to destroy Spanish fascism merely by a formal withdrawal of diplomatic recognition captured the imagination of various left-wing American associations that had long explored methods for the non-violent overthrow of *El Caudillo*. The American Committee for a Free Spanish Republic had underwritten the Spanish republicans' tour, but their most important allies were to be found among the well-funded Friends of the Spanish Republic.[80]

Styling itself a "committee of outstanding Americans," this group could irrefutably boast an impressive membership list: Helen Gahaghan Douglas, Reinhold Niebuhr, Leonard Bernstein, Theodore Dreiser, Albert Einstein, Mrs. Marshall Field, Groucho Marx, Eugene O'Neill, and Drew Pearson were only the most illustrious figures in a lengthy roster of benefactors. Fervently advocating the establishment of a world security organization dedicated to freedom and democracy for all peoples, the Friends of the Spanish Republic submitted that a fundamental step in this endeavor was the barring of "Franco Spain" from the United Nations.[81]

Accordingly, on April 24, 1945, the day before the official

opening of the UNCIO, the committee released a twenty-one page memorandum entitled *The Defeat of the Spanish Republic,* which documented Franco's alleged collaboration with the Axis powers. Vividly tracing the Spanish leader's insidious transformation from a dictatorial wolf, whose defeat of a democratic government was the first step in the fascist drive for world domination, to a seemingly neutral lamb bleating for a seat at the Allied peace table, the text admonished the UN not to allow the Falangists to profit from a victory achieved by Allied blood. Even as the Conference was beginning its work for peace, the paper rehearsed, "14,000 Nazi agents," abetted by Spain, were transferring the accumulated wealth of a decade of Nazi rampage to an undisclosed Latin American location to augment an already extensive cache to fund World War III. To accept Franco's "eleventh hour overtures on their face value," they exhorted, "would be to betray the principles for which this war was fought."[82]

Lest anyone at the United Nations Conference become immobilized with fear at the thought of this satanic fascist conspiracy and thereby neglect the original intent of the memorandum—to ostracize the Falangists—the Friends of the Spanish Republic thought it judicious to release a subsequent document. On April 30, *The Case Against the Admission of Franco Spain,* substantially lowered the Nazi agent tally to 5,000 and focused on perfidious Spanish efforts to secure membership in the world organization.[83]

However ridiculous some of this anti-Franco propaganda now seems, it would be erroneous to assume it was ineffectual. It was, in fact, especially convincing at the UNCIO, which had to deal early on with another allegedly fascist state's admission to the Conference. By early May Richard Pattee was relating to US Catholic leaders, who had long defended Franco, that little by little Spanish membership was becoming a "real issue" in San Francisco. On May 10 William Shirer, chairman of the Friends of the Spanish Republic, had stated that any nation that had given military aid to the Axis after 1939, materially or through personnel, should be excluded from membership.

Pattee understood from his sources that several nations were willing to present this petition to the admissions committee.[84]

By the middle of May Father Conway—who like Pattee was "playing catch-up" on this issue—vainly attempted to convince the American delegates, and any consultants who would listen, that the western democracies had nothing to fear from Spain and that the United States should oppose an anticipated Mexican amendment that somewhat echoed Shirer's membership formula. Mexico, which had earlier proposed a universal-membership amendment to the UN Charter, now submitted a resolution even more restrictive than Shirer's proposal, since it excluded from UN participation all regimes set up with the aid of the Axis. Conway claimed that the only reason for this Mexican motion was that the chairman of its delegation had been censured by Soviet-inspired leftists in his country for supporting Argentina's bid for charter membership. Archbishop Stritch, the chairman of the Bishops' Peace Committee, concurred with Conway that it was a cardinal principle in Soviet foreign policy to "get Franco," but he saw little that could be done to stem the frenzy of the anti-fascist wave at the Conference."[85]

As the vote on Spanish membership drew closer, Pattee strove desperately to bring some sanity to the debate. He declared to the American delegates and consultants that once again the problem of terminology was playing havoc with international relations. Everyone at the Conference stubbornly persisted in believing that the war had been fought for "democracy," which was ridiculous since it was perfectly obvious that the UN did not constitute a democratic bloc. Democracy and fascism had become frivolous terms and the left was profiting from this carelessness. Capitalism, monarchism, and conservatism were dubbed Fascist while liberalism, radicalism, communism, socialism, and all that passed for progressive had taken on the mantle of democracy.[86]

The Soviets were now being seen, even by many persons attached to the American delegation, as belonging to a system that was at least reasonably patterned on the idea of democracy. Furthermore, the popular press directed most of its barbs at conservative Catholic countries that remained neutral during the war: Ireland, Portugal, Spain and Argentina, for example, while socialist Sweden received little criticism, although it had been "forced" into a close collaboration with Germany. This was postwar hysteria and a disservice to clear thinking. Pattee believed, however, that it was tendentious and symptomatic "of the extremely dangerous lengths to which many elements in our population are going to produce confusion and perpetuate hatreds in the name of simon-pure democracy."[87]

It is interesting to note that Thomas Mahony played no part in the debate over the admission of Spain as a Charter member of the UN. His reasons are unknown, since he chose not to reveal them. Even from his advocacy of entry of all "law-abiding" states into the world organization, we do not know his position on the Franco regime, since he never directly categorized it under this label. It might not be stretching credulity, therefore, to conclude that at a moment when the entire American Catholic establishment was roused in support of Spain, the silence of one of its chief spokesmen indicates at least an ambivalence toward that nation.[88]

In the end, however, all Catholic exertions on behalf of Spanish membership were fruitless. Buckling under to intensive lobbying, even the American delegation lined up against Spain. In a climactic last-minute announcement, the United States had declared its "complete accord" with the Mexican amendment and a relieved and exonerated State Department was subsequently deluged with congratulatory telegrams. On June 18, 1945, the UNCIO's Commission on Membership declared that all governments launched with the help of Axis military force were banned from the world organization.[89]

Nevertheless, no one was fooled by this general characterization. The "liberal" *New York Post,* capturing the essence of the triumph in its full-page headline, "Parley Bars Franco Spain From World Organization," declared that the judgment had "brought down the house."[90] On this "dynamic" note, the last membership controversy of the UNCIO came to an end. It also marked a major defeat for the Church in its bid to Catholicize the United Nations.

In surveying the battlefield after the various skirmishes over UN membership, the Catholic Church could not have been pleased with the progress of its crusade for a sympathetic security conference. Its only clear victory, Argentina, had turned out to be a propaganda defeat that directly resulted in Catholic Spain's failure to gain admittance into the United Nations Organization. The Soviets, on the other hand, obtained admission of three communist governments, including the Polish Lublin Committee. Moreover, by its resistance to "fascist" membership in the world body, Russia, the great enemy of Catholicism, portrayed itself as the champion of "peace-loving" peoples everywhere. The Church had now to rethink its strategy in light of Molotov's initial triumphs at San Francisco.

Notes

1. RG 59a 1980, Folder 3, Joseph C. Grew to Mrs. Mary Catlin, [D.C.], March 27, 1945, copy.
2. "Pontifical Mass in Civic Auditorium," *The (San Francisco) Monitor,* April 28, 1945, p. 1.
3. Ibid.
4. ANCWC 13c, "15,000 at Pontifical Mass in San Francisco . . .," Burke Walsh, April 30, 1945.
5. "Mass for Parley Attended by 10,000," *The New York Times,* April 30, 1945, p. 10.
6. Fifty nations would eventually attend the Conference.
7. "15,000 at Pontifical Mass. . . ."
8. ANCWC 13c, "Catholics Number Nearly Half of Delegates at Conference," Burke Walsh, May 7, 1945.
9. Ibid.
10. ANCWC 13c, "Scope of Catholic Participation in San Francisco Conference Analyzed by NCWC Observer," April 30, 1945.
11. Ibid.
12. Ibid., p. 2.
13. "Catholics Number Nearly Half of Delegates. . . ."
14. "Assurances Given to Consultants," *The New York Times,* April 26, 1945, p. 12.

15. AMU Series 6, Box 1, "Report to You From San Francisco," *N.C.C.W. Monthly Message,* June, 1945.

16. ANCWC 11, Pattee to Carroll, [San Francisco], May 15, 1945.

17. Ibid.

18. Neil Middleton, ed., *The I.F. Stone Weekly Reader* (New York: Vintage Books, 1973), p. xi.

19. ANCWC 11, Walsh to Carroll, [San Francisco], April 26, 1945.

20. Ibid.

21. At this time, even within Catholic ranks, opinions on Russia varied widely. In his memoirs Fulton J. Sheen reveals that even the NCWC was sensitive on this issue.

Because of the position Sheen took concerning Russia during the war, his radio talks were carefully monitored. Someone stationed in the booth would cut him off whenever he deviated from the popular position that Russia was a democracy. He sent in a manuscript for one broadcast that contained the line, 'Poland was crucified between two thieves—the Nazis and the Soviets.' He received a telegram from the Bishops' Conference asking him not to say that, because he was implying that one of the thieves was Russia. He answered the telegram by suggesting, 'How would it be to call Russia the 'good' thief?' (*Treasure in Clay,* p. 188)

22. *The Years of Western Domination,* p. 38. In fact, France had agreed to serve as a sponsoring power, but only if French amendments to the Dumbarton Oaks proposals were used as a basis for the Conference on an equal footing with those proposals themselves. The Four were unwilling to concede this, dreading that other countries would ask for comparable treatment. Although France did not become a sponsoring power, soon after the opening of the Conference, its delegation was granted equal status by the other four Great Powers.

23. RG 59b, Folder 5, Press Release, March 5, 1945.

24. The countries qualifying for invitations were those nations that had declared war on Germany or Japan by March 1, 1945 (*Yearbook of the United Nations,* 1946 [New York: United Nations Organization, 1947], p. 47).

25. ANCWC 15, "The Story of the United Nations . . .," p. 9.

26. RG 59a 1991, Folder 1, J. Wesley Jones to Anthony J. Mallozzi, [D.C.], April 23, 1945. "It should, however, be understood that Italian exclusion from the San Francisco Conference does not mean that Italy will for that reason be debarred from participation in the world security organization or from achieving her proper position among the nations. This government's policy has been to work constantly to bring Italy back to full membership in the international community. Much progress has already been made and there is no reason to believe that progress will be arrested."

27. ANCWC 15, Conway to Carroll, "Some Interests of the Church Which May be Involved in the S. F. Conference," [D.C.], April

11, 1945.

28. *The Years of Western Domination,* p. 39. Denmark, unlike most western European nations that had been conquered by the Axis, had no government-in-exile sanctioned by the Allies. However, when Copenhagen was liberated during the Conference, a Danish delegation was immediately admitted to the UNCIO.

29. The nations on this list were: Australia, Belgium, Bolivia, Brazil, Canada, Chile, Columbia, Costa Rica, Cuba, Czechoslovakia, The Dominican Republic, Ecuador, Egypt, Ethiopia, Greece, Guatemala, Haiti, Honduras, India, Iran, Iraq, Liberia, Luxembourg, Mexico, The Netherlands, New Zealand, Nicaragua, Norway, Panama, Paraguay, Peru, The Philippines, El Salvador, Saudi Arabia, Turkey, South Africa, Uruguay, Venezuela and Yugoslavia.

30. RG 59b, Folder 5, Press Release, March 5, 1945.

31. "The opening plenary sessions in the big Opera House were impressive and moving. We felt we were taking part in a great historical event. It is not easy now (1954) to think oneself back into that mood of inspiration and hope, but it was very real" (Virginia C. Gildersleeve, *Many a Good Crusade* [New York: Columbia University Press, 1954], p. 327).

32. President Franklin D. Roosevelt died on April 12, 1945, at Warm Springs, Georgia. Stricken by a cerebral hemorrhage, FDR was 63 years old. He was succeeded by his vice president, Harry S. Truman (Ted Morgan, *FDR: A Biography* [New York: Simon and Schuster, 1985] pp. 763–65).

33. "The Story of the United Nations Conference . . . ," p. 17.

34. *The Years of Western Domination,* pp. 42–43. The work of the Conference was divided among four main commissions: on general principles, on the General Assembly, on the Security Council, and on judicial organization. These were committees of the whole, on which every delegation was represented, and they did much of the actual work of the Conference.

35. Norman Davies, *The Heart of Europe: A Short History of Poland* (Oxford: Oxford University Press, 1987), p. 76.

36. ANCWC 13c, "Russia Remains a Riddle," Richard Pattee, May 7, 1945, p. 2.

37. RG 59a 1980, Folder 3, Department of State to American Embassy, London, [D.C.], March 15, 1945.

38. RG 59a 1980, Folder 3, Joseph C. Grew to Representative Joseph F. Ryter, [D.C.]., March 27, 1945, copy.

39. *E.R. Stettinius, Jr.,* p. 69.

40. RG 59a 1996, Folder 4, Memorandum of Conversation between Stettinius, Molotov, Harriman, Gromyko et al., April 24, 1945, p. 2.

41. Ibid., pp. 4–5.

42. According to William H. McNeill, Molotov's accusation was ironic. McNeill contends that, up to this time, even on the thorny question of Poland, the rights and wrongs of decisions reached took second place in the eyes of the American negotiators to their concern for the effect on the UNCIO if Russia were to become antagonistic (William H. McNeill, *America, Britain, and Russia: Their Co-operation and Conflict, 1941–1946,* [London: The Survey of International Affairs, 1953; reprint ed., New York: Johnson Reprint Corporation, 1970], p. 532).

43. *The Heart of Europe,* p. 74.

44. ANCWC 15, J. Ciechanowski to Carroll, [D.C.], April 28, 1945.

45. ANCWC 13c, "Polish Government in London Asks Security Parley Consider Carefully Claims of Justice," April 30, 1945.

46. ANCWC 15, Carroll to Ciechanowski, [D.C.], April 30, 1945, copy.

47. "Thirty More U.S. Aides at San Francisco."

48. ANCWC 13c, "Peace of World Demands Independent Poland, Archbishop Mitty Warns," Burke Walsh, May 6, 1945.

49. It should be noted that Senator Vandenberg represented the state of Michigan, where many Polish immigrants had settled ("Senator Vandenberg Pledges Support to Proposals in Statements of US Bishops," *The (San Francisco) Monitor,* April 28, 1945, p. 1).

50. ANCWC 13b, "Freedom for Poland," Oscar Halecki, April 17, 1945.

51. AMU, Series 6, Box 1, "Observations On the San Francisco Conference," Thomas H. Mahony, May 3, 1945, p. 2.; ANCWC 11, Conway to Carroll, [San Francisco], May 11, 1945.

52. *The Heart of Europe,* p. 79. This regime, with its famous promise of "free and unfettered" elections, lasted only until July of 1947.

53. *The Years of Western Domination,* pp. 33–35. At first Stalin proposed that each of the sixteen Soviet republics be granted UN membership. Roosevelt, who initially responded to this suggestion by vowing to demand seats for the forty-eight American states, was eventually persuaded by the Russian leader to accept a compromise: membership for the White Russian and Ukrainian Republics. Stalin achieved this by his remarkably frank admission to FDR that his position within the Communist Party on this issue was a weak one and that he needed a concession.

54. RG 59a 1991, Folder 3, Memorandum for the President from Stettinius, April 13, 1945.

55. *The Years of Western Domination,* p. 35.

56. Vandenberg is on record as stating that President Truman was initially opposed to the admission of Argentina to the UNCIO.

(Arthur H. Vandenberg, ed., *The Private Papers of Senator Vandenberg* [Boston: Houghton Mifflin, 1952], p. 178).

57. ANCWC 13c, "America Found Solidified by Soviet Stand Against Admission of Argentina," Richard Pattee, May 7, 1945, p. 1.

58. Under the pliant presidency of General Edelmiro Farrell, Colonel Peron held the office of vice president as well as the portfolios of War Minister and Secretary of Labor and Social Welfare. He also had secured widespread support within most ranks of the military (Joseph A. Page, *Peron: A Biography* [New York: Random House, 1983], p. 87).

59. Ibid., p. 90.

60. George Doherty, "La Grande Argentina," *Commonweal,* 42 (January 12, 1945): 324.

61. Ibid.

62. ANCWC 11, "Report on the United Nations Conference on International Organization convened at San Francisco on April 25, 1945," Richard Pattee, June 18, 1945, p. 8.

63. "Observations on the San Francisco Conference," p. 2.

64. "America's Bloc," *Commonweal,* 42 (May 25, 1945): 131.

65. Ibid.

66. RG 59f, Box 22: "The United Nations Conference as Reported by US Press and Radio Comment," p. 3; Robert A. Graham, "The Open-Door Policy in World Charter," *America* 73 (May 19, 1945): 132.

67. RG 59i, Box 2, Folder: April 14--May, 1945, Everett V. Stonequist to MacLeish, [D.C.], May 12, 1945. p. 1.

68. ANCWC 11, Walsh to Carroll, [San Francisco], May 3, 1945.

69. This theory will be considered in the next chapter.

70. AMU, Series 6, Box 1, "Observations on the International Conference VI," Thomas H. Mahony, May 12, 1945, p. 1.

71. Ibid.

72. Ibid., p. 2.

73. Ibid.

74. AAC 2835H, the Reverend George G. Higgins to Stritch, [D.C.], April 13, 1945.

75. "Open-Door Policy in World Charter," pp. 132–33.

76. ANCWC 15, Conway to Carroll, [D.C.], March 27, 1945, p. 2.

77. "Observations on the International Conference VI," p. 2.

78. ANCWC 13b, "Pope Declares Neutrals Should be Included in World Organization for Peace," Guido Gonella, April 9, 1945, p. 3.

79. "Delegation Asks Ouster of Franco," *The New York Times,* April 20, 1945, p. 11.

80. Ibid.

81. ANCWC 15, William H. Shirer to "The United Nations Conference," April 24, 1945.

82. ANCWC 15, *The Defeat of the Spanish Republic,* April 24, 1945, p. 21.

83. ANCWC 15, *The Case Against the Admission of Franco Spain to the World Organization,* April 30, 1945, p. 3.

84. ANCWC 11, Pattee to Carroll, [San Francisco], May 11, 1945.

85. ANCWC 11, Conway to Carroll, [San Francisco], May 22, 1945, p. 1; AAC 2968C, Stritch to Carroll, [Chicago], January 30, 1946.

86. ANCWC 11, "Some Observations on the San Francisco Conference of the United Nations and the International Situation Since that Date," Richard Pattee, p. 1.

87. Ibid., p. 2.

88. "Observations on the International Conference VI," p. 1.

89. RG 59e, Box 23, Folder 3, Daily Summary of Opinion Studies, June 20, 1945, p. 2.

90. Ibid.

CHAPTER V

The Superpowers at the Conference

Catholic Views on Russia Reconsidered

Even when the NCWC looked ahead to the United Nations Conference on International Organization, it was preoccupied with a parallel concern. Fearful of the resurgence of world Communism in reaction to the horrors of a "fascist war," the Catholic Church in the United States, taking its lead from papal pronouncements, insisted on confronting the seemingly gullible democracies with what it considered to be some embarrassing facts about their loyal ally, Russia. The hierarchy's statement of April 1945 sounded the alarm.

> We have to reckon with the active, cleverly organized and directed opposition of Marxian totalitarianism to genuine democracy. This system herds the masses under dictatorial leadership, insults the intelligence with its propaganda and controlled press, and tyrannically violates innate human rights. Against it, genuine democracy must constantly be on guard, quick to detect and penetrate its camouflage.[1]

Not satisfied with mere words, the NCWC had every intention of uncovering and exposing Communism wherever it was to be found, especially in the US. Consequently, in November of 1945, the hierarchy commissioned a highly classified study of domestic Communist infiltration. For the task, it chose the Reverend John F. Cronin of St. Mary's Seminary in Baltimore.[2] This inquiry was under the supervision of Bishop Karl J. Alter of Toledo, episcopal chairman of the Social Action Department of the Catholic Conference.[3]

Although his report would not be completed until the end of 1945, Fr. Cronin informed the bishops that he intended to uncover the indigenous organization and structure of Soviet communism within the United States and reveal its alarmingly pervasive encroachment on the country's democratic structure. For this purpose he proposed to concentrate on its inroads into labor, "Negro societies," youth, government, foreign language groups, media, liberal organizations, and religious associations. Believing Cronin's preliminary analysis to be "accurate and well-balanced," the hierarchy gave him every support necessary for carrying out such an extensive investigation.[4]

In anticipating the San Francisco parley, therefore, the leadership of the Catholic Church in the United States was skeptical from the outset that anything of note would be achieved in the matter of peace by a world security organization that had the Soviet Union as one of its founding members. Nonetheless it did consider that a constructive reevaluation of international Soviet influence and the Catholic stance on the subject could be useful.[5]

As the Conference began, the NCWC News Service undertook an analysis of Soviet motives with regard to the United Nations. N.S. Timasheff, for instance, a Russian emigré professor in Fordham University's Department of Political Philosophy and Social Science, claimed that Russia did not want the UNCIO to fail, but it did fear isolation within that organization due to its political ideology, which was incompatible with those of the majority. For this reason the Soviets were demanding maximum Security Council veto power and hoped to secure as many votes as possible in the General Assembly.[6]

Timasheff explained that the Soviet Union did not trust the security organization to satisfy its needs for a first line of defense. For that reason it was setting up a buffer zone of eastern European states and developing bilateral coalitions to counter future German aggression. Despite all these suspicions as well as Soviet dislike for the other states in the UN, Timasheff predicted that the Russian people's desire for peace would compel their leaders to join the international organization in order to strengthen their nation's position and prevent world differences from once again reaching the breaking point.[7]

After the debate on the question of Argentine admission to the United Nations, Catholic observers at San Francisco began an examination of Soviet designs. Richard Pattee speculated, with the encouragement of several delegates from Latin America, that there were five primary reasons for Russian behavior at the Conference. Obstructionism was the key Soviet motive, he observed; it had long been a Kremlin ploy to create difficulties at the start of international discussions so that opponents would be thrown off balance. A consensus of the delegates from the western-hemisphere had it that this was again being employed in San Francisco by Stalin's deputies.[8]

Another seemingly indispensable Soviet tactic was the introduction of a fictitious issue into the proceedings so as to exact favorable concessions from other nations. Disappointing no one in this regard, Pattee reported, Molotov acted shamelessly during the Argentine-membership debate by unearthing the specter of an American fascist threat to global peace. On the other hand, general Russian ineptitude was not to be dismissed as an explanation for Soviet conduct, since there had been few recent opportunities for the Russians to participate in diplomatic conferences of the magnitude of the UNCIO. Finally, but not to be forgotten, were Communist propaganda techniques and even a sincere motivation: genuine anxiety over the resurgence of fascism.[9]

In conclusion, although the NCWC consultant thought that there were no intrinsic merits to Russia's case in the matter of Argentina, it had in fact achieved many of its goals in this controversy. For example, the Soviets were successful in correctly pointing out the existence of an American bloc of states and thereby justifying, at least in their own minds, the creation of a sphere of influence in another part of the world. In spite of the Soviet delegation's obvious, self-serving use of the UN Conference so far, Pattee believed that the United States should evaluate potential dangers to the postwar peace and accordingly seek satisfactory relations with the Soviet Union, but not at the price of a reunciation of principles.[10]

Father Conway also probed the speciousness of Molotov's reasoning with regard to Argentina. He was particularly unimpressed with the Foreign Minister's attempt to canonize the sufferings of the Polish people—most of which were presently being caused by the Soviets—in order to contrast the supposed fascism of Argentina and thereby win UN Charter membership for the Communist Poles.

Conway accepted Pattee's assumption that the Soviets were building a bloc both in eastern Europe and at the United Nations. With the inclusion of two other Russian Republics, they could now count on five votes in San Francisco, since Czechoslovakia and Yugoslavia consistently sustained Kremlin policies at the early UN sessions.[11]

Conway, however, had to give Molotov his due, since the wily Foreign Minister accurately assessed the power of the United States coalition. Even the most unbiased observers at the Conference numbered twenty-three sure votes for any American initiative. Up to that time the twenty Latin American states, with Liberia and the Commonwealth of the Philippines, had unwaveringly cooperated with US strategy. It was likewise useless to whine that the Russians had forced two of their not-so-autonomous republics on the United Nations, since the Commonwealth of the Philippines had been granted entrance into the world organization through the good offices of the United States, even though America had yet to grant it independence.[12]

Thomas H. Mahony also had some thoughts on the supposed Russian enigma. Mahony, by now a frequent witness to the complications that Molotov's polemics could create, theorized that a very serious problem was developing. He wondered just how far concessions by the democracies would go in order to prevent a Russian walkout from San Francisco. Asserting that the Soviet Union knew it needed the Conference more than the Conference needed it, the CAIP observer argued that Stalin craved the advantage of collective security, even if just to foster his own aims. Hence Mahony counselled that the United Nations should not render itself impotent by bowing to Soviet demands but it should still look to agreement with all the states in the organization, including Russia, for achieving an ethical world order.[13]

Mahony did not deem Russia quite as paradoxical as many correspondents had painted her. He was convinced that, as a people, the Russians suffered from a national inferiority complex, a fact perpetually on display with Molotov's harping on Soviet equality with the other great powers and his persistent efforts on behalf of the selection of four coequal Conference chairmen. Thus Mahony agreed with *America* that Molotov's "vituperations" in this matter were the tantrums of a seemingly robust and self-assured regime that had a tinge of self-doubt.[14] Finally, he believed that the Soviet Union's attitude toward the UNCIO was condescending but also understandable in view of its experience with the League of Nations, which had refused prior to World War II to listen to Soviet warnings about the Nazi threat. Not only had it ignored her pleas for action, but the League had summarily expelled the Soviet Union when she invaded Finland at the beginning of the war.

Mahony agreed with both Pattee and Conway that Russia feared being "fenced in" by democratic institutions and by the power of the US bloc manifested in the opening days of the Conference. Concluding that the Soviet Union would be a problem at San Francisco, he spoke for all Catholic observers on the scene when he contended that, in spite of everything, the Russians could be dealt with.[15]

The "Soviet Problem"

As agents of the Catholic Church in the United States were conducting their sober analysis of the Soviet Union, they became aware of a change of attitude toward that country on the part of the other Big Powers. While no one would have been startled by Archbishop Samuel Stritch's anti-Soviet comments contained in a May 9 letter to Monsignor Carroll, in which he expounded the conventional Catholic opinion that "Russia will act only on the grounds of expediency and will unilaterally interpret for itself the demands of expediency," the Catholic observers at San Francisco were somewhat surprised to find that this conviction was apparently endorsed by more and more delegations as the UN Charter discussions progressed.[16]

Only four days after Stritch's private remarks, Thomas Mahony sent a report to the headquarters of the Catholic Association for International Peace, in which he outlined what he called a "gradual hardening toward Russia" at the UNCIO. From his meetings with various delegates and consultants, he believed that events in San Francisco and on the world scene caused many states to become impatient with Soviet demands, even while they accepted all of the excuses proffered for its international misbehavior.[17]

Mahony explained that much had changed on the world scene since invitations to the UNCIO had been sent out. Germany's armed forces were in complete disarray and therefore the need for Russian assistance seemed far less compelling now than at the end of 1944. Furthermore, the United States and its allies, the United Kingdom and China among others, had achieved tremendous success against Japan in the Pacific theater without an ounce of Soviet assistance. On the American front, meanwhile, Roosevelt had died and Truman, who seemed less confident than his predecessor that he could control the Russian bear, had curtailed Lend-Lease to the USSR and halted discussions on its postwar credit.

With the German threat practically eliminated, therefore, Russia's position in the world was undergoing a metamorphosis. Because of its earlier role as an accessory to Axis aggression, the Soviet Union was now feared by some as a potential maritime menace to Great Britain and as a continental peril as well, because of extension of its sphere of influence in, or absorption of, Bulgaria, Rumania, Czechoslovakia, Yugoslavia, Hungary, Austria, Poland, East Prussia, Estonia, Latvia, and Lithuania. In addition, it was increasingly criticized for its support of leftist political parties in Greece, Belgium, Italy, and France. Finally, although it had few reliable votes at the United

Nations, some delegates saw an ominous portent in Russia's insistence on the inclusion of two of its republics in the world organization.[18]

Mahony capped his report by stating that he had just heard Churchill's radio address of May 13, in which the British prime minister confirmed that he did not intend to permit "totalitarian or police governments" to replace German despotism in Europe. The CAIP consultant thought that Britain's "hardening" toward the Soviets was a reflection of America's own drift in that direction.[19]

As early as January of 1944 the State Department informed the NCWC General Secretary, Michael J. Ready, that all relations with the Russians were extremely difficult. Since Molotov and his assistants were arbitrary in their methods of diplomacy, American intermediaries were instructed to show a firm hand in any dialogue with the Kremlin or all would be lost. The Administration still professed to believe, nonetheless, in the sincerity of Soviet declarations on the necessity for international cooperation in order to achieve a true peace.[20] By late April of 1945, however, indications were that the United States no longer credited these Soviet protestations. Many observers at the Conference—including the Catholic consultants and correspondents—now assumed that the US was leading the opposition to the Soviet Union's expansionist policy in Europe and shifting its policy from retreat in the face of Soviet demands to selective diplomatic contention.[21]

Catholic rebellion against this stance was centered in the weeklies *Commonweal* and *America* as well as in a few scholarly periodicals. *Commonweal* urged that a *modus vivendi* be worked out between the Soviets and the Western allies. "Without equilibrium," it editorialized, "we cannot accomplish that which it is our duty to try to accomplish." Elaborating on this, *Commonweal* quoted an article in the *Historical Bulletin* of May in 1945 by Jesuit George Dunne:

> The world which will emerge from this war and from the peace settlement, will in many respects fall short of the ideal

of perfect justice: not only because of Poland and the Baltic States, but because of the American Negro and the tens of thousands of Americans with insufficient health care and food; and because of the tens of thousands of political prisoners languishing in Franco's jails.[22]

Even that unyielding foe of Communism, John LaFarge, S.J., struck a similar note in an article in *America* entitled "Russia Challenges the Allied Conscience."[23] A genuinely "liberal and democratic-minded" West had no need to appease the Russians or go to war with them. If the democracies could provide sound government at home and in Europe, and if they could solve their own basic social problems, then no "Red Danger" need be feared. LaFarge concluded by stating that Soviet successes in Eastern Europe "were gained not so much because of inherent Russian strength but because of the weakness, political, social or ideological, of the countries in which the Moscow methods had triumphed."[24] Although his views were to be proved sorely wrong, LaFarge's opinion did epitomize the unofficial liberal Catholic consensus at the time of the San Francisco Conference.

The Conference Presidency

The first direct confrontation between the two postwar superpowers had occurred even before the early UNCIO controversies over Argentina or Poland. In a memorandum prepared for President Truman on the UNCIO, dated April 13, 1945, the day after FDR's death, Secretary of State Stettinius informed him that the United States had a problem with Russia over the presidency of the Conference.[25] Because President Roosevelt had instructed him to maintain the US position that one "responsible chairman" was sufficient for the Conference, Stettinius displayed the new "hardened attitude" toward the Russians with his opposition to Molotov's demand that the heads of the four sponsoring delegations should serve as rotating cochairmen. "We feel that if we yield to the Soviet position it might set an undesirable precedent for future Conferences and even for the organization itself."[26] In this, the new Chief-Executive fully concurred.[27]

The Soviets, however, were not ready to voluntarily relinquish their new equal status with America at a global conference on the government of the postwar world. At the same April 24 encounter at which Stettinius and Molotov discussed the topics of Poland and the two Russian republics, the Soviet Foreign Minister insisted that the issue of the Conference presidency be the leading question on the agenda. Asserting that four chairmen from the sponsoring powers would serve as a visible symbol of Great Power equality, he refused to back down in the face of US obstinacy. Once again, Stettinius patiently, if somewhat condescendingly, attempted to explain to Molotov the American rationale on this issue. For the first time, nonetheless, he held out the possibility of a US concession whereby all four nations would share in an honorary chairmanship in the absence of the permanent chairman. Disregarding this attempt at appeasement, the Soviet Foreign Minister inquired whether this meant that the United States had no intention of reaching an authentic agreement on the issue. The Secretary informed him that he was only following instructions and that the matter would have to be decided by the Steering Committee, a grouping composed of the chairmen of all delegations.[28]

It was at the end of this particular meeting that the Soviet Foreign Minister made the sagacious remark that he noted a change in the atmosphere between the US and the USSR since the Yalta discussions. Pattee may not have had as privileged a vantage point as Molotov, but by the second day of the Conference the NCWC consultant was likewise able to discern a distinct chill in superpower relations. Not surprisingly, this occurred as the Soviet Union was making its first bid to exert a dominant influence at the UNCIO.[29]

This Russian stratagem came in the Steering Committee in reaction to a motion by Ezequiel Padilla, Minister of Foreign Affairs of Mexico, which would have designated Stettinius as permanent Conference president. Pattee asserted that the recommendation would have passed without comment if Molotov had not risen to declare that the fundamental principle of equality of the sponsoring powers was endangered. In making his statement he also found time to accuse Padilla of being a willing tool of the international interests of the United States. With this speech what had been a private disagreement among the Big Three became a controversial Conference topic.[30]

The chairman of the French delegation, purporting to have no bias in the matter, in spite of the fact that his country had recently concluded a bilateral security pact with the Soviet Union, now submitted a counter proposal that each of the foreign ministers of the sponsoring powers be given a turn at the presidency. Since this approach was little more than a rehash of the Soviet position, the committee's final decision to accept the French suggestion was, in Pattee's words, "a hit in the opening inning" for the Soviets. It also revealed an initial Soviet strategy at San Francisco: firm adherence to a position in the hope that the Conference would sustain it.[31]

Father Conway saw this squabble in a somewhat different light. In his view both the United States and the Soviet Union were being intransigent over a minor matter. While certainly not ignoring that "the stocky, broad-faced man from Russia" was trying to keep the Conference off balance by his tactics, Conway appreciated the counsel of Anthony Eden, the chairman of the British delegation, who had acted as an informal moderator in the discussions on this procedural matter. The delegates were in San Francisco to set up a world organization, the British Foreign Secretary reflected. If they worked efficiently, and focused on the central issues, they would be able to achieve this. Taking Eden's advice, a majority of the delegates decided accordingly not to press the issue and acceded to the Russians in this case.[32]

This controversy in the UNCIO plenary sessions was quickly written off by most observers, such as Conway, as nothing more than a "lesser crisis." According to this theory Russia was branded, correctly or otherwise, as a brute and a bully, willing to pout its way through the Conference; its behavior, however, was not to be interpreted as an affront to the United States, a personal insult to Secretary of State Stettinius, or the harbinger of a more serious superpower schism.[33]

Richard Pattee, on the other hand, was considerably more astute in his evaluation. His familiarity with the Latin American representatives gave him a different perspective. Intensely involved in the activities of the nineteen Latin American delegations, he could see that they had a darker view of this "minor" altercation. The whole issue of the "presidency crisis," at least for the Latin Americans, revolved around the fact that their initial motion at the Conference had been proposed by a small nation, Mexico, in alliance with the United States, a large state, and that motion had been summarily rejected by another large (and unfriendly) nation, Russia. This only confirmed all the anti-Soviet anxieties that these delegates had brought to San Francisco and reaffirmed their intention of collaborating with the US.[34]

American Continentalism Versus European Nationalism

On April 21, 1945, four days before the opening session of the UNCIO, a telling scene was played out at the San Francisco Municipal Airport. A dozen Latin American Ambassadors arriving for the Conference were discovered by reporters to be closely shepherded by their "good neighbor," the US Assistant Secretary of State for Latin American Affairs, Nelson Rockefeller. Professing optimism over the prospects for the UN parley, Rockefeller would comment to journalists' queries on the meeting only by saying that everything was "swell." Nonetheless, he did not interfere with the heads of the Latin delegations who were quite anxious to relate what was on their minds. To no one's astonishment, the various ambassadors voiced their unanimous hope that the United States would take control of the leadership of the San Francisco Conference. Guillermo Belt, Chairman of the Cuban delegation, was even more specific. In his remarks, he made it absolutely clear that the nations of the Americas were placing all their trust in the prestige of the United States to carry out a western-hemispheric plan for world order.[35]

If Catholics in the United States had been paying attention to their diocesan newspapers in the weeks before the UN Conference, they would have been quite familiar with this program. The NCWC News Service had supplied the nation's more than two hundred Catholic weeklies with its "Spotlights on San Francisco" series, topped off by two articles by Latin Americans who had been present at the meeting of the Republics of the Pan-American Union at Mexico City from February 21 to March 8, 1945. Philosophical in nature, the two columns provided a glimpse at the western-hemisphere's end-of-the-war optimism, which stemmed from its belief that it alone possessed the intellectual and moral stamina indispensable for future world peace.[36]

The first of these commentaries was written by Dr. Alceu Amoroso Lima of Brazil, a professor of sociology at the Catholic Institute in Rio de Janeiro. Amoroso Lima claimed that, although the tide of Nazi imperialism was waning, the poison of totalitarianism was still potent and could affect the peace. He reminded his American readership that even after the all-but-certain defeat of Germany and Japan, the Soviet Union would still be a menacing presence on the global scene. Although the USSR had belatedly enlisted with the two outstanding democracies of the day, the United States and Great Britain, to defeat the Axis powers, it was the heir to the outmoded tradition of "statism" that caused the war. It could not reasonably be looked on, therefore, as a pillar on which the postwar world could sensibly construct a peaceful future.[37]

Amoroso Lima recounted that this form of old-world nationalism had been born in Europe with the Renaissance reaction to a Catholic continentalism that was the cornerstone of medieval civilization. By the seventeenth century it had developed into an imperialistic ideal fed by the discoveries of "lands beyond the seas." Serving only the purposes of European colonizer nations, this variety of internationalism reached its extreme, up to that time, in the Nazi Third Reich. Amoroso Lima posited that the threat from this system would not necessarily pass with the death of Hitler. Britain still possessed its Empire, and more significantly, Pan-Slav imperialism was perceptibly on the rise.[38]

There were, nonetheless, prospects for tomorrow. If Europe was the cradle of the destructive nationalism of the past, the Americas were the home of the rebirth of "continentalism." The idea of encouraging neighborliness among the free countries of a continent to prevent avarice and hostility from developing was the first victory over nationalistic imperialism. This Pan-American ideal, which began with the liberation of the thirteen American colonies from the British Empire and had most recently been expressed at Chapultepec, marked the first great contribution to a new phase of civilization. On this model a universal community could now be built based on the example of Christianity, which offered to an exhausted world a love of liberty, justice, and truth.[39]

Dr. Victor Andres Belaunde, a former Peruvian Minister of Foreign Affairs and a member of his country's delegation to the UNCIO, picked up this theme from Amoroso Lima's article and developed it in his own "Catholic Spotlights" column. In the final installment in that NCWC series, Belaunde criticized the pantheism inherent in the creed of European nationalism, which had perceived the state solely as a self-serving entity freed from all ethical and juridical principles.[40]

The Reformation, the child of the Renaissance, had disrupted a thousand years of Catholic unity, which had spawned, among other things, Spanish theologians and jurists who formulated a basis for consitutional and international law. Germany, the center of the Protestant Reformation, had shunned this tradition and formed a culture of "nationalistic particularism." In contrast to universal civilization and religion, the *Volkgeist* or national soul was proclaimed by Hegel and Spengler. In this system religion was subservient to the wishes of the nation-state. Germanic racism and autocracy were the results.

Other nations such as Communist Russia had also placed all aspects of their culture, including religion, under the dominion of the state. In the Soviet Union a nationalistic, undemocratic insularism, combined with Marxism, an extreme form of positivism, resulted in the primacy of the economy and in a militant secular materialism. This unfortunate amalgamation produced a political model antithetical to, and useless for, republican world organization. As an antidote for global confusion Belaunde held up instead an Anglo-Latin ideal based on the Christian conception of life. In his hypothesis Belaunde unquestionably saw the United States as the present champion of the Anglo-Saxon tradition, while the "Ibero-American" nations represented true Catholic universalism.[41]

Not surprisingly, Amoroso Lima and Belaunde were advancing, in these statements, the sentiments of delegates from the American Republics who had met at Chapultepec for the Inter-American Conference on Problems of War and Peace. In a resolution unanimously approved at that hemispheric conference, the United States and its Latin American allies suggested that certain points be considered in the formulation of the United Nations Charter. Since this document was signed by all the states that Belaunde had catalogued as subscribing to his Anglo-Latin ideal, one could conclude that the plan for this "ethical universality" was laid out there for all to see.[42]

In fact, universality was the very first hope expressed for the new world association by the Inter-American signatories. They exhorted the delegates to the United Nations Conference to spell out the principles and purposes of the organization in order to better achieve this goal. In the same vein, the conferees labelled the UN General Assembly the "fully representative organ of the international community." They also called for amplification and clarification of its powers so that these could be effectively harmonized with those of the Security Council. Their resolution went on to express a desire for extension of the juridical competence of the World Court and creation of an international agency to promote intellectual and moral cooperation among nations.[43]

Finally, the American delegates suggested that the general international organization look to the Pan-American Conference and "inter-American methods and procedures" in the solving of western hemispheric matters. This closing point, unlike those that preceded it, was backed by a concrete resolve of the twenty republics represented at Mexico City. In a document entitled the "Act of Chapultepec," also signed on March 8, 1945, coercive action by the Pan-American Union had been mandated against any state committing an aggression against the western hemisphere.[44]

In all this the states of the Americas were undeniably trying to influence the debates that were to occur in San Francisco, but their deliberations were more than merely utilitarian. They honestly believed that their tradition of republicanism—which in certain cases was reverenced more in theory than in practice—was a valuable contribution to international peace and security. However, as Thomas Mahony was to remark, the fiercest debate at the UNCIO was not over the Pan-American Union's vague perceptions of the United Nations Organization and its vision for world peace. Far more contentious was the crucial problem of whether such a regional organization should be tolerated at all. Under the Dumbarton Oaks proposals, all enforcement actions by such organizations were to be renounced or put under the supervision of the Security Council.[45]

The Regional Arrangements Debate

On his return from Mexico City after the Inter-American Conference, Pattee confided to his superiors at the NCWC that he was at a loss to explain the absence of any discussion by the United States and its Latin American allies of a formula to adjust their regional agreement to the United Nations Charter. Aside from general statements of principle, there had been no attempt to reconcile the Act of Chapultepec with the overall framework of the international organization as stipulated by the Dumbarton Oaks proposals. This was particularly evident in the matter of hemispheric defense as spelled out in these documents.

The Dumbarton Oaks proposals maintained that the Security Council should use and even invite the use of regional agencies, both for peaceful resolution and for enforcement when appropriate. These regional organizations could not be used for enforcement, however, without the explicit authorization of the Council. At Chapultepec the Latin Americans and the US—which should have known better—determined on a regional system based on the principle that each member was obliged to defend the others when under attack.[46] Nonetheless it came as a great surprise to the State Department when protests quickly mounted within the international community that the republics of the western hemisphere had undermined the effectiveness of the UN through their regional security pact. In Pattee's words, it was painfully obvious that at Chapultepec "nothing was done to foresee this eventuality."[47]

To counter this rising tide of criticism, the State Department issued a secret directive, dated March 19, 1945, which instructed Administration officials on the proper diplomatic approach to America's policy toward Inter-American arrangements in relation to the UN. To be emphasized were the facts that the Chapultepec signatories unanimously endorsed establishment of a United Nations based on Dumbarton Oaks, that no regional bloc had been created, and that a coordinated relationship was envisioned between the Inter-American system and the proposed world organization. The "governing paragraph" of the Act of Chapultepec was to be stressed: the Monroe Doctrine had been reaffirmed at Mexico City and the states of the Americas intended only to protect their "peace, security, sovereignty, and independence."[48]

This directive interpreted the significance of Chapultepec as an effort by the nations of the Americas to consult with one another in a case of aggression against any one of their number and take necessary steps so that world peace could be maintained. This would be done, of course, only with the "encouragement" of the international organization and within settlements compatible with its principles and goals. With these guidelines the Administration intended to present a picture of a loosely bound group of nations attempting to reorganize an association that had been allowed to fall into disarray during the previous fifty years. These State Department efforts notwithstanding, a general impression at the San Francisco Conference was that the American states had created a "tight regional system."[49]

As the UNCIO discussions progressed, it soon became evident that the subject of regional arrangements would be among the most factious at the Conference. Thomas Mahony saw that the controversy aligned the parties to the Act of Chapultepec against those interested in bilateral security. The model for the latter was a recently-concluded treaty between the Soviet Union and France based on mutual fear of a resurgence of German militancy.[50] Mahony as the CAIP consultant related that there was a serious debate within UN circles whether either of these security pacts conformed to the Dumbarton Oaks proposals.[51]

Since the State Department's directive of March 19, however, it was evident that the US would insist that the Pan-American states could not act against an aggressor without the previous sanction of the Security Council. Therefore it came as a shock to its Latin American allies when on May 4 the United States proposed an amendment to the UN Charter that precluded the United Nations from barring coercive measures by European nations to prevent "aggression by a state now at war with the United Nations." This exclusion clause—which for all practical purposes permitted bilateral treaty nations to do exactly what it forbade to the Inter-American states—was proposed as a favor to the USSR, England, and France. It was meant also to take some pressure off the US, which was identified as the anointed leader of an increasingly controversial regional arrangement. Through this exemption the Great Powers could, individually or as a group, prevent the Security Council from functioning in a particular combat situation.

The South and Central American states registered strong objections to this US motion. Adding to their humiliation was the fact that the supposed leader of the Pan-American bloc proposed such an amendment to the Charter. Why, they wondered, was the USSR given preferential treatment with its bilateral treaties, which were construed by Latin Americans as nothing more than regional arrangements?[52]

Thomas Mahony discovered in his discussions with some of the Republican members of the American delegation, such as Harold Stassen and Arthur Vandenberg, that there was a serious rift on this point within the delegation.[53] A majority, led by Secretary of State Stettinius, insisted upon the maintenance of the superior authority of the international organization, but a substantial minority—including Dulles, Representatives Bloom and Eaton, and Rockefeller—sided with Inter-American solidarity and the Monroe Doctrine. Mahony reported, however, that the latter group was not likely to press the issue in public debate.[54]

Pattee claimed to be unable to find any ethical reasons for American willingness to exempt Soviet treaties but not the Chapultepec agreement from the application of the UN Charter and he publicly stated such sentiments to anyone who would listen. Of all the Catholic observers, Pattee was to become most passionately engrossed in the discussions surrounding this issue.

The Consultants And Latin America

Prior to the San Francisco Conference, the leaders of the American Catholic Church were advised by some of its specialists to beware of regional arrangements. A report by one such expert, Father Paul Tanner, delivered after the bishops' April statement, insisted that, although on paper the Pan-American Union looked like an ideal group, it could easily develop into an isolationist arrangement. If the western hemisphere were now to be seen merely as a US sphere of influence, this account advised, then any good that the Act of Chapultepec might achieve would have to be weighed against its destructive effect on world organization.[55] In this same vein, Conway, in his memorandum on Catholic interests at the UNCIO, assumed that, at least theoretically, hemispheric agencies were in accord with Catholic thought. But practical questions existed, such as the "consecrating of Russia's hegemony in Eastern Europe." Most Catholic doubts of the salutary impact of the Pan-American Union seem to have been put aside by late April of 1945.[56]

In one of the earliest evaluations of the Act of Chapultepec, the Polish Government in London issued a memorandum on world organization, which included a glowing endorsement of that agreement. This statement was given official approbation by the NCWC and was widely disseminated by its news service. Comparing the agreement at Mexico City favorably to the Dumbarton Oaks proposals, the Catholic Poles alleged that the Latin American delegates had established international relations on a basis of "justice, law, the respect of treaties, the equality of States, a good neighbor policy, noninterference in internal and external affairs of states, and the non-recognition of territorial acquisitions by force." The document boldly suggested that the UN Conference scrap the results of the Dumbarton Oaks Conversations and adopt the Pan-American document as a model for its own charter.[57]

The most obvious reason for Polish devotion to the accord reached at Chapultepec was that it allowed unencumbered self-defense in matters pertaining to hemispheric security. On its terms, no outside power with the veto in the Security Council could stop the Pan-American Union from defending what it perceived to be its own interests. Since this act recognized the principle that every state was objectively entitled to political independence and to respect of its territorial integrity, the Poles hoped that this would be an adequate UN safeguard against Russian imperialism in eastern Europe.[58]

Although American Catholic observers at San Francisco were not quite as amenable to the decisions reached at Mexico City as were the London Poles, nonetheless, by the end of the membership debates on the two Soviet Republics and Argentina, they were prepared to work in support of at least recognition by the UN of the Inter-American organization's right to defend itself. There were, however, some differences of opinion on the nature and timing of such a defense.

By May 4, the date on which the United States submitted its amendment to the Dumbarton Oaks proposals, Pattee had determined that the US was now deterring the American republics from formulating an adequate regional defense strategy by its refusal to license western-hemispheric enforcement actions without the previous authorization of the Security Council.[59]

Pattee sympathized openly with the Latin Americans' frustration and irritation at their ally's willingness to exempt Soviet security but not theirs from the UN Charter. Even the League of Nations had made specific mention of "such agreements as the Monroe Doctrine." Pattee concluded that with one act the United States had seriously damaged Inter-American solidarity, thrown into question its support of the principles of the Monroe Doctrine, and rendered South and Central American defenses suspect. Now there could be no swift response to aggression in Latin America.[60]

Pattee's Latin American friends were not merely expressing their grave reservations to him alone. They bombarded Stettinius with a host of complaints on the matter and entreated him to find some compromise formula that would not vitiate the Act of Chapultepec and leave them at the mercy of a Russian veto in the Security Council. By his May 14 meeting with the American consultants, this pressure was beginning to have some effect. In answer to a question of Thomas Mahony, Stettinius insisted that the western-hemisphere would not be left defenseless, nor was Russia being given *carte blanche* in security matters. Even under her bilateral treaties, he protested, the Soviet Union could act only against a resurgence of German or Japanese aggression.[61]

Furthermore, the Secretary felt confident that the UNCIO delegates would be able to find a solution whereby the Charter would recognize the self-defense of the western hemisphere. Off the record, he informed the consultants that if the Security Council failed to act when an armed attack occurred, then the American republics would "have the right . . . to act collectively along traditional lines of relationship within the American system."[62] With such assurances, which were being repeated to its Latin American allies, the United States was able to calm its hemispheric partners.

The final solution to the problem of regional arrangements was reached on May 20, when the Soviet Union agreed to an American proposal that would eventually become Article 51 of the Charter.[63] This article conceded to regional organizations such as the Pan-American Union that collective self-defense against armed attack would not be censured until the Security Council had taken "all necessary measures." Mahony reported that from his discussions with Latin American delegates, the Chapultepec signatories were interpreting the final part of this statement to mean that nothing in the Charter impaired the intrinsic right of regional self-defense in the event that the Security Council did not maintain international peace and security by preventing or repelling an armed attack against a member state. He agreed with this conclusion, but stressed to these delegates that the nations of the Pan-American Union had an obligation to demonstrate to the other members of the UN that they recognized the supremacy of the Security Council in matters concerning the exercise of force, even in their own region.[64]

Neither Pattee nor Mahony, however, was gratified by this compromise. In Pattee's opinion, this resolution was not satisfactory. How could a regional organization such as the Pan-American Union act autonomously and at the same time be subservient to the Security Council? Moreover, the text as agreed on did not provide for anything that would conceivably guarantee the necessary universality of the United Nations, nor did it secure for regional organizations the assurance of supremacy in their respective parts of the world. Both associations had lost something essential in the debate.[65]

Adding to the confusion in this dispute was poor leadership that the US Secretary of State demonstrated. In Pattee's opinion, Stettinius, who was under great pressure from all sides, seemed to vacillate from day to day in his statements on regional arrangements. In an "entirely off the record" meeting with the consultants to the American delegation on the morning of May 14, he stated that no matter how important the Latin American system was, no exceptions could be made for it that would weaken the international community.[66] On another occasion, Pattee related, the "tragic weakness" of the American position was evidenced by the Secretary's public admission that the Pan-American Union had nothing to fear from Security Council intervention, since the US veto in that body would always be used "to obstruct any action (by the United Nations) in the Americas. Pattee was deeply disheartened by the apparent lack of principle exhibited in these statements.[67]

Mahony agreed with Pattee that discussion of regional arrangements had not really settled anything. The relationship between the two organizations was still unclear and would probably cause much difficulty in the future. Mahony believed that a rational solution would be to have a particular region resolve its own martial crisis unless that conflict threatened the rest of the world. But nothing was defined in these terms and a public display of compromise was all that the UNCIO delegates seemed to require.[68]

Pattee and Mahony were nonetheless in a distinct minority in their dissatisfaction over the regional arrangements compromise; the vast majority of observers breathed a sigh of relief when the outcome was announced. Though Robert A. Graham, S.J., concurred with the two Catholic consultants that regional problems should be left at least in part to the regions for solution, he was entirely satisfied with the Big Power resolution of the problem. Writing in *America,* he saw the settlement of May 20 as an ironic victory for the Latin Americans—and therefore the small nations—and a tactical defeat for the Big Five and a Security Council manipulated through their veto. "The center of gravity," Father Graham professed, "both as regards enforcement action and as regards peaceful settlement of disputes" was now shifted "to the region and its juridicially equal member states." Gleefully Graham predicted that regionalism would be the wave of the future and would reduce the likelihood that the Great Powers would play an indispensable part in conserving the postwar peace. In this he woefully misunderstood the future complications that such a trend would beget.[69]

With trepidation and keener insight, commentators of a distinctly different stripe were envisioning an identical outcome. Though I.F. Stone did laud Stettinius for allegedly keeping Pan-Americanism in its place at the UN parley through his compromise settlement, the journalist urged that there be no more rationalizations for "splitting the post-war world into hostile blocs."[70] *Commonweal* agreed. Unlike Graham, it deemed regionalism one of the "unfortunate happenings" at the Conference. Far from lessening the influence of the Great Powers, the phenomenon of "America's Bloc" had only convinced the Soviets that real authority must be lodged in the Security Council, on which they held a permanent seat with full veto powers.[71]

In fact, while this understanding between the United States and the Soviet Union on a "regional arrangements' compromise" was receiving general support across the country, American opinion was beginning to look with disfavor on even the concept of regional groupings. This viewpoint held that hemispheric associations such as the Pan-American Union were dimming the chances of a Big Power solution to the problems of the world, prompting attention to focus on rivalries within the Big Three. Stone in particular believed that the whole matter of Chapultepec had produced an unnecessary superpower crisis. In his estimation, the meeting at Mexico City should have been convened after the UNCIO, since the United States and its many Latin American allies were seen to have used the meeting as a strategy session in preparation for the San Francisco Conference.[72]

Compromise was indeed the order of the day in San Francisco. The Soviet Union and the United States, two powers that earlier thought to contest each other at every turn of the Conference, determined after the regional-arrangements debate, which had actually been a surrogate squabble over their spheres of influence, that it was to their mutual benefit to compromise as much as possible on the UN Charter. As Pattee reported, even the United States' allies in Latin America, sensing a return to the spirit of Yalta, never again carried a rebellion against the United States to such lengths or provoked Big Power disunity, even when this entailed forsaking "small power interests."[73]

In The Spirit Of Compromise

After the discussions at Yalta in early February of 1945, the American State Department went out of its way to emphasize the importance of unity among the Great Powers. Claiming that this policy would be the strongest means of preserving the peace, the Administration either proposed or acceded to measures such as the voting formula in the Security Council and the "freezing" of previously arranged treaties, two topics that will be discussed in the next chapter.[74] In the interests of Great Power solidarity, therefore, stability for the Big Three was deemed essential.[75]

Far from challenging the premise underlying this type of alliance, the American press and public seemed to accept it without demur. Accordingly, by the time of the UNCIO, the most sensational news coverage was directed at the theme of US-Soviet relations, especially their differences of opinion. It was generally assumed in the media that the success of the United Nations Conference, and of the projected organization itself, depended on absolute superpower cooperation; any disagreement, however insignificant or transitory, was depicted as an ominous threat to international security.[76]

Reading the daily papers, one could have concluded that all Conference "crises" resulted from discrepancies between the American and Soviet delegates. No matter where blame for a specific dilemma was ultimately cast, the theme of requisite good relations between the superpowers was always thrust to the fore. The problems of Poland, Argentina, and the Soviet Republics were examples of such crises, but the matter of regional arrangements, with its one uncomplicated factor, i.e., a sizable and cohesive "US bloc," was made to order for this issue. As with the other questions mentioned above, the general view here was that the United States had to stand firm with the Soviets on matters of principle—a maddeningly elusive assertion never satisfactorily explained—while at the same time being sympathetic and patient. In this, of course, the press was only echoing the State Department's pre-Conference position.[77]

A typical example of this was reported to the Department by correspondents from the Office of War Information after the Argentine membership debate. Scouring the country for opinions on this controversy, these agents certified that there was much distress over the reversal of US policy, which now appeared to support "fascism" in South America, while dangerously departing from the whole concept of the organization of international security based on the unity of the Great Powers. Unbelievably, the OWI representatives found that for many citizens Argentina was perceived "as a much greater danger to the peace and democratic future" of the world than the Soviet Union. From this standpoint the fact that the US had to contest this issue with Russia, with whom unity was "vital," created wide alarm.[78]

The perception of public confidence in the trustworthiness of the Soviet Union on the matter of postwar peace was confirmed by a poll conducted after the Argentine debate. A confidential State Department survey released to officials on May 11 found that only 30 percent of the American people thought that the USSR was not to be relied on to cooperate with the US when the war was over.[79]

Most Catholic views on this subject differed markedly from the general mood of the country. Don Luigi Sturzo, a famous Italian priest and statesman, deferred to those who held little hope for any global security mechanism except a united Big Three.[80] He nonetheless considered it unfortunate that these states would have an inordinate influence in determining most of what happened at the San Francisco Conference. In his opinion these nations would be left, because of their power and influence, to repair the international order as they saw fit.[81]

Bishop Paul Yu-Pin likewise disparaged the concept of a necessary unanimity among the Great Powers as the central mode of operation for the world organization. His criticism of this method was based on the assertion that underlying this idea of a United Nations was the ridiculous notion that one of the permanent members of the Security Council could never be an aggressor state. Since most of the world's might was concentrated in these states, it seemed to the bishop that the "impeccability" of these powers was a hazardous principle on which to build international security.[82]

It was left to Richard Pattee to put a particularly American Catholic twist on this point of view. He indicated that the US bishops had warned against any permanent global arrangement that was *de facto* little more than an alliance of the Great Powers. In spite of the NCWC's statement *On International Order,* Pattee believed that the US had been converted to the Soviet assumption that, unless the powers were in absolute agreement on UN proposals and actions, the chance for peace was faint. To admit that the Soviet Union, the United States, and possibly Great Britain had to agree on a line of conduct and policy, or else there would be no possibility for peace, was to concede that the smaller members of the United Nations, at least half of whom were Catholic, had little more than secondary status within the organization.[83]

Pattee likewise acknowledged that the structure of the world organization was beginning to encompass principles that were practically irreconcilable. The fact that the United Nations Charter was being constrained to recognize an equilibrium among the Great Powers, which permitted them to shun UN decisions, while professing its superiority to any sovereign state or regional grouping—as had happened in the regional arrangements compromise—was, to say the very least, "a disappointing trend." Those who had hoped for a genuine world body could not but be disappointed. In Pattee's opinion the Charter was being formed with recognition accorded only to current political exigencies and not to the long-term objectives of future peace and security.[84]

Mahony had to admit reluctantly that, so far at least, the

Great Powers had all but ruled the Conference, and their self-serving cooperation, possibly out of fear and jealousy of other members as well as of one another, had prevailed in the main. Nevertheless, he hoped that, during what remained of the parley, their flagrant prerogatives would be greatly offset "by the general and equal ability of all nations to discuss, recommend," and guide future global peace.[85]

Two major impending deliberations at the UNCIO, the question of the veto power in the Security Council and the altercation over what came to be called the "Vandenberg Amendment," were to establish which of these interpretations would prove correct.

Notes

1. *On Organizing World Peace,* p. 2.

2. John F. Cronin was born in Glens Falls, New York, on October 8, 1908. He studied for the priesthood and was ordained in 1932, entering the Sulpician Order the next year. He received a Ph.D. from the Catholic University of America in 1935 and taught for many years at St. Mary's Seminary in Roland Park, Baltimore. After his 1944–45 study of Communism in the United States, he became a staff member of the Social Action Department of the NCWC from February 1946 until his retirement in June of 1967. In this capacity he served as the hierarchy's expert on Communism (Joy Anderson, gen. ed., *American Catholic Who's Who, 1980–1981* [Washington: National Catholic News Service, 1979] p. 159).

In the 1950s, Cronin would unsuccessfully attempt to redirect Senator Joseph R. McCarthy toward a less sensational investigation of American Communism by providing him with detailed material on actual Communist subversion. Cronin eventually criticized McCarthy's methods, citing his lack of veracity and improper procedures (Donald F. Crosby, S.J., *God, Church and Flag* [Chapel Hill: University of North Carolina Press, 1978], pp. 56–57, 199–200)

3. ANCWC 2a, Cronin to Monsignor Michael J. Ready, [Baltimore], November 17, 1944.

4. ANCWC 2b, *Report on the Investigation of Communism,* the Reverend John F. Cronin, S.S., December 31, 1945; Karl J. Alter to "Your Excellency," [Toledo], December 4, 1945.

5. ANCWC 21, MAB 29, November 16, 1944.

6. ANCWC 13b, "Soviets Will Keep Differences at San Francisco from Becoming a Break," N.S. Timasheff, April 16, 1945, p. 2. Mr. Timasheff was the author of *Religion in Soviet Russia.* He was a

member of the Russian Orthodox Church.

7. Ibid.

8. ANCWC 13c, "Molotov's Motives Analyzed," Richard Pattee, May 3, 1945, p. 4.

9. Ibid.

10. "Report on the United Nations Conference. . . ," p. 8.

11. ANCWC 13c, "Russia Remains a Riddle," Edward A. Conway, S.J., May 3, 1945, p. 3.

12. Ibid.

13. AMU Series 6, Box 1, "Observations on the San Francisco Conference," Thomas H. Mahony, May 3, 1945. p. 1.

14. "Russia and San Francisco," *America* 73 (April 14, 1945): 35.

15. Ibid.

16. AAC 2964C, Stritch to Carroll, [Chicago], May 9, 1945.

17. AMU Series 6, Box 1, "Observations Upon the Conference III," Thomas H. Mahony, May 13, 1945, p. 1.

18. Ibid.

19. Ibid., p. 2.

20. ANCWC 6, Memorandum of Conversation between James Clement Dunn and Michael J. Ready, January 5, 1944, p. 3.

21. RG 59e, Box 23, Folder 1, Daily Summary of Opinion Developments, May 22, 1945, p. 2.

22. "Russian Developments," *Commonweal,* 42 (June 8, 1945):179.

23. John LaFarge was born in Newport, Rhode Island, on February 13, 1880, the son of the famous artist, John LaFarge. He was educated at Harvard and entered the Jesuits in 1901. He taught at Loyola College in Baltimore and later worked for fourteen years in Leonardtown, Maryland, where he strove to improve the conditions of Afro-Americans and opened eight schools for Afro-American children. He became assistant editor of *America* in 1926 and remained on its staff for thirty-seven years until his death in 1963. He founded the Catholic Interracial Council in 1934 and was for decades the leading Catholic spokesman on racial issues. He wrote ten books, including his autobiography, *The Manner is Ordinary* (1954), (*The Dictionary of American Catholic Biography,* "La Farge, John,").

24. John La Farge, "Russia Challenges the Allied Conscience," *America* 73 (June 9, 1945):191.

25. Edward Reilly Stettinius, Jr., was born on January 10, 1900. He joined the State Department as Undersecretary in October of 1943 and, after the resignation of Cordell Hull, was named Secretary of State by President Roosevelt on November 27, 1944. President Truman accepted his resignation on June 27, 1945 (*E.R. Stettinius, Jr.,* p. 1); *The Private Papers of Senator Vandenberg,* p. 171.

26. Memorandum for the President from Stettinius, April 13, 1945, p. 2.

27. Truman recounts, with undisguised satisfaction, his initial diplomatic reaction to Soviet non-compliance. At the President's insistence, Molotov was instructed to stop in Washington for two days of talks before the opening of the San Francisco Conference. Mr. Truman, in front of a stunned Stettinius, used very graphic language to tell the Soviet Minister of his irritation over Russian failure to live up to agreements. "I have never been talked to like that in my life," Molotov said. "Carry out your agreements and you won't get talked to like that," Truman replied (Harry S. Truman, *The Truman Memoirs,* vol. 1: *Years of Decision* [Garden City, New York: Doubleday, 1955], p. 82).

28. Memorandum of Conversation between Stettinius, Molotov, et al., April 24, 1945.

29. ANCWC 13c, "Molotov's Stand in Dispute Over Permanent Head Causes Profound Reaction Among Latin American Delegates," Richard Pattee, April 30, 1945, p. 1.

30. Ibid., p. 2.

31. Ibid.

32. ANCWC 13a, "Thoughts on a Momentous Occasion," Edward A. Conway, April 30, 1945, p. 1.

33. RG 59f, Box 22, The United Nations Conference as Reported by US Press and Radio, July, 1945, p. 3.

34. Ibid.

35. "Latin Envoys Look to Our Leadership," *The New York Times,* April 22, 1945, p. 28.

36. ANCWC 13b, "Brazilian Savant Evaluates Conference," Frank Hall, May 21, 1945, p. 1.

37. ANCWC 13b, " 'War Will Have Been Lost' Unless Victorious Democracy Finds New Concept of Life," Dr. Alceu Amoroso Lima, May 21, 1945, p. 3.

38. Ibid., p. 2.

39. Ibid., p. 3.

40. ANCWC 13b, "Latin America Destined to be Important in Peace," Victor Andres Belaunde, May 30, 1945. p. 1.

41. Ibid., p. 2.

42. Pan American Union. *Final Act of the Inter-American Conference on Problems of War and Peace,* Mexico City, 1945, XXX, pp. 73–75.

43. Ibid.

44. "Observations Upon the Conference III," p. 2.

45. AMU Series 6, Box 1, "Observations Upon the Conference VIII," Thomas H. Mahony, May 19, 1945, p. 1.

46. *The Years of Western Domination,* p. 52.

47. "Report on the United Nations Conference. . . ," June 18, 1945, p. 13.

48. RG 59i, Box 1, Folder 1, "United States Policy Towards Inter-

American Arrangements in Relation to General International Organization," March 19, 1945, p. 2.

49. Ibid., p. 3.

50. Russia had concluded such treaties also with the United Kingdom, Czechoslovakia, and Yugoslavia.

51. ANCWC 15, "Observations Upon the Conference IV," May 14, 1945, p. 1.

52. Ibid.

53. AMU, Series 6, Box 1, Observations Upon the Conference VIII, May 19, 1945. p. 1.

54. *The Private Papers of Senator Vandenberg,* p. 188. "After Stettinius circulated my letter, 'Hell' broke loose. Even Stassen felt my proposal would gut the international power (of the UN) by emphasizing regional authority."

55. "Ideological Notes," p. 2.

56. ANCWC 15, "Catholic Interests in the San Francisco Conference," Edward A. Conway, April 11, 1945, p. 1.

57. ANCWC 15, "On Some Aspects of a World Security Organization. . . . ," April 19, 1945, p. 3.

58. Ibid., p. 4.

59. ANCWC 13c, "Latin Americans See Threat to Chapultepec," Richard Pattee, May 14, 1945, p. 2a.

60. Ibid., p. 3.

61. RG 59a 2001, Folder 2, Minutes of Consultants' Meeting, May 14, 1945, p. 8.

62. Ibid.

63. This statement, presented by Stettinius on May 16, 1945, advanced three principles. Its first aim was recognition of "the paramount authority of the world organization in all enforcement action." The second acknowledged the "inherent right of self-defense, either individual or collective" in the event that the Security Council did not maintain international peace and security and an armed attack against a member state occurred. The final purpose of the compromise was to insure that the regional agencies would be looked to "as an important way of settling local disputes by peaceful means" (Robert A. Graham, S.J., "Will Regionalism Be UNCIO's Answer?" *America* 73 (June 2, 1945):171–72).

64. *The Private Papers of Senator Vendenberg,* p. 186; "Observations Upon the Conference VIII," p. 2.

65. "Report on the United Nations Conference. . . , p. 13.

66. RG 59a 2001, Folder 2, Minutes of Consultants' Meeting, May 14, 1945, p. 3.

67. Report on the United Nations Conference. . . ," p. 13.

68. ANCWC 15, "The San Francisco Conference," Thomas H. Mahony, July 11, 1945, p. 16.

69. "Will Regionalism Be UNCIO's Answer?" pp. 170–71.

70. RG 59e, Box 23, Folder 2, Daily Summary of Opinion Developments, May 24, 1945, p. 2.

71. "America's Bloc."

72. Ibid.

73. ANCWC 11, "The American Bloc," Richard Pattee, June 18, 1945, p. 1.

74. *America, Britain, and Russia,* p. 505.

76. RG 59f, Box 22, The United Nations Conference as Reported by U.S. Press and Radio Comment, "US-Russian Relations," July, 1945.

77. Ibid.

78. RG 59i, Box 2, Folder 2: April 14–May, 1945, Everett V. Stonequist to MacLeish, [D.C.], May 12, 1945. p. 2.

79. Rg 59e, Box 23, Folder 1, Daily Summary of Opinion Developments, May 11, 1945, p. 1.

80. Luigi Sturzo was born in Caltagirone, Sicily, in 1872. In 1919 he founded the Popular Party, which attempted to introduce Catholic ideals, especially the social teachings of Leo XIII and Pius XI, into Italian political life. In 1924, with the rise of Fascism, he was forced to leave Italy, but he continued his crusade for Christian social justice in other countries (ANCWC 13b, "Don Sturzo Discusses Golden Gate Meeting," Frank Hall, May 23, 1945, p. 1).

81. ANCWC 13b, "Principles of 'Spheres of Influence' in Peace and War Implicitly Accepted by 'Big Three,' " Don Luigi Sturzo, May 23, 1945, p. 2.

82. ANCWC 13b, "Peace Must be Based on True Collective Security," Bishop Paul Yu-Pin, May 14, 1945, p. 2.

83. ANCWC 11, "Deficiencies of Charter Declared Not Justifying its Outright Rejection," Richard Pattee, June 11, 1945, p. 1.

84. Ibid.

85. AMU, Thomas H. Mahony, *The United Nations Charter* (Washington: The Catholic Association for International Peace, 1945) pp. 6–7.

CHAPTER VI
Change or Stasis

At the outset of the UNCIO, Christopher Dawson, a British Catholic philosopher, crusaded against those who argued that the formal principles on which world organization was established were of secondary importance. To the contrary he maintained that there was a vast moral and psychological difference between a structure in which the nations of the world accepted the sovereignty of law and worked together equitably for a common measure of justice, and a system that simply depended on the element of power and coveted security through global military and economic power. To Dawson this point seemed of such overwhelming importance that it must overshadow all matters of technical or procedural policy. In his opinion the public debate on the formation of a United Nations Charter, which had concentrated on these questions, had gone astray. The vital consideration was not who had power or how much power, but what were the ends for which it would be used.[1]

To some delegates and observers at the San Francisco Conference it was evident that these two elements, power and ends, had to be intertwined in the draft of the UN Charter. They saw a moral imperative in the advancement of a system that could apportion justice through proper international procedures. Some of the most ardent disputes at the UNCIO, therefore, centered on two tactical issues viewed by many as inseparably tethered to the question of justice. These problems were the privilege of veto power for the permanent members of the Security Council and the pacific settlement of disputes. Since the latter topic, which concerned the UN General Assembly, was in part a reaction to the final compromise on the modification of the "veto power", we will first discuss this Security Council suffrage controversy.

139

The Veto Power

In the opinion of Richard Pattee, the issue of the Big Five veto in the Security Council "was the crux logically of the whole business."[2] Because of its central prominence in the discussions at the UNCIO, we have already had occasion to refer to the veto confrontation several times in this study.[3] Therefore I will forgo repeating the complete background and many particulars of what came to be called the "Yalta Concession." The following inquiry, therefore, will concentrate on the debate over the issue itself and on reactions to its outcome.

Throughout the conference this topic lingered as the foremost preoccupation of the delegates. This was so because their respective governments were, at the end of a seemingly interminable war, riveted by the problem of international security. At Dumbarton Oaks the Great Powers had taken on the common burden of thwarting or at least restraining war through a "security council," although specific procedures had been left to the subsequent Big Three deliberations at Yalta.[4]

The Crimea conferees' determination to secure for themselves a veto in the Security Council was widely challenged at San Francisco. Whereas, in the aftermath of the two world wars, the preservation of peace was recognized as one of the key responsibilities of the Big Five, the lesser powers were nonetheless distrustful of any such total control over warfare deterrence. The Great Powers claimed to be baffled by this conference opposition to their Yalta formula, which mandated a "unanimity rule" in the Security Council by which any one of them could prevent an action being taken. After all, it was nothing new in world diplomacy for a government in a global parley to reserve to itself matters affecting its own interests.

The more astute smaller nations, however, immediately retorted that there was a significant difference in this circumstance. A new wrinkle had been introduced into this international principle when it had been applied to Security Council balloting; in this instance the Big Five were refusing to all other members of the UN the freedom of reservation that they were arrogating to themselves. For these minor powers the question was viewed as one of bias, "of drawing a line of privilege between nations." Moreover, it signified a lessening of sovereignty for some states but not for the designated few—something even the League of Nations had endeavored to shun. Finally, the veto power seemed to counter all the professions of equality among nations that had been repeated in various pacts and deliberations during the war years.[65]

In rebuttal the permanent members of the prospective Security Council, who had self-consciously appropriated for themselves the epithet "realists," were quick to point out an awful truth. The sovereignty of the lesser powers had already been reduced in fact; this was demonstrated by their relative defenselessness in the two world wars. Not only had a profession of neutrality been futile for any particular country in the path of aggression, but the united approach to security fostered by the League of Nations had disintegrated under the ultimate test of force.[6]

American Catholic opinion was solidly inclined toward the position of the smaller nations. For Pattee, the rule of consensus meant plainly that the UN would be, in effect, an alliance of the Great Powers. In such a confederation the lesser powers would not be able to get beyond the debating stage in the Security Council. And even this was in doubt early at the conference, since the Soviet Union was questioning the right of Security Council discussion of any topic in the face of a Big Power rebuff. Since the role of the lesser states had been restricted in the General Assembly to merely that of bystanders with the advantage of dialogue,[7] Pattee argued that the participants at San Francisco might as well confess that if the Yalta agreement were put into the Charter, it would be an indication to all the world that aggression by a large state, or one of its clients, could not be prevented.[8]

To illustrate this point Pattee turned to a hypothetical situation that was to become a cliché of the veto debate: "Suppose Bulgaria were to attack Turkey?" First proposed by James B. Reston in *The New York Times* of April 20, 1945, this scenario indicated that, if Turkey appealed to the Security Council for protection, it was inevitable that Russia would exercise her veto in favor of the aggressor nation. Furthermore, if another member-state attempted a solitary action against Bulgaria, Russia could veto this as well. This would place the rescuer-nation in peril of violating the principles of the organization and conceivably of destroying the UN itself. While all this was going on, Pattee predicted, the world organization would be able only to stand by helplessly and watch.[9]

Thomas Mahony agreed that it was evident that any of the permanent members could, by its veto, stay the request for military sanctions against an aggressor state, and even more confidently, it could avert implementation of such an authorization against itself if it resolved on a course of militancy. Furthermore, if the Big Five and only two other members of the Security Council voted to apply such sanctions against another state, all other member states, whether minor powers or lesser nations, had to commit forces to a suppression of that other state's action. This would be true even if the balance of the states, the temporary members of the Security Council, voted unanimously against supporting such a ratification. For this reason, along with others already indicated, Mahony strongly advised either a limitation of the Great Power veto or an expansion of the authority of the non-permanent members of the Security Council.[10] Mahony's parent organization, the Catholic Association for International Peace, had likewise spoken candidly on this subject. The CAIP accused the Security Council of being its own court of arbitration and yet "the most partial body conceivable."[11]

As we have seen in previous chapters, opposition to the "veto power" by the bishops of the Catholic Church in the United States was forceful and public. In their April statement they argued that whatever concessions must be made to the Great Powers in light of their expenditures during the war and of their prevailing power in its aftermath, it still seemed "inequitable and dangerous to give any nation in perpetuity a virtual veto . . ." over all other nations of the world.[12]

Catholic aversion to "the rock of Big Five unanimity" generally took the form of a censure of the lack of equality in the Security Council. Though no one in the Church intended to deny the Great Powers a superior influence in the United Nations, Guido Gonella stated in his "Catholic Spotlights" article that the "veto power" was being challenged because it assured that an undemocratic spirit would prevail in all discussions.[13] For the same reason Conway, one of the authors of *Goals for San Francisco,* urged that no one nation should be granted a veto in any confrontation.[14]

Other suggestions on the permanent-member veto were plentiful, but examples of the two most prevalent were offered by Gonella and by Jan Ciechanowski, the ambassador to Washington from the London-based Polish government-in-exile. Gonella proposed a middle course between unanimity of all Security Council members and the Great Power privilege of a veto. He recommended that a clear majority of Council members be required for any weighty decision; in fact, he favored a two-thirds vote of the permanent and non-permanent members. Ciechanowski, on the other hand, took a more drastic approach. He advised a radical revision of the UN Charter that would mandate that all decisions of the Security Council be taken by a simple majority vote of its members.[15]

These Catholic innovations had all been set forth either before the opening session of the UNCIO or soon after. Along with many others, they would be discussed during the most contentious debate of the conference—one that, more than any other, would determine the nature of the prospective world organization.

"The Test of the Conference"

By opting to concentrate on one issue, the "veto power," in their assault on the prerogatives of the Big Five, the smaller nations were able to gain the attention of the American press and radio and even win their sympathy. However, these weaker states, realizing that it would be necessary to give the Great Powers some special rights, did not press their case in the media with doctrinaire obstinacy, or try to exact the entitlement that they had possessed in the League of Nations. What they did urge was that a differentiation between great and small powers should not be sustained in the introductory processes. In other words, a preliminary discussion of security issues should not be blocked by a Big-Power veto in the Security Council.[16]

It was on this point that the Yalta Agreement was appealed to, and a dilemma of conflicting interpretations ensued.[17] In this clash the American and British rendition of the Yalta accord, as well as those of China and France, was found to be similar to the connotation of the smaller powers. On May 24 Undersecretary of State Joseph Grew gave the official American interpretation of the Yalta formula: it was his "Government's understanding that under these voting procedures [the Yalta Agreement] there is nothing which could prevent any State from bringing to the attention of the Security Council any dispute or any situation which it believes may lead to international friction or may give rise to a dispute."[18]

The Soviet Union implicitly repudiated this stance by insisting that it had never meant to give any such acknowledgement to the authority of the non-permanent members. Andrei Gromyko, the Soviet representative who had taken Molotov's position as head of the Russian delegation, insisted at the beginning of June that a Great-Power veto in the Security Council had to stand. Furthermore, he insisted, it must apply to discussion and even consideration of any subject that might come before that body. He also decried the lack of Big-Five unity in this "test of the Conference" and exhorted the Great Powers to persevere as a unit in all enterprises undertaken by the Council.[19]

From Conway's discussions with American delegates and other participants at the Conference, he believed that by this stance Stalin might have "overplayed his hand." By asserting that the permanent members of the Security Council must have the power to veto, and thereby prevent, even discussion of a dispute, the Kremlin leader was taking a position from which he would later be willing and able to retreat in order to get what he really wanted.[20]

Various pundits informed Conway that what Stalin really begrudged the non-permanent members was not the first stage of the process in the pacific settlement of disputes, but the second. In their opinion he was hoping to retain Big-Five authority to halt formal investigation of a conflict, whether any of the Great Powers was involved in it or not. A preliminary discussion of the matter was of no concern to him. By this ploy the Soviets would be able to point to the fact that they had yielded to the smaller nations, and this "concession" would be used to demand a reciprocal compromise on the part of these lesser powers, which still bitterly opposed any veto power over investigation of disputes and recommendation of settlements.[21]

It was at this moment that President Truman intervened by dispatching to Moscow two Americans in whom Stalin had demonstrated broad trust: Harry Hopkins, the administration's foreign-policy trouble-shooter, and Joseph E. Davies, former American ambassador to the Kremlin. Hopkins's visit would result in the Russian delegation's surrender of a right of veto on all preliminaries in the pacific settlement of disputes—reserving this Big-Five option for formal Security Council inquests and military enforcement. At the time, however, rumors were rife in the media that there was some willingness on the part of the Americans to precipitately extend a compromise to Russia in order to shatter the superpower impasse on this issue. Reacting to this hearsay, Conway made approaches to the senior Republican on the American delegation, Senator Arthur Vandenberg.[22]

Father Conway's request for a meeting was granted almost at once. He met the senator and his chief advisor, John Foster Dulles, in the Vandenberg hotel suite on the afternoon of June 5. Conway straightaway communicated the disquiet of the NCWC over reports of an American giveaway and advised the senator that it would be difficult to gain Catholic support for the Yalta agreement, even as interpreted by the US. It would, however, be almost impossible to justify the hierarchy's support of a clarification that would impede even the presentation of a dispute before the council.[23]

Vandenberg reassured Conway that the Americans would not recede an inch from their stand expressed in a cable sent to Stalin on Sunday, June 3, in which they and the other three Great Powers rejected the Soviet position. He vowed to Conway, furthermore, that if any other compromises were made in the face of Soviet posturing, the Republicans would walk out of the US deputation. Conway gathered that the senator had made all the allowances he possibly could in the interests of delegation unanimity.[24]

Vandenberg told Conway that on Saturday, June 2, the US committee had drafted what he called "a glorious reaffirmation of the traditional American doctrine of freedom of speech," which the Senator believed had been completely spurned by the Soviet proposal. He averred that on Monday, June 4, he had requested that Stettinius counsel the president to release this declaration in order to demonstrate to the world that the United States was still a patron of ethical international policies.[25] Truman refused, believing that the release might endanger the sessions then going on between Hopkins and Stalin. The senator was convinced, however, that in this crisis the smaller countries were looking to see which of the two superpowers would prevail. For this reason the US should use all resources at its command to make its position on this subject known. It was Vandenberg's opinion that the side that won the day on veto interpretation would be able to sway the course of the United Nations and consequently the postwar world.[26]

At this point in the interview Conway inquired whether it would help if Achbishop Mooney, as chairman of the NCWC Administrative Board, sent a telegram to President Truman setting forth Catholic sentiments on this matter. Vandenberg and Dulles were enthusiastic in their encouragement. Accordingly the three immediately set to work on drafting such a communication. First of all, they believed that Mooney should applaud the president on his backing of the efforts of the American delegation. They likewise thought it would be politic to congratulate the White House on its defiance of Soviet pressures in the "veto power" controversy, since by these actions the president had reaffirmed America's commitment to freedom of speech and had thereby prevented the evisceration of the United Nations. It was agreed that the second half of the telegram should be a request for a "crystal clear" statement of the US position in the matter so as to counter Soviet propaganda.[27]

After this session Conway returned to his hotel to telephone Archbishop Mooney and convey the details of his discussion with the two Republicans. Mooney conceded the first point on which the conferees had agreed, but thought that Truman was correct in not permitting the publication of the American statement while the Moscow negotiations were proceeding. However, the NCWC chairman suggested that in place of a formal American communiqué, the United States "take a leaf out of the Russian book" and "leak" the US statement to the press.[28]

Conway then contacted Vandenberg, transmitting the gist of his conversation with Mooney. The senator approved the archbishop's proposals but repeated his recommendation that Mooney send his telegram to the president immediately so as to forestall further capitulations on the part of American diplomacy. Conway again shuttled Vandenberg's message to the archbishop, adding his own recommendation that Mooney enroll Archbishop Stritch, chairman of the Bishops' Committee on the Pope's Peace Plan, in his bid to outline the official Catholic viewpoint.[29]

Although the chairman of the Administrative Board would forward his telegram to Harry Truman denouncing the "gag rule" veto in the Security Council, and that communication would be duly noted and publicly acknowledged, historians such as James T. Shotwell are generally of the opinion that the administration never really considered sacrificing its position on the "veto power" in order to appease Stalin.[30] Harry Hopkins had, of necessity, been unyielding with the Kremlin leader, maintaining that the US could not go against its allies within the bloc of smaller nations, much less the Republican minority in both the American delegation and the United States Senate. It is likewise agreed that Hopkins achieved one of the greatest diplomatic strokes in American history by forcing Stalin to back down from his posture that the Big Five should be permitted to exercise their veto in the council on topics of debate.[31]

Father Conway continued to believe, however, that Stalin had positioned himself to make just such a strategic retreat, thereby obliging the smaller powers to do the same through a tacit acceptance of the Yalta formula, a move that they initially hoped to avoid. Furthermore, the Jesuit believed that this settlement had been a propaganda victory for the Soviets. Seen as a Soviet concession, it was regarded as proof that Stalin really wanted to cooperate in UN affairs and, even more important, that the Soviets were willing to collaborate in Big-Three policy decisions and thereby to guarantee that the Great Powers could successfully work out their differences.[32]

After some inordinately bleak days in early June, during which the pervading mood in San Francisco had been one of pessimism because neither the Soviets nor the Americans would yield on the veto issue, a settlement was reached on June 7. It was accompanied by an excessive demonstration of joy. In spite of all this exhilaration, however, there were, even at the State Department, cooler heads that saw the true picture. An interdepartmental press report conceded that even with this celebrated arrangement, the veto question actually stood precisely where it always had been: where the Soviets wanted it.[33]

"Quis Custodiet Ipsos Custodes?"[34]

The weekly *America* claimed to readily understand Soviet reluctance to submit all disputes to free discussion and inquiry before a Security Council dominated by what the Russians saw as "Anglo-American morality and imperialism"; nonetheless, along with *Commonweal, America* found it difficult to envisage how the UNCIO could ever have contemplated extending to a permanent Council member the power to stop discussion of a matter affecting world peace.[35] Both periodicals therefore exulted in the final veto solution, emphasized "the very friendly and cooperative spirit between the United States and the Soviet Union," and gave little coverage to how much the small nations insisted upon keeping for themselves.[36]

The official Catholic Church's reaction to the settlement of the "veto power" debate was not so sanguine, muted as it was by the fact that, although its representatives had worked for the Russian concession, it could never celebrate an achievement that was seen as a part of a far more objectionable overall veto settlement.

Richard Pattee's opinion was typical. He thought that the real problem was evident in the fact that he had to ask himself whether the total veto arrangement was better than nothing at all. He thought it was, though complete responsibility for world peace had been inadvisably put into the hands of the Great Powers. He could never be satisfied as long as authentic Security-Council partnership for the smaller powers was being denied to them.[37]

Additionally he was not ready to place all the blame on the Soviet Union. Right from the start, the position of the Big Five had been to stand by the Dumbarton Oaks proposals and to allow as few changes as possible. It seemed clear to him that in the basic issue of the veto—whether the Great Powers should each have a controlling hand over discussion and enforcement in security matters—the Soviets had been "running interference for the Senate." He deemed it unlikely that the Senate would have accepted any provision leaving the use of American troops contingent on the verdict of a majority vote of any assembly of foreign states. The US concept of sovereignty had been the ground for the parallel American determination to uphold the unanimity clause. Therefore, for motives not dissimilar from those of the USSR, the Administration had pressed for retention of undisputed authority over any allocation of its military or other resources.[38]

For his part, Conway agreed with an assessment by Thomas Mahony that the rigid interpretation of the Yalta formula on voting procedure in the Security Council, condoned at San Francisco, was one of the major failures of the UNCIO.[39] With Pattee, moreover, he refused to limit culpability to the Soviets. After all, Conway recalled, it was Tom Connally of the United States Senate, speaking for the Big Five, who steam-rollered the agreement through the Conference. And it was Connally who tendered the ultimatum to the "Little 45" that it was a choice of having an international organization with the veto or having none at all.[40]

Therefore Conway's hero in the "veto power" debate was not an American or a delegate from any of the Great Powers. He was not even a Roman Catholic. Instead, the subject of the Jesuit's admiration was Herbert Vere Evatt, the Australian Minister for Foreign Affairs and the leader of the small and middle nations opposed to the veto provisions of the Charter.[41]

In an "exclusive interview" with Father Conway, Vere Evatt promised that when the world security organization began to function he would challenge the Great Powers every time they exercised their veto and would press for its early revision. He contended that this was necessary because the veto was a real threat to the possibility of mediating disputes in the Security Council. From the start these matters would have to be settled by the Big Five "in dark corners," and these surreptitious goings-on would undoubtedly become intolerable to the majority of delegates at the UN, who would consequently insist on veto repeal. Therefore, the Australian regarded his defeat in this controversy as a temporary one.[42]

Conway did not fail to mention to the National Catholic Welfare Conference that the Foreign Minister was a friend of the Catholic archbishops of Sidney and Melbourne and that he expressed nothing but praise for the Administrative Board's April 15 declaration on world organization. His views on the veto clause, for instance, were in perfect harmony with those voiced by the American hierarchy in that document. It was also noted that the other member of the Australian delegation was Francis Michael Forde, the Catholic Deputy Prime Minister, who had worked hand-in-hand with Vere Evatt. In fact, no one recapitulated American Catholic sentiment at the end of the "veto power" debate more succinctly than this Protestant from Australia. In words that Conway trumpeted to the Catholic press, Vere Evatt insisted that "if disputes could be brought without let or hindrance before the Council, there would be a chance at least for their settlement according to the rules of justice and equity. But if peaceful conciliation and other measures are vetoed, disputes will have to be settled by political dealings. . . ."[43]

It is all the more curious, therefore, that after the failure of the veto debate, Father Conway could still put forward the fiction that acceptable headway had been made in work on the proposed Charter to bring it in line with his *Goals for San Francisco.*[44]

The closer the Security Council came to being the preserve of the Great Powers, the more important became the so-called "Vandenberg Amendment" on peaceful change, which would have allowed the General Assembly to promote legislation for the non-violent resolution of global crises that it judged likely to impair international well-being. But once again the question at hand was whether the Big Five would give the other members of the United Nations the right to interfere in matters that these inviting powers considered part of their cherished autonomy.

The Vandenberg Amendment

It was the thinking of the Conference that the supreme lesson of the two world wars was that it was too late to stop a conflict after it had begun. Any police action, even one inaugurated by a world organization, could not be seen as anything but an exercise in force. Therefore, the only sure way of maintaining the peace was to anticipate violence by instituting measures of pacific settlement. This was most imperative in the correction of treaties and pacts that contributed to hostile relations among the various states and therefore were permanent irritants to worldwide accord. If stipulations for this alternative were not written into the Charter of the security organization there would be no possibility of a permanent peace. Although the threat of force by the United Nations was not to be excluded as an ultimate formula for restoring harmony, it was obviously a paradoxical method for a global association of "peace-loving" nations.[45]

The American political figure most concerned with the development of peaceful means for the solution to world predicaments was Arthur Vandenberg, the Republican senator from Michigan and the senior minority member of the Senate Foreign Relations Committee. Even before he received President Roosevelt's formal invitation to serve on the American delegation to the UNCIO, Vandenberg accordingly quizzed the Assistant Secretary of State for Congressional Relations, Dean Acheson, on whether decisions such as the one regarding Poland—which was then in the process of development under the general plan of the Dumbarton Oaks proposals—were subject in any way to revision by the United Nations.[46] Since the Polish arrangement had already caused serious international dissatisfaction, and would most probably continue to do so, Vandenberg was persuaded that such an unwelcome settlement should be examined by a yet-to-be-determined mechanism of the prospective United Nations.[47]

On March 19 Stettinius reported in a secret memorandum to FDR that Senator Vandenberg was willing to go along "100% on the world security organization" only if the American delegation could work into its proposals two points that he considered essential. The first was the inclusion of more language into the Charter on the concerns of justice; the second, which went hand-in-hand with the first, was the insertion into the document of a provision empowering the United Nations to review and possibly to make recommendations on past arrangements between governments. If this amendment were not forthcoming, then the senator was confident that the new international association would in effect freeze the *status quo* existing at the end of the war and would thereby solidify a balance of power that resulted from decisions made in the name of military expediency and without regard to justice.[48]

In an important speech on the floor of the Senate of the United States on April 2, 1945, Vandenberg delivered his celebrated "straightjacket" indictment of the Dumbarton Oaks interpretation of the United Nations. Contending that permanent peace was inconceivable if the new league attempted to arrest the state of the world at the cessation of hostilities, he alleged that, especially in light of the veto given to the permanent members of the Security Council, a "peaceful change" amendment for the UN Charter was crucial to its success. The small states in particular, since they were most in need of protection, deserved to be reassured that the Big Power search for security would have some regard for fairness and morality. In the senator's words, the world organization needed a "soul."[49]

Professing to have found the spirit required, Vandenberg anticipated adding the following paragraph to Chapter Eight, Section A of the UN Charter, which dealt with international compacts. "If the Security Council finds that any situation which it shall investigate involves injustice to peoples concerned, it shall recommend [to the General Assembly] appropriate measures of adjustment which may include the revision of treaties and of prior international decisions." Calling this sentence a "direct escape clause from 'injustice,' " the senator recommended that its sentiments, although possibly implied in the Dumbarton Oaks proposals, be spelled out in the Charter in order to avoid all misunderstandings.[50]

Upon reading Senator Vandenberg's comments, Father Conway remarked that they recalled the convictions of Pius XII in his Christmas allocution of 1939. In that address, which launched the Pope's Five-Point Peace Program, the pontiff had declared that since it was improbable that the nations of the world could foresee every eventuality and could safeguard against every menace at the instant when treaties were signed, it was mandatory to erect a juridical institution that would assure implementation of the terms of just arrangements and would revise and correct any acknowledged deficiencies.[51]

Taking their cue from the Pope's Peace Plan, the Catholics at San Francisco welcomed Vandenberg's attempt to place justice at the hub of the regulation of international settlements. Conway stressed that the doctrines of peaceful change and of revision of onerous treaties were two of the cardinal points of *Goals for San Francisco.* In that document, quotations from the American Catholic bishops' statement of November 1944 had been prominently highlighted. The hierarchy had maintained that the life of nations, like that of persons, was not static. Therefore, the United Nations Charter had to provide for revision of treaties in the interest of equity and of the common good of the international community. In anticipation of the San Francisco Conference, the bishops had reaffirmed these sentiments in their April 1945 declaration, *On Organizing World Peace*.[52]

The "Vandenberg Amendment" In San Francisco

The path of Senator Vandenberg's amendment to the UN Charter was a protracted and tortuous one. At the beginning of the United Nations Conference it was introduced to the other three sponsoring powers by the American delegation. By that time, however, it had undergone changes since Vandenberg introduced it in the Senate. Now, instead of vesting the power of review in the General Assembly as the original amendment specified, this new version merely proposed the power to recommend revision.[53]

Great Britain and China agreed to advance the American recommendation, but only if this modification was attached to the original motion. Russia, however, requested more time to study its ramifications. With the deadline for submitting amendments to the Charter approaching and the Soviets unwilling to make up their minds, the US delegation was compelled to introduce the amendment on its own. Subsequently, the Soviets did agree to co-sponsor the revised proposal—but at a price. It was therefore formally registered as a four-power revision of the Charter.[54]

In Conway's opinion, what was still called the "Vandenberg Amendment" on peaceful change had emerged from these Big Four conversations looking like "a survivor from a Nazi torture camp." As we have seen, the senator had asked that the Charter provide explicitly for review by the Assembly of unjust "treaty obligations" and "other international arrangements which might cause friction and lead to war." Now it was offered only the right of "recommendation." Moreover, at Molotov's insistence, another important change in the wording of the proposal was made.[55] No mention of treaties remained in the four-power rendering of the amendment; the word "situations" supplanted it. The phrase "revision of treaties" was replaced by a more general phrase: "peaceful adjustment of any situations, regardless of origin."[56]

In a major press conference in early May, Senator Vandenberg warmly defended this new phraseology and expressed the belief that the word "situations," though a broader term than "treaties," definitely included them. The rest of the American delegation likewise professed to believe that "situations" was an excellent term and that it included unjust treaties and all settlements growing out of World War II or any other war. Father Conway remarked that if this US interpretation was correct, a point he frankly questioned, then one of the major demands of the American Catholic Church had been met.[57]

But on the day after Vandenberg's optimistic briefing, Molotov, in his final press conference before returning to Moscow, presented a quite different interpretation of the resolution. By claiming just as unequivocally that in the discussions of the Big Four on this amendment, "naturally, the question of revising treaties was rejected as untenable," he exempted all such international arrangements from the purview of the United Nations. Vandenberg quickly countered this denial with a May 7 press release in which he persisted in seeing little difference between himself and Molotov. The Soviet delegate, he inferred, meant by treaties only "the controls which we intend to fasten on the enemy states." All other situations, however, would be legitimate subjects for inquiry and recommendation by the General Assembly.

For Conway, however, the situation was obvious. Molotov left a big question mark in the matter of "peaceful change." It was true, as Vandenberg stated, that the Foreign Minister had initiated his press conference by discussing only the settlements to be imposed on the defeated aggressor nations and the Soviet bilateral treaties, which had been exempted from UN review. He ended, however, with the categorical statement that, in the Big Four discussions, the revising of all treaties was repudiated. In Conway's view, Molotov was a wily character—

he had never been wilier than in this performance—but what did the American delegates hope to achieve by so intently refusing to accept this predicament? Feigning disbelief would not solve the problem of an obvious superpower difference of opinion over the "rubber word," "situations."[58]

Conway soon found an answer to his query. The public assertions by the senator and his colleagues in the American delegation were, Conway discovered, just a ploy to cover up a bitter backstage battle between the United States and the Soviet Union. Fearing a breakup of the Conference over an issue that the Americans hoped to resolve behind closed doors, they were determined to give the impression of a united Big Power front no matter how ridiculous the justification.[59] In a righteous huff over this conspicuous charade, Conway reported to Monsignor Carroll that the bishops should do all in their power to drag this hidden conflict into the open. Only in that way could an agreement be reached on the meaning of the irritating word "situations." No arbitrary deadline, furthermore, should prevent the ventilation of this question, as had happened with several other issues. However, the NCWC observer soon was far less certain of his passion for openness, at least on this issue.[60]

After Molotov's departure from San Francisco, the Russian delegation secretly informed the British and Americans that they would never agree to any provision, such as the "peaceful change amendment," that might allow the Germans to secure a lightening of the controls to be placed upon them. In this the French were in complete accord with the Kremlin. These two countries believed that American big business wanted not only undemanding controls upon the Axis nations but even a further lightening of these regulations after a brief interval. The very practical goal of this scheme was more and more business with Germany and her former allies.[61]

The French theorized that representatives of American big business had been sent to San Francisco specifically to lobby for this policy. These agents of Wall Street were now in consultation with Senator Vandenberg and other Republican politicians close to the business community, especially John Foster Dulles, to find a way of resisting the Russian demands. The French had heard, moreover, that this Republican-business combine decided to use the religious argument that all the faiths in the United States were demanding the "peaceful change" provisions. In this hypothesis, Dulles was seen as the man most likely to deliver this "grand combination" of denominations for the American delegation in its attempt to require a wider interpretation of the Vandenberg Amendment.[62]

This revelation caused Father Conway to reevaluate the status of the Catholic observers at San Francisco and that of the Catholic Church in the United States. He had consulted frequently with John Foster Dulles on many issues, and now he thought that, before proceeding in the matter of "peaceful change," he had better find out if he was being used.

The Catholic Dilemma Over "Peaceful Change"

Conway's source of information on French and Soviet intentions in the "peaceful change" quarrel was an unnamed radio broadcaster who was "close" to members of the French delegation. This commentator was privy to daily discussions in which they rehearsed the day's events at the Conference. Although many participants in these exchanges were intimates of Georges Bidault, Foreign Minister of France and chairman of his country's delegation, it was reported that the diplomat himself had remained aloof from these dialogues and, in Conway's words, was "lying low, trying hard not to take sides between Russia and the United States." Caught in the middle of this controversy, Bidault was sympathetic to the Soviet position, at least regarding Germany, but he also recognized the peril in letting the Soviets get away with "freezing" all the settlements it had made, particularly the Polish convention. For purely political reasons, Bidault was, at the moment, supposed to be counseling Paris not to oppose the USSR, at least for the present.[63]

Conway reported that, at the request of the French, the top

men of the Big Five delegations were then meeting to review "peaceful change" options. Therefore, in view of what he recounted, he wrote that he was most anxious for precise instructions from the hierarchy on this matter.

First of all, given that it was certain that American mercantile interests were lobbying for a rapid redevelopment of the Axis states, did the NCWC accept the contention that the business community, with Dulles as its contact, was actually using religious documents such as *Goals for San Francisco* in a cynical and manipulative way? If so, should Conway, as an emissary of the Catholic Church at the UN Conference, let the former Federal Council of Churches official know that he was aware that the French believed he had the whole religious bloc in his pocket? Moreover, should Conway take the trouble to emphatically deny to Dulles that he could control the Catholic "vote" or orchestrate its use for the pleasure of his associates on Wall Street? If the reply to these questions was in the affirmative, should another step then be taken?[64]

Conway did not think that Dulles, with his familial and administrative background in organized Protestant affairs, would consent to be little more than a paid henchman for Big Business. The Jesuit did believe, however, that Dulles was using the religious bloc for his own purposes. He deduced from information he had compiled that Dulles was playacting at four roles: official advisor to the American delegation and personal consultant to Vandenberg, representative of the interests of Big Business and international finance, self-appointed spokesman for all three faiths, and agent for American Protestantism. In this final incarnation, Conway conjectured, Dulles could potentially be most dangerous to the Church, since he would be able to advance several Protestant objectives at the expense of Catholic interests. Accordingly, Conway preferred to let Dulles know that Catholics reserved the right to dissent from his arguments and would freely use this autonomy as a bargaining chip at some future time.[65]

If this technique was too forceful, then Conway assured his NCWC superiors that he could undertake an indirect approach. The Jesuit alleged that he always had a standing engagement with Vandenberg's secretary, who often worked in tandem with Dulles. Since this man was an old friend, Conway would simply discuss, in regular conversation, the application that was being made of the potentialities of religious groups in securing amendments. Such a tête-à-tête would get back to Dulles almost immediately. In this way, the US advisor would still be made to understand that, as a minimum, Catholics wanted to be consulted in any exercise of a religious-bloc threat. If this simple courtesy was not forthcoming, then Dulles would be informed that he could not count on Catholic public support when the UN Charter came before the Senate.

In conclusion, Conway wondered if the NCWC should bring pressure to bear on Bidault to line him up with the British and Americans on this issue. He assumed that the French would do nothing to endanger their security pact with the Russians as long as there was any chance that the UN would be too easy on Germany. They would need strong assurances before they would vote against the Soviet Union on a major point such as this.[66]

Caroll immediately sent copies of Father Conway's letter to several of the most important prelates in the nation, including Archbishops Amleto Cicognani, Apostolic Delegate to the United States, Edward Mooney, and Samuel Stritch. Although the Delegate made no reply, Stritch and Mooney, who were good friends, had a conversation on May 15 in which they considered Conway's report and expressed their mutual doubts about the trustworthiness of John Foster Dulles.[67]

Stritch had received an account from a Catholic journalist according to which Dulles had informed the newsman that he did not agree wholly with the Pope's Peace Program. The US advisor was furthermore, in Stritch's opinion, a representative of Wall Street and big finance. Comparing Dulles with John D. Rockefeller, "a Protestant who never forgets his business interests," and who probably regarded the Catholic Church as an inconsequential establishment, he exhorted Mooney to inform Dulles discreetly and indirectly that he "may not speak for us." Accordingly, Mooney instructed Conway that he was to be circumspect and prudent in whatever he had to say. He also notified Monsignor Carroll that he should let their direct contacts at the State Department know how the Catholic Church stood on this important topic.[68]

With regard to the issue under discussion, Stritch was quite favorable to Vandenberg's proposed amendment—even in its revised form. It was, he concluded, in accord with Catholic thought and at least it expressed the mind of the UN as against the freezing of arrangements already made or being made at that time. But he admitted that his expectations were as low as they could be. It was very clear from world events that it would be impossible to form any workable world organization without Russian cooperation; but with its participation one could anticipate nothing but inexorable contention. Finally, the members of his committee on the Pope's Peace Plan were generally in agreement with the proponents of the "peaceful change" amendment, but they did not want John Foster Dulles to presume to represent them.[69]

In spite of Carroll's wire commending a prudent indirect approach to Vandenberg's secretary, Conway declined to take immediate action with regard to Dulles. Instead he straightway sought further instructions in the light of additional information he had just received. The Jesuit had obtained confirmation of the French view of the "Vandenberg Amendment," as well as further intelligence that revealed that the Vatican was being seen by France as a collaborator with Dulles in his attempt to secure an early relaxation of the controls to be imposed on Germany. In summary Conway said that the French delegation was clustering the Republicans, international financiers, and American religious groups, together with the Vatican, into a steadfast hostile alliance, opposed to all demands for an unbreakable rein over Germany.[70]

This was an all-important question for the French and was the real reason, Conway discovered, for Bidault's temporary absence from the Conference. The priest had to confess that the new data in his possession contradicted some of his prior information on Bidault. Far from staying on the sidelines in the "peaceful change" dispute, the head of the French delegation was in the thick of the conflict.

On his way to consult his government in Paris, the French Foreign Minister had stopped off in Washington to disclose to Truman, who the French were convinced would not emulate FDR's bipartisan foreign policy, what "the republicans were doing." Conway said that Bidault proposed to the president a separate control pact over Germany under the supervision of, among other nations, France and Russia. This compact would be completely outside the world organization; since in French opinion the American delegation was under Republican control, no attempt had been made to present this proposal to it.

At first inclined to bitterly oppose the "peaceful change" amendment, which as interpreted by Vandenberg would have covered absolutely all situations that might cause trouble, the French would now rely on Truman and the Democrats in the delegation to support a separate control pact. With this in place, they would no longer need to oppose the adoption of the amendment. Conway was led to believe that the Russians were in complete accord with this strategy.

Going into the final round of this baffling crisis, therefore, Conway accurately advised the leadership of the US Catholic Church that it had been put in a most difficult position. In view of the papal insistence on terms for the revision of treaties, the absence of such provisions would make it extremely hard to defend the UN Charter as in accord with Vatican thought. On the other hand, insistence on the specific proposal that was now being identified with the Republicans would align the NCWC with those alleged financial schemers who were being denounced as potential saboteurs of world peace.[71]

The "Peaceful Change" Solution

In spite of the inherent dangers that existed in a promotional campaign for the "peaceful change" clause, the National Catholic Welfare Conference ultimately opted for this course. In a bold lobbying effort, inspired in part by Father Conway's suggestions, it launched a month-long drive for incorporation into the UN Charter of an effective juridicial mechanism for the revision of international treaties.[72]

Catholic agents in San Francisco and Washington were made to understand that, as far the Church was concerned, the word "situations" omitted no treaties; Russia's security pacts as well as the peaceful settlements to be imposed on Germany and Japan were all open to UN review. Furthermore, in spite of French and Russian antagonism, the NCWC defended the principle that, in the not-too-distant future, a German recovery should be facilitated by the rapid withdraw of postwar sanctions. This action was advocated not in deference to big business, but from a desire for justice and liberty for the German people.

Finally, through some of its governmental connections in Washington, the NCWC approached President Truman to "set him straight" on the policy of the Church in all matters relating to the "peaceful change" amendment. This effort was aimed at assuring Truman that Catholic mediation in this case was not to be construed as indicating that it was in sympathy with some of the ulterior purposes that were being ascribed to "Republican international financiers."[73]

For several weeks, during which the NCWC conducted its crusade for the "peaceful change" amendment, the controversy over this addition to the UN Charter lay dormant. But the question of interpretation erupted again in mid-June, during the final sessions of the Committee on the Political and Security Functions of the General Assembly. During these discussions Senator Vandenberg, as spokesman for the Big Five, was put in the awkward position of having to oppose a recommendation that suggested a more specific definition of the word "situations." Even as he was doing so, Gromyko was denying the competence of the General Assembly in matters of revision of treaties.[74]

When the Senator was asked whether he and the Soviets were in agreement on the interpretation of the clause, he admitted publicly for the first time that they were not. Calling the Soviet position a unilateral one, Vandenberg claimed that the overwhelming weight of opinion was on the side of the American rendition. However, this was not quite the case and the senator from Michigan knew it.[75]

The minutes of several meetings of the American delegation, which Vandenberg attended, indicate that the Americans were aware that they were in a minority on this issue. Moreover, even many State Department officials were not anxious to see the spirit of Vandenberg's original language become the official UN explication of the amendment.[76] Nelson A. Rockefeller, as Assistant Secretary of State for Latin American Affairs, was adamantly opposed to such an interpretation. He had been informed by all the Pan-American delegates that the initial version would unduly complicate the situation for Latin American diplomats who hoped to avoid opening existing treaties for revision, because of the numerous border disputes on their continent. Therefore, owing to these factors, Vandenberg was knowingly tolerating the probable sacrifice of his amendment on the altar of ambiguity.[77]

Because of Latin American opposition to a serious "peaceful change" clause, Pattee, who was very close to these delegations, remained outside the center of the debate. Not wishing to contest the NCWC stance on this point, he limited his commentary to a few meager observations. For Pattee, however, it was obvious that in time there would be a need to introduce changes into treaties then in existence. He believed that to freeze the present system would be disastrous. Therefore, in an attempt to bridge the chasm between the views of the NCWC and of his Latin American friends, he proposed a fundamental principle that would revise treaties and other agreements only when such action was required by justice and by the good of the world community. In this way most South American border disputes would be overlooked.[78]

Conway was satisfied that only time would determine whether it might have been better to precipitate a crisis—"just as acute as that over the veto issue"—as the NCWC policy would have done, than to adopt an amendment the meaning of which was open to contradictory explanations. The Jesuit neatly summarized Catholic thought on this point by predicting that when Vandenberg would be asked during the ratification debate in the US Senate whether his "peaceful change" motion had been accepted, he would not be able to give an unequivocal response. He would be able to state only that the General Assembly now had the power to recommend the revision of unjust "situations"—whatever that meant.[79]

The final compromises on "veto power" and "peaceful change" reflected several stated goals of the US Catholic Church, but the overwhelming opinion of the Catholic consultants and observers held that the Big Five had preserved the preponderance of the "Yalta Concessions" for themselves. They believed, furthermore, that this predicament could only spell disaster for democratic procedures and policies in the United Nations.[80] Nonetheless, it was hoped by many Catholic representatives that, at least, ethical constitutional principles would be inserted in the San Francisco Charter. Such fundamental tenets would, they anticipated, go far in the direction of a viable moral framework on which a gradual UN reform could be based.

Notes

1. ANCWC 13b, "Assertion of Moral and Juridical Principles," Christopher Dawson, April 30, 1945, p. 2. Christopher Dawson was born in 1889 in Yorkshire, England. He was converted to the Roman Catholic faith in 1914. Educated at Winchester and at Trinity College, Oxford, he lectured for many years in philosophy at Liverpool University, and in the history of culture at University College, Exeter. He was the author of numerous books in the fields of history and religion. He edited the *Dublin Review* and was active in the British Catholic peace organization, *The Sword of the Spirit* (ANCWC 13b, "One of the Great News Stories of History," Frank Hall, April 2, 1945, p. 1).

2. "Report on the United Nations Conference. . . ," p. 15.

3. See Chapter I, pp. 18–19; Chapter II, pp. 21–22; Chapter III, pp. 69, 74–76, 87, 102; Chapter V, pp. 152, 182–86.

4. ANCWC 15, James T. Shotwell, "Charter of the Golden Gate," *Survey Graphic,* July 1945, p. 311. This was the fifth in a series of six articles written for *Survey Graphic* by Shotwell under the general title "Bridges to the Future."

5. Ibid.

6. Ibid., p. 312.

7. On June 4, 1945, the famous "penthouse meeting" of the Big Five occurred, at which the United States, Great Britain, China, and France agreed, against the appeal by Andrei Gromyko of the Soviet Union, that the General Assembly of the United Nations had the power to discuss questions "in the sphere of international relations," even those "dealing with the maintenance of peace and security" (ANCWC 15, Report of Interview with Senator Arthur Vandenberg and John Foster Dulles, Edward A. Conway, [San Francisco], June 5, 1945, p. 4, copy).

8. "Report on the United Nations Conference. . . ," p. 15.

9. "Fear 'Big Five' Veto As Aggressor Aid," *The New York Times,* April 20, 1945, p. 13.

10. "Observations Upon the Conference VIII," p. 2.

11. "Implementing the World Court," *The New York Times,* March 9, 1945, p. 18.

12. *On Organizing World Peace,* p. 1.

13. ANCWC 13b, "Rights of Small Nations Must Be Considered, Says Authority on Papal Program for Peace," Guido Gonella, April 9, 1945. p. 2.

14. *Goals for San Francisco,* p. 1.

15. ANCWC 15, Memorandum on Some Aspects of a World Security Organization. . . ," Conway to Carroll, [D.C.], April 19, 1945, p. 4.

16. "Charter of the Golden Gate," p. 312.

17. "2. Decisions of the Security Council on procedural matters should be made by an affirmative vote of seven members. 3. Decisions of the Security Council on all other matters should be made by an affirmative vote of seven members, including the concurring votes of the permanent members; provided that . . . a party to a dispute should abstain from voting" (*Yearbook of the United Nations, 1946–1947* [Lake Success, New York: Department of Public Information, United Nations, 1947], p. 9).

18. ANCWC 11, "Soviets Seen Overplaying Their Hand in Showdown Over Veto Interpretation," by E. A. Conway, S. J., June 5, 1945, p. 7.

19. *E. R. Stettinius, Jr.,* p. 71; "The Charter of the Golden Gate," p. 312.

20. "Soviets Seen Overplaying Hand in Showdown Over Veto Interpretation," p. 7.

21. Ibid.

22. *E. R. Stettinius, Jr.,* p. 71.

23. Report of Interview with Senator Vandenberg and John Foster Dulles, June 5, 1945, p. 1.

24. Ibid.

25. "I was proud of my country when I heard the Stettinius mes-

sage. It is in the best American tradition. It left no room for doubt that the United States cannot join an international organization in which the doors are shut upon free speech and free discussion. After that message, it would be impossible for us to yield, or even compromise, if we ever expect Stalin to have the slightest respect for our American word again" (*The Private Papers of Senator Vandenberg,* p. 202).

26. Report of Interview with Senator Vandenberg. . . , p. 2.

27. Ibid.

28. Ibid., p. 3.

29. Ibid. The telegram read as follows:

President Truman
White House
Washington, D.C.

"Deeply appreciate your support of American U.N.C.I.O. Delegation in refusing to write into Charter an interpretation of veto power that will allow one nation to prevent Security Council from discussing any dispute or situation threatening international peace. Those of us who have worked wholeheartedly for effective international organization could not in good conscience endorse Charter sanctioning gag rule interpretation of a voting agreement which in itself is far from ideal.

Archbishop Edward Mooney
Chairman, NCWC Admin. Board"

30. In 1945 James T. Shotwell was a Professor of History at Columbia University and director of the Division of Economics and History of the Carnegie Endowment for International Peace. He was, moreover, a consultant at the UNCIO for the Carnegie Endowment ("Charter of the Golden Gate," p. 309).

31. "Charter of the Golden Gate," p. 312.

32. RG 59f, Box 22, "The U.N. Conference as Reported by U.S. Press and Radio Comment," July 1945, p. 3.

33. Ibid.

34. "Who will guard the custodians . . . ?"

35. "The Veto Solution," *America* 73 (June 16, 1945):214; "The Veto Crisis," *Commonweal* 42 (June 15, 1945):204.

36. "World Organization as a Forum," *America* 73 (June 2, 1945):166.

37. "Report on United Nations Conference. . . ," p. 15.

38. "Some Observations of the San Francisco Conference. . . ," p. 18.

39. "The San Francisco Conference," p. 4.

40. ANCWC 11, "Satisfactory Progress Seen in Proposed Charter

Toward *Goals for San Francisco,*" Rev. E. A. Conway, S. J., June 25, 1945, p. 8.

41. ANCWC 11, Memorandum of Conversation, Conway and Herbert Vere Evatt, [San Francisco], June 25, 1945, p. 1.

42. Ibid.

43. Ibid., p. 2.

44. "Satisfactory Progress Seen in Proposed Charter Toward *Goals for San Francisco,*" p. 8.

45. "Charter of the Golden Gate," p. 312.

46. Shirley Hazzard, *The Defeat of an Ideal* (Boston: Little, Brown, 1973) p. 7.

47. R.G. 59a 1977, Folder 1, Memorandum of Conversation between Arthur Vandenberg and Dean Acheson, [D.C.], February 19, 1945, p. 2.

48. R.G. 59a 1980, Secret Memorandum for the President on Senator Vandenberg, [D.C.], March 16, 1945.

49. U.S. Congress. Senate, Speech of Senator Vandenberg on the United Nations Organization, 79th Cong., 1st sess., April 2, 1945, *Congressional Record* 91:4584.

50. Ibid.

51. *Pius XII and Peace, 1939–1940,* "Christmas Message, December 24, 1939," p. 39; ANCWC 11, Enclosure with "Those Big Four Amendments," Edward Conway, May 13, 1945.

52. *On Organizing World Peace,* p. 1; RG 59b, Box 191, Folder 6, Summary of Statement Issued by the Archbishops and Bishops of the NCWC, April 14, 1945.

53. ANCWC 11, "Peaceful Change Clause of Charter Remains Open to Varying Interpretations," E. A. Conway, S. J., June 18, 1945, p. 20.

54. Ibid.

55. "Those Big Four Amendments," p. 1.; *The Private Papers of Senator Vandenberg,* p. 172.

56. ANCWC 11, Memorandum *re* Vandenberg Amendment on "Peaceful Change," Conway to Carroll, [San Francisco], May 13, 1945, p. 1. The amendment now read: "Subject to the provisions of paragraph I of this Section, The General Assembly should be empowered to recommend measures for the peaceful adjustment of any situations, regardless of origin, which it deems likely to impair the general welfare or friendly relations among nations, including situations resulting from a violation of the Purposes and Principles set forth in this Charter."

57. "Those Big Four Amendments," p. 2.

58. Ibid.

59. Memorandum *re* Vandenberg Amendment on "Peaceful Change," p. 1.

60. ANCWC 11, Conway to Clarence Enzler, [San Francisco], May 19, 1945, p. 3.

61. Ibid.

62. This interpretation of events is corroborated by the memoirs of Georges Bidault (*D'une Résistance à L'Autre,* [Paris: Les Presses du Siècle, 1965], pp. 97–101).

63. Memorandum *re* Vandenberg Amendment on "Peaceful Change," p. 2.

64. Ibid., p. 3.

65. Ibid.

66. Ibid., p. 4.

67. AAC 2966M, Stritch to Mooney, [Chicago], May 15, 1945, p. 1, copy.

68. Ibid., p. 2.

69. Ibid.

70. AAC 2967C, Conway to Carroll, [San Francisco], May 19, 1945, p. 1, copy.

71. Ibid., p. 2.

72. Memorandum *re* Further Developments in Big Power Discussions of Vandenberg Peaceful Change Amendment, p. 3.

73. Ibid.

74. *The Private Papers of Senator Vandenberg,* p. 212.

75. "Peaceful Change Clause of Charter Remains Open to Varying Interpretations," p. 20.

76. *The Private Papers of Senator Vandenberg,* p. 214.

77. *General: The United Nations,* pp. 906–07.

78. "Some Observations on the San Francisco Conference. . . ," p. 19.

79. "Peaceful Change Clause of Charter Remains Open to Varying Interpretations," p. 20.

80. In reviewing the first ten years of the UN, Luard supports this contention of the Catholic consultants. He believes that though the powers of the Assembly had been marginally increased in the area of security, neither the basic structure of the organization nor the general subordination of the Assembly to the Security Council in matters of peace and security had been significantly altered (*The Years of Western Domination,* p. 57).

CHAPTER VII
The Juridical Order

On May 28, 1945, Father Raymond McGowan, Executive Secretary of the Catholic Association for International Peace, congratulated its consultant, Thomas H. Mahony, for his labors on behalf of the Peace Association at the San Francisco Conference. McGowan had been advised beforehand by Catherine Schaefer that Mahony had been extraordinarily effective at UNCIO in matters of international law, the International Court of Justice (ICJ), and an International Bill of Rights. His influence was particularly felt within the American Bar Association, which was exerting a significant, if not always successful, influence on the United States delegation. This circumstance was all the more remarkable, since Mahony, in his dealings with the legal establishment at the Conference, made no effort to conceal that he was espousing "Catholic opinions" on these subjects.[1]

In his letter to the CAIP representative, an obviously delighted McGowan said that although the conference was far from over—the UNCIO would not conclude its work for another four weeks—"even if the whole thing doesn't go through," Mahony's work had been a fine piece of Catholic "apologetics." In McGowan's mind, this should have demonstrated to members of the American delegation and to other consultants the necessity and worth of cooperation with Catholic agencies.[2]

Mahony would have been the first to concede that he was aided in his efforts at San Francisco because the Catholic Church approached the UNCIO with a considered position on the nature of the postwar juridical order. Although abetted by this logical, matured framework, he and other Catholic agents were nonetheless confronted by a Big-Power bloc—including the United States—far more eager to secure world peace through armed might than through creation of an equitable codification of international law.[3]

Security Versus Justice

Even during the carnage of World War I, Pope Benedict XV had urged a democratic, juridical, and universal world organization. Pius XI and his successor, Pius XII, persisted in this plea, even in the face of the failure of the League of Nations and the approach of another global conflict. Continuing in this vein, the American bishops stressed throughout World War II—along with Protestant and Jewish groups—the importance of such an association. The bishops stated that the preamble to its charter should provide acknowledgment of the supremacy of moral law. Its statutes must likewise arrange a codification and development of international law and prohibition of arbitrary exceptions to adjudication of disputes. Finally, regulations to certify proper revision of treaties and protection of the political and economic rights of small nations, a pledge that would guarantee their adequate participation in the activities of the UN, and suitable administration of mandated areas (trusteeships) in the interest of the political and economic advancement of their non-self-governing peoples, had also to be formulated by the new league.[4]

The Dumbarton Oaks proposals, on which the UNCIO intended to base its organizational charter, visualized that the international association would furnish collective security for its members and maintain peace primarily through the overwhelming power of the United States, the United Kingdom, and the Soviet Union, as well as through the nascent military capacities of China and France. These propositions implied that, as these Powers alone possessed the major force, and therefore the major obligation, to prevent or overcome aggression likely to endanger peace, little more needed to be said about "world jurisdiction."[5] Accordingly, no specific references to the sovereignty of moral law in relations among states, or in codification of international law, were included in the Dumbarton Oaks proposals.[6]

Father Conway was the first Catholic spokesman to depre-
cate this underlying doctrine of Dumbarton Oaks. It was not
the pope or Catholic leaders, he said, who were asking, "What
is the use?" (of upholding international law and the "reign of
justice"). In the face of wartime anarchy, he believed, many
leaders determined to stabilize the international situation only
through use of military arms. The peoples of the world recognized the evil of disorder, however, and they would turn to good
government if it was clearly presented to them. Pius XII's
"Peace Program" established that the natural habitat for social
beings was an orderly society, operating under law and legal
international institutions. This, Conway affirmed, was what the
pope meant by juridical order and institutions.[7]

In their statement of April 15, 1945, the bishops of the
Administrative Board echoed these sentiments and disparaged
the Dumbarton Oaks solution as little more than a surrender to
the "spirit of paralyzing fatalism." Labelling it an "Alliance
between the Great Victorious Powers" and not a plan for organization under law, they challenged the UNCIO to amend the
"flawed" document and to get on with the business of establishing a new era of genuine peace and progress.[8]

The controversial CAIP document, *Judging the Dumbarton
Oaks Proposals,* which professed to welcome what was good
and to criticize what was defective in that compact, targeted as
Dumbarton's greatest failure its inability to produce a formula
for codification of international law. Such an index, the Peace
Association asserted, should have registered not only matters
of custom and procedure that had grown out of standard international practices, but also a clear statement on innate human
rights.[9] By early April, Father Conway, as a member of the Post
War World Committee that had ratified this CAIP declaration,
was likewise making this point. Advocating the development
and impartial enforcement of international law in his tri-faith
statement, *Goals for San Francisco,* he cited the statement of
the Federal Council of Churches' report of January 1945, which
championed the "progressive subordination of force to law."[10]

Conway's most complete pronouncement on this subject,
and the most comprehensive public stance taken by a Catholic
up to that time, came even before *Goals.* In a radio broadcast of

March 11, 1945, made in Indianapolis for the "Indiana Committee for Victory," Conway enumerated a series of juristic propositions to be considered by the UNCIO. The preamble of the UN Charter, he stated, should commit the signatory states to acknowledge that "they are subject to a law that takes priority over their individual wills." The Big Five organizers of the San Francisco Conference needed, in addition, to proceed at once to form a commission for development of international law. Finally, commissions on human rights, on non-self-governing peoples, on minorities and small nations should likewise begin immediately to ensure that these legal guarantees would be incorporated into the constitution of the world organization. Only in this way would proper, constructive steps be taken toward international jurisdictional collaboration.[11]

The Catholic Church's pre-conference theories on a "cornerstone" for postwar peace were summarized by Christopher Dawson, editor of the *Dublin Review*. Writing for the "Spotlights on San Francisco" series, he noted that the principle of security, as perceived and practiced by the Big Powers, had been responsible for some of history's most heinous crimes. A preoccupation with security alone would lead inevitably to a subordination of international law to political interests, whereas a sovereign international legal system would eclipse political interests and address the concerns of both large and small nations.[12]

Dawson posited that it would not be possible "to create instantaneously, by a sort of international social contract," a true world-society with an effective legislative and jurisdictional system, but that the foundations for such a structure could be laid and its aims defined at San Francisco. It was therefore essential that the UN Conference rebuff all positions that were incompatible with these paramount objectives and that could tempt the conferees to relinquish a fitting juristic arrangement simply to gain short-term political advantages.[13]

A Boston Lawyer In San Francisco

In 1945 the Catholic Association for International Peace scheduled its annual weekend "Study Conference" at Trinity

College in Washington, D.C. for April 2 and 3 to consider the Dumbarton Oaks recommendations in light of Catholic teachings. Because of an Office of Defense Transportation order that restricted the holding of conventions, however, the Executive Council of the CAIP was forced to cancel the event. Thomas Mahony was listed as the opening speaker at the symposium, and although his intended remarks are not extant, the title of his address, "Development of International Law and Extension of International Jurisdiction," gives every indication of its content. There can be little doubt that Mahony had already given much thought to the topic of this discourse, and was therefore well prepared for the deliberations on these questions at San Francisco.[14]

Only three weeks later, in the earliest phase of the Conference, Mahony was already acknowledged as one of its most enlightened and influential legal authorities. With several other lawyer-consultants he had set up an *ad hoc* committee to discuss matters relating to codification of world law. This circle of legal specialists, composed mainly of consultants from the American Bar Association and the National Lawyers Guild, had held several sessions by early May. Boasting such distinguished members of the profession as David Simmons, president of the ABA, Professor James T. Shotwell of Columbia University, and Judge Joseph M. Poskauer of the American Jewish Committee, this group captured the attention of the American delegation through its recommendation that the United States submit an amendment to the UN Charter establishing a commission to codify fundamental principles of international law. The delegation, however, did not follow this recommendation.[15]

Mahony had been instrumental in the fast-paced effort to develop such a revision, but he was not fast enough. Midnight on Friday, May 4, was the deadline for filing all amendments to the Dumbarton Oaks proposals. Any American revisions needed approval by the other sponsoring Powers before that hour. The lawyer-consultants hoped that the United States would amend Dumbarton Oaks by calling for establishment of a codification commission, but neither the United States nor

any other Big Power came forth with such a motion. In other
words, no commission or agency to formulate principles of
general international law to guide relations between member
states, or to control decisions of the International Court in
adjudication of disputes, was to be established.[16]

Mahony would not give up, however. Insisting that all was
not lost, he pointed out that the Chinese delegation had suggested an amendment to the Charter that provided that "the
[General] Assembly should be responsible for initiating studies
and making recommendations with respect to the development
and revision of the rules and principles of international law."
This proposal, endorsed by the other members of the Big Four,
was assured of approval, and was in Mahony's opinion a significant improvement over Dumbarton Oaks. Urging his fellow
consultants to work with like-minded associates within the
delegations of smaller nations, he mobilized a lobby intent on
improving the Chinese amendment.[17]

These improvements to the Chinese amendment encom-
passed granting the General Assembly power-of-appointment
over a permanent commission to formulate principles of international law for submission to the organization and to its members for adoption. The consultant also proposed giving the
Assembly authority from time to time "to propose modifications, extensions, abrogations of, or additions to, such principles."[18] Defeated by time once before, Mahony realized that
here again there was a necessary air of emergency in all this.
These substitutions must be incorporated into the amendment
before it reached the plenary session of the Conference at
which it would be debated and voted on. The UNCIO committee to which all such emendations were submitted was called
"Committee IV-2." With the help of American consultants,
several delegations had, my May 11, submitted to this body
additions to the Chinese amendment.

Mahony favored one introduced by the Egyptian delegation.
That panel's modification stipulated that it was advisable to
promulgate a code of international law subsequent to the UN-
CIO, either by creation of a special agency under the General
Assembly or through the projected Economic and Social Coun-

cil. Either way, it declared, rules of international law and morality must be "determined, defined, codified and developed."[19]

In his defense of the Egyptian proposition, Mahony had recourse to remarks of Pius XII and of the Catholic hierarchy of the United States. It was of the first importance, the pontiff stated, to erect some global juridical institution that would guarantee the unfailing fulfillment of the conditions accepted by the united nations of the world: one that would, in case of recognized need, revise and correct its ordinances. The CAIP consultant also rehearsed the Catholic bishops' statement of November 1944, which recommended that an essential condition for right functioning of an International Court was appropriate development and codification of international law. Inasmuch as law was dynamic, Mahony summarized, it must be adequate for changing times and conditions—even though it was based fundamentally on the immutable natural law. An agency or agencies should be set up to formulate principles of international law that would apply to the judicial determination of disputes of a legal character and would recommend changes in such laws when required.[20]

Not willing to stand passively awaiting the decision of Committee IV-2 or the plenary session of the UNCIO, on May 24 Mahony outlined a draft for a resolution that encouraged members of the American delegation to uphold a more flexible method of amending the UN Charter. This blueprint advocated specifically the convening of a constitutional convention at the end of five years, as well as a commission to formulate principles of international law for acceptance by member states.[21]

Mahony was determined, however, to follow a policy of "indirect action" in this case—at least in the matter of publication of the resolution. For tactical reasons he preferred that it be drafted by David Simmons of the American Bar Association. The CAIP consultant thought that the memorandum would receive more support if it were advanced by a legal organization rather than by the Catholic Peace Association. Catherine Schaefer thought this was a wise decision. And indeed, when the smoke finally cleared at the end of the UNCIO, Mahony could claim this as one of his successes.[22]

Since the Dumbarton Oaks proposals made no provision for formulation or modification of the principles of international law, the fact that the UN Charter ultimately did so had to be deemed a victory. It further provided for application of that law in various sections of the Charter dealing with subjects such as "justice as a purpose and principle," individual rights, and the International Court of Justice. Mahony counted as a partial victory the plenary session's approval of the Chinese Amendment. With regard to the functions and power of the General Assembly, the UNCIO had incorporated into the Charter this rider that affirmed the right of the Assembly to "initiate studies and make recommendations for the purpose of . . . encouraging the progressive development of international law and its codification."[23]

Of course, there were also defeats. The Egyptian revision and the ABA resolution had been shunted aside. In functioning under the Chinese amendment (Article 13, Section 10), the General Assembly could not fashion any recommendations legally binding on the members of the UN. H. G. Nicholas, in *The United Nations As a Political Institution,* stated that one could call this prerogative "quasi-legislative," since it had the form but not the force of law. For this reason, the feeling was still strong that, like the Dumbarton Oaks proposals, the Charter did not show enough regard for law as a basis for international organization. These failures, Mahony believed, were glaringly evident, and unfortunately went to the very heart of sound jurisprudence.[24]

In addition, Mahony noted that the UN Charter would contain no specific reference to the sovereignty of the moral law. It did not provide, therefore, for recognition of its supremacy in principle, much less of its rule over relations among states or of citizens within those states. There was no stipulation that exercise of national sovereignty by any state need defer to the rights of the international community, nor did it provide limitations on this national sovereignty. Finally, Mahony ruefully recounted that the Charter failed to give any agency power to legislate on international relations, international rights, and international obligations, as the Egyptian revision mandated.[25]

The Tranquility Of Order?

Mahony believed that without law to control the relations of a global society, world order would be impossible for any length of time. Quoting St. Augustine, he argued that peace was inconceivable without world order. This reaction to the San Francisco Charter was shared by most Catholic participants, observers, and journalists.[26]

In a letter to *The New York Times,* Father Conway stated that for thousands of years the world had learned that wherever government by law endured, peace could exist; where there was no government by law, conflict was a constant reality. By maintaining the absolute sovereignties of rival nation-states, the UNCIO had prevented the creation of a superior standard in world relations. In this failure it resembled nothing so much as the old "*Articles of Confederation* of the thirteen original American republics." Conway posited that no "league system" ever attempted in human history had prevented conflict among its members. He therefore called for an all-out effort for a "Federal Constitution of the world, a working worldwide legal order."[27]

This did not mean that Conway advocated rejection of the UN Charter. To the contrary, he fully intended that "men of good will" should work with what the UNCIO furnished. What the conference furnished was the Chinese Amendment, which permitted the General Assembly to "encourage" the development and classification of international law. Through this vague instruction, Conway detected, too optimistically, the opportunity eventually to amend the Charter so that the General Assembly could establish a corpus of international law as the bishops of the United States advocated.[28]

With regard to the media's reaction to the issue of the development of international law, the State Department's Office of Public Opinion Studies was no doubt correct in its concise evaluation that "the press and radio paid scant attention to judicial matters."[29] This was not true, however, of at least one Catholic periodical, *Commonweal.* In their espousal of the rights of small nations, the magazine's editors claimed that the only hope for the peoples of these states—and for the peoples of the world—was the establishment of an effective United Nations with a fully developed and universally accepted code of law. What had unfortunately occurred in San Francisco, they believed, was the establishment of principles and laws without adequate punitive agencies to enforce them, and the setting forth of idealistic preambles in the face of "realistic and hard-boiled new devices of power politics." *Commonweal,* however, was up to the challenge. The cynics could sneer at the vague quixotic formulas of the Charter, but the democratic forces of the world—those who believed in freedom—had to make these canons real. "The hard work for freedom starts from here and is defined here," the editors proclaimed.[30]

All this bravado provoked the American Labor Party to issue a sarcastic pamphlet entitled, *Angels Could Do It Better,* attacking *Commonweal* for its "perfectionist" crusade. Protestant leaders at San Francisco as well as the weeklies *Life, Time,* and *Liberty,* however, rallied to *Commonweal's* defense. Although the fervor at its Madison Avenue headquarters was certainly not dimmed by the Labor Party's mockery, *Commonweal's* editors still spoke darkly of an "overload" of work to be done.[31]

Mahony ended his comments on the settlement of the international law dispute in a similar vein. After stating reassuringly that the Charter did contemplate amendments and permit general discussion, he listed two melancholy pages of UNCIO juridical failures. Fortunately, that inventory did not include an International Bill of Rights.[32]

An International Bill Of Rights

On March 26, 1945, the "Text of the Appeal of H.[is] E.[xcellency] Archbishop Sapieha to the American Hierarchy and to the Catholic Bishops of the World," reached Washington. Dispatched through the "Polish Underground Army," this plea for the "defense of Polish Christians" censured Soviet authorities for "ruthless might, deportations and executions" directed at "Holy Church." Claiming that the Russians intended nothing less than the utter and cynical destruction of the Roman Catholic Church in Poland and throughout the world, the archbishop enumerated various atrocities that "the Bolsheviks" had perpetrated, including the deportation of Catholic teachers and children into Russia, the execution of seminary professors, and the "liquidation" of entire communities of religious priests and nuns.[33]

Because of the impossibility of communicating openly with the Vatican and with the rest of the world, Sapieha begged the American hierarchy to speak for him "in the name of all martyred Poles," to inform Pius XII of this matter, to issue a petition for justice for Poland, and to address themselves to competent authorities in the United States who could put pressure on Stalin to restore religious freedom in Europe. Two days after this entreaty was delivered to NCWC headquarters, the Catholic Conference initiated a correspondence with O. Frederick Nolde, Executive Secretary of the Joint Committee on Religious Liberty of the Federal Council of Churches—and a future UNCIO consultant—in order to effectively coordinate the activities of independent sectarian committees that advocated a "Commission on Human Rights in the World Organization Charter."[34]

The dying Franklin Roosevelt had realized substantial success in making the Yalta Decisions on Eastern Europe palatable to dubious American Catholics. The Big Three, he reminded them, had pledged that Poland would have free elections and that the Baltic peoples would not suffer the imposition of unrepresentative regimes. There was to be freedom, independence, and peace in the region.[35] The NCWC had always been skeptical of FDR's optimism and had said so publicly. Now, however, the US Catholic leadership's disquiet in the face of incontrovertible proof of the absence of religious and civil well-being in Poland goaded the Church to actively embrace the cause of human rights at the UNCIO.

As the Conference began, Thomas E. Kissling, a staff writer for the NCWC News Service, warned that it was still far from inevitable that religious freedom and liberty of conscience would be given anything more than a perfunctory endorsement by the UN Charter. If history was any indication, the UNCIO of 1945 might well resemble the Paris Peace Conference of February 1919. At that assembly, a strong bid was made to include a "religious freedom clause" in the proposed Covenant of the League of Nations, but in the end it was the only article deleted from the original draft.[36]

Indeed, an interested bystander from the United States, in Paris at the time of the Peace Conference, left an account of the demise of the proposed Article XIX, which would have granted free exercise of religion. Writing in 1939, in his book *The Bishop Jots It Down,* Francis Clement Kelley, bishop of Oklahoma City and Tulsa, observed:

> It was held by some that the liberty of conscience article would have been fatal to the League. The exact contrary is true; it might have saved the League. The first blow given the League was the refusal of the United States to enter it. One of the arguments in support of that action was based on the fact that the Covenant did not safeguard liberty of conscience.[37]

Not wishing to witness another global failure on the order of the League of Nations, the Catholic Church in the United States had long undertaken to prepare itself for postwar deliberations on the various human freedoms—including religious enfranchisement. For example, in 1942 the Catholic Association for International Peace commissioned Wilfrid Parsons, S.J., to compose a Catholic version of "An International Bill of Rights." The results were, unfortunately in the words of Archbishop Stritch, ". . . too porlix . . . too indirect," and did not stick to accepted Catholic expressions on the matter.[38]

A far more productive and beneficial contribution to this enterprise was Father John Courtney Murray's *Notes on the Theory of Religious Liberty,* a lengthy memorandum on freedom of religion and of conscience with respect to the state and its temporal powers. Commissioned by the Administrative Board in early April 1945, this study by the noted Jesuit theologian was seminal to informed US Catholic opinion at the time of the UNCIO.[39]

The reverberations from Murray's research were felt almost immediately through the Administrative Board's pre-Conference statement, *On Organizing World Peace*. Professing that no country had the right to violate the inalienable rights of its citizens, the declarations stated the obligations of nations to the international community. Violations of the rights of minorities and denial of civil and religious liberties, the Board affirmed, had been throughout history the real dangers to world peace. To remove these dangers, the UNCIO ought to adopt an International Bill of Rights in which human beings everywhere were guaranteed their inherent freedoms. Moreover, the hierarchy concluded, if a regime declined to subscribe to a global Bill of Rights specifying these liberties, then its active participation in the world organization was unthinkable. How could a regime that did not secure these rights for those it governed strive honorably and sincerely for the maintenance of world peace and mutual cooperation?[40]

The struggle for recognition of this principle was one of the enduring legacies of World War II—at least on paper. The Atlantic Charter of 1941 called for a peace in which these rights would be reiterated and expanded, and the Dumbarton Oaks Conference pledged that the United Nations would promote respect for human rights and fundamental freedoms.[41]

Father Conway now proselytized actively for the transposition of these sentiments into a UN Charter that would tangibly secure human rights for "all the citizens of the world." *Goals for San Francisco,* of which he was the primary author, advocated not only an International Bill of Rights but also "a commission or commissions to protect and further the rights and liberties of persons and of racial, religious, and culural groups, especially those uprooted by war and oppression."[42] Citing other sectarian documents, such as the Federal Council of Churches' Cleveland Conference Report of January 1945 and *Pattern for Peace*—another document he had composed—Conway gave radio speeches and wrote essays that championed the dignity of these UN citizens. He claimed that if this verity were not spelled out in an international declaration of rights, with all its essential implications, then the establishment of the global organization could never be justified, and its failure would be foreordained.[43]

Taking these words to heart, the Catholic consultants to the UNCIO moved naturally to collaborate with other sympathetic representatives from the diverse American associations at San Francisco when the challenge arose to develop a comprehensive rationalization for inclusion of human rights into the UN Charter.

Relevance To The Charter

In early May, Conway remarked that although no one could deny that the preamble of the Covenant of the League of Nations was "a pretty sad affair," Chapter I of the Dumbarton oaks proposals—which dealt with principles—made that preamble look flawless by comparison. Likening the latter to the decrepit elevators at the San Francisco Palace Hotel, he launched a crusade to persuade the UNCIO conferees to try their hand at some improvements.[44]

To this end Conway favored a "most attractive draft" submitted by the seventy-seven-year-old Marshal Hans Christian Smuts, chairman of the South African delegation and Prime Minister of the Union of South Africa.[45] It was the purpose of the United Nations, Smuts wrote, to reestablish faith in fundamental human rights, the sanctity of human personality, the equal rights of men and women and of nations large and small, and so to promote social progress, better standards of living, tolerance, justice, and the obligations of international law. Certainly, Conway asserted, the Church could have no argument with this, and he reported that the Catholic consultants were already urging the Conference's Committee on the Preamble to include Smuts's text in that introduction to the Charter.

Although the Commission on General Principles, which oversaw the operations of the Preamble Committee, was chaired by a delegate from the Ukrainian Soviet Socialist Republic, Conway did not doubt that the Smuts preamble would triumph, since he correctly predicted that Russia dared not oppose so popular an affirmation of human rights. Accordingly, on the matter of the UN Charter's preamble, the Catholic representatives at San Francisco had their work done for them. However, not all rights endeavors were to be so effortless or so successful.[46]

On May 2, after only one full week of Charter debate, twenty-two of the forty UNCIO consultants—in reaction to US delegation inaction—formally submitted recommendations to that delegation for alterations to the Dumbarton Oaks proposals. The essential premise of these amendments was that "the ultimate inclusion of the equivalence of an International Bill of Rights in the functioning of the Organization is deemed of the essence of what is necessary to preserve the peace of the world."[47]

This modification was a response to an event of the day before. On Monday, May 1, at a regularly scheduled consultants' meeting, Dean Virginia Gildersleeve declared, in substance, that the United States delegation would not introduce any amendments on human rights or on the establishment of a commission to deal with their protection. On the other hand, it would support such suggestions if they came from other delegations. It was thus made apparent to the assembled consultants that the Truman Administration did not aspire to be in the vanguard of the fight for a UN Bill of Rights.[48]

Bewildered by this insensitivity toward human freedoms by representatives from the "Cradle of Liberty," a committee of consultants, consisting of Joseph Proskauer, James Shotwell, O. Frederick Nolde, and Jane Evans of the National Peace Conference, blithely ignored the delegation's apathy and drafted some potent equal-rights amendments. Circulated among the consultants, the solicitation soon garnered sufficient signatures and was presented to the Secretary of State Stettinius, who under the circumstances received it with "grace."[49]

The authors of this exhortation had a purpose, a principle, and a plan. The purpose was "to promote respect for human life" and the principle concerned the dignity and inviolability of persons as the cornerstone of civilization. The consultants therefore advised that assurance of "life, liberty and the pursuit of happiness," and the end of persecutions and infractions against human rights, were absolutely essential to international peace. The world organization must accordingly guarantee that each member state would treat its own population in a way that would not violate the dictates of humanity and of justice. This could be achieved only through an International Bill of Rights backed by a Human Rights Commission.[50]

The effectiveness and power of this proposal went beyond the mere statement of its principles and goals. Its final paragraph spoke of the innate "relevancy" of American leadership to the crusade for universal human rights. Although the authors understood that the primary objective of the UNCIO was to devise a structure for the new world-organization, it would come as a grievous shock if the constitutional framework of the United Nations failed to make adequate provision for the ultimate achievement of fundamental freedoms. The Atlantic Charter, the Four Freedoms, and the Declaration of the United Nations, as well as other proclamations made during the war, had given the peoples of the world the right to expect that the UN would expand international law to meet the anticipated progress toward peace with freedom. All indications were that the United Nations allies and the US population had assumed that America would be the deliberate patron of liberty in this cause. Sponsorship of this rights project would therefore undoubtedly receive enthusiastic support of the American people. For these reasons, both ethical and pragmatic, the consultants insisted that the US delegation take a position of leadership in this vital field.[51]

The reaction to their efforts must have been gratifying. The customarily diffident Stettinius—presumably in shock after his first taste of a consultant onslaught—almost immediately took up the proposal with the other members of the US delegation, and with apparent good results.[52] On May 2, at another meeting with the consultants, Archibald MacLeish announced that the principle of the May 2 petition and the plan for a commission on human rights would be included in formal amendments to be submitted to the Big Powers. He further conceded that the action of the consultants had an impact on the American position. At this same meeting, Commander Stassen "waxed eloquent" on the necessity of affirming human rights in the Preamble and of providing a commission to sustain those rights.[53]

Thomas Mahony and Richard Pattee had, of course, voluntarily signed the consultant petition, criticizing only one feature of the text during its final formulation. In the second section of the document, entitled "Principles Involved," they objected to the term "barbarous" in the statement "Hitlerism has demonstrated that persecution by a barbarous nation throws upon the peace-loving nations the burden of relief and redress." They noted that the NCWC Administrative Board had recently contended that the German people as a whole could not be held responsible for atrocities perpetuated by the Nazis. Although their unsuccessful protest was sincere and forceful, they did not think this one negative point to be important enough to outweigh the resolution's many positive attributes.[54]

Though Father Conway agreed unquestionably with the two consultants on this minor point, he was otherwise thoroughly dissatisfied with their lack of overall effectiveness in this "Human Rights Affair." Realizing his first bitter taste of frustration at the UNCIO, he resented being forced to stand far back from even the periphery of policy development, while other, more privileged Catholic representatives failed to capitalize on their positions. Hastily he looked around for some way to bring his connections, experience, and expertise to bear on the human rights debate.

By Pattee's admission, the opening days of May saw the human rights "angle on fire" in San Francisco, generating more interest than any other juridical issue. Unlike other legal questions, the "rights cause" could readily be identified with people and their needs. Conway thought, however, that Protestants and Jews—most notably Proskauer and Nolde—had "stolen the ball" on human rights. Grandiloquently, the Jesuit envisioned that they would go down in history as the champions of universal liberty while the "R.C's," that is Catholics, would be seen as inconsequential endorsers. In spite of this perceived setback, Conway was not vanquished. Without prior knowledge or assistance of Pattee and Mahony, Conway chose to employ the full authority and influence of the NCWC to persuade the US delegation that they should do all in their power to push for an even more extensive endorsement of individual freedoms.[55]

Though Stettinius promised the consultants that the US would take up their motions in the delegation's resolution— "the equivalence of an International Bill of Rights in the functioning of the Organization" as well as a UN Commission—the consultants had never made a direct connection between their vague concept of human rights and the scope of the projected commission. They hesitated to introduce such an explicit link that might circumscribe the framers of the Charter. Moreover, even their most optimistic colleagues failed to predict that the members of the American delegation would accede so readily to their counsel. For these reasons many details were left out of a proposal most thought doomed to failure. However, now that two thirds of the human rights goals were endorsed by the delegates, Conway resolved to seek the balance.[56]

On May 3, after hearing that the US delegation had acquiesced in the consultants' advice, Father Conway telephoned Archbishop Edward Mooney to inform him that it looked as though all mention of human rights would be restricted to Marshal Smuts's Preamble and that no concrete provision for the creation of a definitive International Bill of Rights would be specified in the body of the document. He advised, at this "crucial moment," that a telegram to the members of the American delegation could help win the day for an equitable and just peace for all. The archbishop concurred.[57]

Introducing his May 4 telegram with a frank reminder to the delegates that the need for firm international commitments on human rights had been strongly emphasized in recent Administrative Board statements, Mooney insisted that this criterion could not be met adequately by a mere declaration in the preamble of the Charter. A UNCIO commission to formulate a list of these rights stipulated in the Charter was the least that would satisfy such a requirement. Support for this was expected of a nation that sincerely aspired to maintain a just peace in a free world. Anything less would be accurately inter-preted "as mere lip service to democratic ideals." Certainly, Mooney hoped, the American delegates would uphold the pri-mary objective of safeguarding and implementing human rights.[58]

The reactions to this telegram were virtually instantaneous; tangible results were, however, another matter. In a letter to Carroll the next day, May 5, Pattee confirmed that Mooney had sent a copy of the telegram to him, along with a note that made it perfectly clear that Conway's was "the line to take on the matter of human rights." That morning, however, the consul-tants gathered to hear the Secretary of State present the pro-posed American amendments. The mimeographed text con-tained no mention of a Commission or Bill of Human Rights to be included in the Charter. Pattee had been told that this represented the agreement of the Big Four, and although it did "not go as far as some," i.e. Conway, "would like," it was the most that the US delegates were inclined to ask.[59]

Putting the best face on this situation, Conway reported that Mooney's telegram "did good." But even he had to confess that all was not going well. There were indications that the Ameri-cans were now "playing with the idea" of adopting the Cana-dian draft of the section on the Economic and Social Council, which, like the American amendment, did not contain a provi-sion for a Commission on Human Rights.[60] The drafts of both amendments must have been bitter reading for Conway. Al-though they contained endless repetitions of the phrase "human rights," ensuring these rights was left to vague locu-tions such as "effective collective measures" and "promotion and encouragement." Ironically, it was the slow and steady work of consultants such as Pattee and Mahony that would produce further additions to the final draft of the Charter and yield some explicit modifications in favor of human rights.[61]

Results And Reactions

On May 19 Catherine Schaefer confided to Father McGowan that Conway had approached her to solicit her support for his campaign to be named CAIP associate consultant, now that McGowan, who was officially listed as an associate, no longer intended to come to San Francisco. Schaefer believed, however, that such an appointment was not a good idea. True, Conway's *modus operandi* was "more assertive" than that of any other Catholic representative, but she did not suppose that switching to his techniques would be "the wisest thing if results and not publicity (even the elevated kind that goes down in history books) are what we are after."[62]

In Schaefer's opinion Mahony was doing an excellent job; although his major preoccupations were in the areas of the International Court and codification of international law, he was also working steadily for the eventual creation of a Commission on Human Rights. Richard Pattee also received some praise. Through his efforts every American delegate and consultant had received a copy of the bishops' April statement. He was pointing out tirelessly, to anyone who would listen, the contention of the NCWC that the Dumbarton Oaks proposals had not given sufficient recognition to the "fundamental God-given character of human rights" or adequate provision for their ultimate protection.[63] Through his painstaking labors and those of other religious consultants, the US delegation was prepared by the middle of May to consent to a provision enabling the Economic and Social Council to set up eventually a Commission on Human Rights. On this point, Mahony confided, a post-Conference establishment of the commission was unavoidable and not merely a Big Power ruse, since to consider such an intricate proposal at the conference, especially in light of the wide discrepancies between the Soviet Union and the other powers present, would extend unacceptably the life of the Conference.[64]

Pattee cautioned discretion for those who might be overly eager to see Christian principles incorporated into the Charter. Catholics had to comprehend that at San Francisco there were large numbers of Moslems, Hindus, atheists—not to mention divergent Christian groups. Furthermore, the Soviets and other nations did not extend even a minimal guarantee of human rights within their territories. It had required several months and an extraordinary degree of persistence to get even a few inadequate words on human rights into the Dumbarton Oaks proposals. Six weeks at San Francisco would not be adequate to devise a declaration that would reflect the thinking of all the delegates. For this reason, Pattee said, it was sound policy to urge that a Rights Commission be created, which could proceed more leisurely with the task of drafting such a bill. In this way the chance of creating something real, and not mere lofty illusions, was enhanced. On the advice of Pattee and Mahony, therefore, the NCWC decided to rescind its demand for immediate action on a UN Bill of Rights.[65]

The final American amendments to the UN Charter were a credit to the collaboration of all twenty-two consultants who signed the initial human rights resolution, but especially to the effectiveness of the religious organizations and their consultants—including the Catholic representatives, who were not, it is true, the pacesetters in this enterprise.

These US amendments, which were due to the emphasis that the above-mentioned associations placed on the principle that human rights existed independent of any governmental grant, were seen as a great improvement over the Dumbarton Oaks proposals, which provided solely that the United Nations "should promote respect for human rights and fundamental freedoms." Now one of the "inherent purposes" of the UN was declared to be their promotion. The General Assembly was entrusted with the power to study and recommend how it could assist member nations in fulfilling this rationale for world organization. Finally, the Economic and Social Council would provide machinery and procedures whereby such rights might be adequately protected.[66]

The Vatican daily, *Osservatore Romano,* approved these innovations in the UN Charter, which, it claimed, made that document superior to the pact of the League of Nations and to the Dumbarton Oaks proposals. In an article of June 14 it praised the guarantee and defense of the fundamental liberties of persons and of states. In this way, it declared, the creation of a direct bond between "peoples and the community of nations could be the beginning of an evolution which if resolutely followed through could open up the prospect of rapid and secure progress."[67]

In spite of his disappointment at the inactivity on a Human Rights Commission, Father Conway in his NCWC column gave much praise to the Conference's "human rights efforts," especially to the Economic and Social Council's mandate to form such a commission. He concluded nonetheless that it was too soon to determine the effectiveness of these "paper provisions." What would the declaration of rights contain? Would all the nations of the UN agree to incorporate such a declaration into their basic laws? These were questions that needed answers. The Jesuit noted also that the bishops' demand for a guarantee in law and a respect for innate human rights as a condition of United Nations membership had not been acceded to, partially because Archbishop Mooney's condition for creation of a UNCIO commission to frame such a Bill of Rights had not been promoted.[68]

Even before the debate on these matters, *America* stated that an International Bill of Rights was "the greatest of all questions to be discussed at the Conference." Its editor, Father John LaFarge, proposed that the human rights issue be inserted into the UNCIO agenda and kept there until the delegates fashioned a sound international political structure that ensured "effective, sincere, morally and spiritually motivated" guarantees: in other words, real freedoms and not mere abstractions.[69]

America's recommendation that an explicit human-rights clause be inserted into Chapter Two of the document had been rebuffed by the UNCIO. That proposal would have confirmed that

All members of the Organization, accepting as a matter of international concern the obligation 'to defend life, liberty, independence and religious freedom, and to preserve human rights and justice in their own lands,' shall progressively secure for their inhabitants without discrimination such fundamental rights as freedom of religion, speech, assembly and communication, and to a fair trial under just laws.[70]

By the end of the Conference, nevertheless, the editors were content to await anxiously ratification of the Charter and formation of the commission by the Economic and Social Council, so that the business of drafting such an International Bill of Rights could get under way.

Commonweal had likewise taken a keen interest in these discussions. It was in sympathy with the prevalent Catholic conviction that endorsement of such a bill of "inalienable rights" should be required for active participation in the world body.[71] In addition, it argued that some sort of "Bill of Rights" should be incorporated into the Charter—especially in connection with freedom of information. Professing displeasure at the "pious passages" on liberties substituted for actual measures that would bring them about, the editors nevertheless hoped that these sections would at least serve as blueprints for the construction of a substantive UN Bill of Rights.[72]

All in all, most Catholic pundits thought that the words of the Charter on this question were "impeccable" and that the way had been paved for an eventual International Bill of Rights. Much faith was placed in the Economic and Social Council's capacity to help the peoples of the world and their rulers to recognize "that mankind has a conscience." After this success, many Catholics anticipated that the International Court, buttressed by a UN Bill of Rights, would be a permanent legal instrument of conscience for the new organization.[73]

A Supreme Court For The United Nations

Flying east from San Francisco on the day after the closing ceremonies of the UN Conference, President Truman, speaking in Kansas City, volunteered that

It will be just as easy for nations to get along in a republic of the world as it is for you to get along in the republic of the

United States. Now when Kansas and Colorado have a quarrel over the water in the Arkansas River they don't call out the National Guard in each State and go to war over it. They bring a suit in the Supreme Court of the United States and abide by the decision. There isn't a reason in the world why we cannot do that internationally.[74]

Unfortunately for Mr. Truman and the UN, such comments in late June of 1945 were water under the bridge. There existed one appalling reason why two international litigants would never be able to plead such a republican claim before the universal seat of justice of the United Nations. The UNCIO had refused to institute a legal tribunal with compulsory jurisdiction to constrain obedience to its orders—powers delineated in the mandate of the Supreme Court of the United States.

"Teeth" For The International Court

Richard S. Childs in *The New York Times* on March 9, 1945, seconded the contention of the Catholic Association for International Peace that in light of the Big Power veto the Security Council would apparently become its own court of arbitration. Where, he wondered, was the independent tribunal of eminent persons at which decisions were to be rendered "in conformity with generally accepted principles of justice and equity?"[75] And what had become of the International Court contemplated by Anthony Eden at the Moscow Conference of October 1943, when on Churchill's instructions the British Foreign Minister promoted compulsory jurisdiction bolstered by an "armed force capable of implementing its decisions"?[76] The new game appeared to be hide-and-seek.

None of these Big Power shenanigans surprised the Catholic Conference. In the Administrative Board's statement of November 1944 the NCWC turned a dubious gaze toward the juridical blueprints of the Big Four. The new international organization would not be complete, the bishops contended, unless an International Court were given more than the advisory authority contemplated by the UN's founding members. The tribunal must be granted the judicial prerogative of referring its decisions to the Security Council, not for appeal or review but for enforcement. In April the Board developed this point. To establish such a bench and subsequently deny it competence to direct the execution of its decrees or make their administration subject to the whim of the Council "was a manifest denial of a prime attribute of a juridical institution." Nations that refused to acknowledge this or declined to submit disputes to the International Court, actions that would constitute a threat to the peace of the international community, were to be treated as miscreant states.[77]

What brought about this apprehension over the status of the new International Court of Justice was the painful memory of the Hague tribunal affiliated with the League of Nations. This "Permanent Court of International Justice" was intended by the Versailles Covenant of 1919 to be neither an inherent part of the League nor a bar to which litigants could apply for compulsory adjudication. During the 1920s and 1930s it was unable, therefore, to mediate the very predicaments that brought World War II into being. The NCWC anticipated that the memory of this long and frustrating experience would condition the Allied nations to submit their legal disputes willingly to the new Court. This was not to be. Although the Dumbarton Oaks conferees had affixed an "International Court of Justice" to the UN structure and constituted it "the principal judicial organ of the Organization," the proposals made scant reference to its functions. For example, would its statute be a new one or the edict of the League's Permanent Court adopted in 1920? Because the Catholic Church had categorized the latter alternative as a continuation of the debilitating "optional jurisdiction" of the prewar years, Mahony, Pattee, and Conway all worked diligently to secure the former.[78]

In conversation after conversation with members of the American delegation Pattee tried to demonstrate that the enervating problems that developed between the wars were caused by member states' failing to relinquish the right of final recourse to an impartial international jury. To tolerate once again an International Court without compulsory jurisdiction would be a "serious and possibly dangerous compromise" that would sacrifice principle for the expediency of politics. The heart of the "court question," Pattee believed, was its operation; if it was not given legal "teeth"—to quote the bishops—it would be flouted entirely.[79]

The conference was almost equally divided on this issue, with many smaller nations, including the Latin Americans, in solid support of the principle of compulsory jurisdiction. A Committee of Jurists, which met immediately before the UN-CIO, was likewise split. But the five Great Powers, all of whom had delegates on this committee, gave their blessing to what was euphemistically labeled the "optional clause." This famous proviso stipulated that nations could choose whether "to bind themselves to accept the Court's decisions." Confusingly titled, the clause gave states opportunity of signing a declaration whereby they recognized "as compulsory, *ipso facto* and without special agreement, in relation to any other state accepting the same obligation, the jurisdiction of the Court in all legal disputes." Though all this sounded promising in principle, in fact members were permitted to add seemingly endless reservations, about either specific topics or general matters such as "domestic jurisdiction." What was infuriating to Mahony about this Big Five stance was the candid admission that the principle of "compulsory jurisdiction" was a sound one; the proposition was denounced, nonetheless, as "unrealistic at the present time" and prejudicial to prompt ratification by the major powers.[80]

"Beating the bushes" around the American delegation, Pattee did uncover a few sympathetic listeners—mostly Republicans—who were uncomfortable over this situation. Senator Arthur Vandenberg and Commander Harold Stassen, with their principal advisor, John Foster Dulles, spoke in delegation meetings of the need to accept the challenge of "rising above the immediate dictates of politics and convenience." They were, however, outvoted by the majority, which agreed with Senator Tom Connally that any UN Charter licensing an International Court that could dictate to the United States of America would be assured a cool reception in the US Senate. When pressed on this matter by Pattee, even Vandenberg had to admit that the fight for a "real court" would be ticklish—but worth the chance.[81]

Conway had been doing his best to lobby for the principle of juridical supremacy. Talking to delegates from the South American countries, including Manuel Gallagher, chairman of the Committee of Jurists and a delegate from Chile, he discovered that numerous persons among them were willing to oppose the Big Five on this issue. Gallagher apprised Conway, however, that it was unlikely that the solid wall of opposition erected by the Great Powers and their allies could be overcome.[82]

In this quest Conway attempted to illustrate not only that this judicial dilemma centered on the fact that the Court would not be given the power it needed, but also that the Security Council was given broad discretion in enforcement of juridical decisions.[83] Article 94 of the proposed Charter was to declare that "if any party to a case fails to perform the obligations incumbent upon it under a judgement rendered by the Court, the other party may have recourse to the Security Council, which may make recommendations, if it deems necessary, or decide upon measures to give effect to the judgement." Once again, Conway maintained, the final say was to be given to the Security Council, which held veto powers. If any of these nations chose to block an official action by the International Court, it could do so effortlessly in the Council. This would indisputably render the Security Council the *de facto* Supreme Court of the United Nations, but not its conscience or court of justice.[84]

The Verdict

In a casual valediction to the International Court, Assistant Secretary of State Archibald MacLeish remarked to Walter Kotschnig of the US State Department, "The jurisdiction of the Court is Not Compulsory unless accepted as such by member states."[85] In Article 94 of the UN Charter the same fact had been proclaimed in a more circuitous way. Thomas Mahony, however, went beyond mere recitation of the facts to level a *J'accuse* at all would-be offenders. If a state refused to comply with a verdict of the tribunal, he maintained, this resistance "would suggest some ulterior purpose."[86]

Once he had a chance to compose himself, however, Mahony took time to assess the new Court. He was pleased that it was established, at least in theory, as the principal organ of the UN, which implied an underlying worldwide judicial system. He was satisfied also that its statute was an integral part of the Charter and that it could apply to the Security Council for that chamber's discretionary enforcement of its decisions. Finally Mahony admitted that the San Francisco Conference had gone much further than the League of Nations Covenant or the Statute of the Permanent Court by indicating its intent that the United Nations should uphold the Court.[87]

Though the Charter and the statute of the new bench did not provide for compulsory jurisdiction over international disputes, Mahony was convinced that the voluntary-jurisdiction clause was not so retrograde a step as it might appear. The UNCIO document now conceded—beyond the League of Nations' mandate—that the jurisdiction of the Court included more than cases that "the parties refer to it and all matters specially provided for in treaties and conventions in force." To indicate this, the San Francisco delegates added to the tribunal's statute all the situations indicated in the Charter of the United Nations.[88]

Mahony was encouraged by the fact that, although both world organizations' statutes contained similar "optional clauses," some nations that voluntarily recognized the compulsory jurisdiction of the League's Permanent Court now signaled their intention to continue to do so under the new system. Furthermore, some of the twenty-two members of the current United Nations who either were non-signatories to the League of Nations Covenant or as members had not recognized the Permanent Court's compulsory authority, were now expected to do so if the United States would sign the "optional clause" (Article 36) and would try to get others to follow suit. Such, of course, was a barren hope, but Mahony, caught up in the same blush of UNCIO optimism that had entrapped many, including President Truman, was resolved to trust in universal good faith and world cooperation. The Catholic press, on the other hand, was not so confident.[89]

Commonweal applauded the bishops for their defense of a strong International Court; the Administrative Board's April 15 statement asserted that it was crucial to give the International Court of Justice power to modify peace agreements and other settlements "as might be dictated by past errors or altered circumstances."[90] *Commonweal,* however, was skeptical that the Great Powers would ever grant such leverage to the international bar and thereby relax their stranglehold over the UN. By the end of the conference the editors were vindicated; no such political altruism of the permanent members of the Security Council had been forthcoming. In fact, *Commonweal* professed, what was positively startling about the new court was the comparisons it brought to mind with the tribunal of the League of Nations: both its general framework and the "optional clause" as defined in Article 94 had a disappointingly "familiar ring."[91]

America focused on a statement by Harold Stassen, who, at a San Francisco press conference, pointed out that although many aspects of the Permanent Court would belong to the new tribunal, its membership roles would not. All neutrals and Axis powers could be excluded, since only "peace-loving states" were to be admitted to the UN. The editors, reminding their readers of this significant detail, criticized the San Francisco Charter for failing to set up a sound universal organization for peace, justice, and security.[92]

Reflecting on the UN's role as a "peace-enforcing agency," Edgar R. Smothers, S.J.,[93] wrote in *America* that because of the perpetual need for unanimity among the Veto Powers, the UN was as seriously flawed as the Maginot Line. Speaking for most Catholic commentators at San Francisco, Smothers remarked wistfully, "It is regrettable that the executive effect of peace-enforcement under such a charter is not subject to some jurisdiction competent to declare justice."[94]

The motive of the Church's positions on juridical matters was anxiety for the postwar liberties of smaller nations, minorities, and persecuted populations. Following their admittedly limited achievements in international law at the UN Conference, Catholics now determined that the best avenue for international social reform would be through two new quasi-independent agencies of the UN, which would be charged with matters in these areas of concern: the Economic and Social Council and the Trusteeship System.

Notes

1. AMU Series 6, Box 1, McGowan to Mahony, [D.C.], May 28, 1945.
2. Ibid.
3. Franz B. Gross, gen. ed., *The United States and the United Nations* (Norman, Oklahoma: University of Oklahoma Press, 1964), "Introduction," Robert Struasz-Hupe, p. 5.
4. "The San Francisco Conference," p. 2.
5. Sumner Welles, *Seven Decisions That Shaped History* (New York: Harper, 1950), pp. 191–92.
6. Ibid., p. 3.
7. "Catholics and the Dumbarton Oaks Proposals," p. 3.
8. *On Organizing World Peace,* p. 1.
9. *Judging the Dumbarton Oaks Proposals,* p. 2.
10. *Goals for San Francisco,* p. 3.
11. ANCWC 15, "Your Role in San Francisco," E. A. Conway, S.J. Text of a broadcast made in Indianapolis, March 11, 1945, p. 2.
12. ANCWC 13b, " 'Assertion of Moral and Juridical Principles' is Key Question Confronting United Nations at World Meeting," Christopher Dawson, April 30, 1945, p. 3.
13. Ibid.
14. AMU, Series 1, Box 1, "Tentative Topic Suggestions, Dumbarton Oaks and Catholic Teaching," [D.C.], April 2–3, 1945, p. 3.
15. AMU, Series 6, Box 1, Memorandum on Matters Being Discussed and Acted on by United States Consultants, Catherine Schaefer to Carroll, [San Francisco], May 4, 1945, p. 3.
16. AMU, Series 6, Box 1, "Observations on the San Francisco Conference," Thomas H. Mahony, May 7, 1945, p. 1.
17. Ibid., p. 2.

18. Ibid.

19. ANCWC 15, "Observations Upon the Conference V," Thomas H. Mahony, May 11, 1945, p. 1.

20. Ibid.

21. ANCWC 15, McGowan to Carroll, [D.C.], May 25, 1945.

22. AMU, Series 6, Box 1, Schaefer to McGowan, [San Francisco], May 19, 1945, p. 1.

23. Article 13, Section 1, *United Nations Charter:* "The General Assembly shall initiate studies and make recommendations for the purpose of (a) . . . encouraging the progressive development of international law and its codification; (b) . . . assisting in the realization of human rights and fundamental freedoms for all without distinction as to race, sex, language, or religion" (*The Charter of the United Nations, 1945* [Lake Success, New York: Department of Public Information, 1946], p. 68).

24. H. G. Nicholas, *The United Nations As A Political Institution* (London: Oxford University Press, 1959), p. 104; "The San Francisco Conference," p. 8.

25. Ibid., p. 3.

26. "Observations at San Francisco," p. 2.

27. "Peace by Law Our One Hope," *The New York Times,* October 10, 1945, p. 20.

28. "Satisfactory Progress Seen in Proposed Charter. . . ," p. 1.

29. RG 59f, Box 22, The U.N. Conference as Reported by US Press and Radio Comment, *General Summary,* July, 1945, p. 2.

30. "Prospect for the Small Nations," *Commonweal* 42 (June 22, 1945):227; Max Ascoli, "The Test of San Francisco," *Commonweal* 42 (June 15, 1945):212.

31. RG 59g, Daily Summary of Opinion Developments, May 24, 1945, p. 2.

32. "The San Francisco Conference," Thomas H. Mahony, p. 5.

33. ANCWC 15, "Text of Appeal of H.E. Archbishop Sapieha to the American Hierarchy and to the Catholic Bishops of the World," March 24, 1945, p. 1.

34. ANCWC 15, O. Frederick Nolde to Carroll, [New York], March 28, 1945.

35. John Lewis Gaddis, *The United States and the Origins of the Cold War: 1941–1947* (New York: Columbia University Press, 1972), pp. 164–65.

36. ANCWC 15, "How Religious Freedom Clause Was Eliminated from the League of Nations Covenant," Thomas E. Kissling, June 4, 1945, p. 6.

37. Francis C. Kelley, *The Bishop Jots It Down* (New York: Harper and Brothers, 1939), p. 256.

Francis Clement Kelley was born in Vernon River, Prince Edward Island, Canada, on November 24, 1870. He trained for the priesthood at Nicolet Seminary at Laval University, Quebec, and was ordained for the diocese of Detroit in 1893. In 1905 he founded the Catholic Church Extension Society of the United States to serve the needs of home missions. He was its president for nineteen years. Often serving as an ecclesiastical envoy, he represented the Mexican bishops at the Paris Peace Conference of 1919 and was Vatican envoy to England in 1921, at which time he negotiated on problems concerning German and Austrian missions. He was appointed bishop of Oklahoma (later Oklahoma City-Tulsa) in 1924; there he continued his mission efforts and battled the Ku Klux Klan. He wrote numerous books, including several novels. He died in Oklahoma City on February 1, 1948 (James P. Gaffey, *Francis Clement Kelley and the American Catholic Dream,* 2 vols. [Bensenville, Illinois: Heritage Foundation, 1980], vol. 1, pp. xix–xxix).

38. Wilfrid Parsons, S.J., *American Peace Aims* (Washington: CAIP, 1942), Appendix C, "An International Bill of Rights," pp. 41–45. "We hold these truths to be, if not self-evident, then certainly based on that natural law which is the eternal Law of God as discovered by human reason. . . ."

39. Murray's analysis of this issue was examined at length in Chapter III, "Preparing for San Francisco," pp. 19–26.

40. *On Organizing World Peace,* p. 1.

41. Sir John Wheeler Bennett and Anthony Nicholls, *The Semblance of Peace: The Political Settlement after the Second World War* (New York: St. Martin's Press, 1972), p. 415.

42. *Goals For San Francisco,* p. 4.

43. ANCWC 15, Conway to Carroll, [D.C.], March 27, 1945, p. 4.

44. ANCWC 13a, "That All Important Preamble," May 7, 1945, p. 1.

45. Smuts was the only veteran of Versailles at San Francisco.

46. ANCWC 13a, "That All Important Preamble," May 7, 1945, p. 1.

47. ANCWC 15, Text of U.S. Consultants' Resolution, [San Francisco], May 2, 1945, p. 1, copy.

48. AMU, Series 6, Box 1, "On Matters Being Discussed and Acted on by United States Consultants," Schaefer to McGowan, [San Francisco], May 4, 1945, p. 1.

49. Ibid.

50. ANCWC 15, Text of suggestions for Human Rights Amendments by United States Consultants, [San Francisco], May 2, 1945, p. 1.

51. Ibid., p. 2.

52. Norman A. Graebner, ed. *An Uncertain Tradition: American Secretaries of State in the Twentieth Century* (New York: McGraw-Hill, 1961), "Edward R. Stettinius, Jr.," by Walter Johnson, p. 219.

53. ANCWC 15, Schaefer to McGowna, [San Francisco], May 4, 1945, p. 1; "That All Important Preamble," p. 2.

54. Ibid.

55. AMU, Series 6, Box 1, Schaefer to McGowan, [San Francisco], May 19, 1945, p. 1.

56. ANCWC 11, Conway to Carroll, [San Francisco], May 11, 1945, p. 2.

57. ANCWC 11, The Reverend John A. Donovan to Carroll, [Detroit], May 5, 1945.

58. ANCWC 11, Mooney to Stettinius *et al.,* [Detroit], May 4, 1945, copy.

59. ANCWC 11, Pattee to Carroll, [San Francisco], May 5, 1945.

60. ANCWC 11, Conway to Carroll, [San Francisco], May 11, 1945.

61. ANCWC 11, Text of U.S. Delegation's Amendments to Charter, May 5, 1945, pp. 1–2, copy.

62. AMU, Series 6, Box 1, Schaefer to McGowan, [San Francisco], May 19, 1945, p. 1.

63. ANCWC 11, Pattee to Carroll, [San Francisco], May 3, 1945, p. 1.

64. "Observations on the San Francisco Conference," May 3, 1945, p. 1.

65. ANCWC 13c, "Special Commission Proposed to Draft Human Rights Bill. . . ," Richard Pattee, May 14, 1945, p. 2.

66. "Observations on the San Francisco Conference," May 7, 1945, p. 1.

67. ANCWC 13c, "Article in Vatican Paper Says World Organization Plan Contains Perplexities," June 18, 1945, p. 4.

68. ANCWC 13c, "U.S. Bishops' Recommendations Seen Substantially Reflected in Charter of U.N.," Edward A. Conway, S.J., July 2, 1945, p. 2b.

69. John LaFarge, S.J., "World Freedom Demands Human Rights," *America* 73 (May 12, 1945):109–11.

70. "Stating It Plainly," *America* 73 (April 21, 1945):45.

71. "An International Bill of Rights," *Commonweal* 42 (April 27, 1945):35.

72. "What Was Done at San Francisco," *Commonweal* 42 (July 20, 1945):324.

73. RG 59e, Box 23, Folder 1, "Daily Summary of Opinion Developments," May 18, 1945, p. 1.

74. "Peace by Law Our One Hope."

75. "Implementing the World Court," p. 42.

76. *The Semblance of Power,* p. 105.

77. *Pastoral Letters. . . ,* vol. 2, *On International Order,* November 16, 1944, p. 2.

78. *Yearbook of the United Nations, 1946,* Chapter 7, p. 6.

79. "Some Observations on the San Francisco Conference. . . ," p. 8.

80. *The United Nations As a Political Institution,* pp. 143, 144.

81. Ibid.

82. ANCWC 11, Conway to Carroll, [San Francisco], May 11, 1945, p. 1.

83. *The Years of Western Domination,* p. 67. The old and involved system of elections to the Court was maintained. Membership in the Court had to be approved first by the Security Council, where any permanent member could veto a nominee, and then by election in the Assembly.

84. "U.S. Bishops' Recommendations Seen Substantially Reflected In Charter of United Nations," p. 2b.

85. R.G. 59a 2006, Folder 4, MacLeish to Kotschnig, [San Francisco], June 25, 1945, copy.

86. "Each member of the United Nations undertakes to comply with the decision of the International Court of Justice" (*Charter of the United Nations,* Chapter XIV, Article 94, 1).; "The San Francisco Conference," p. 16.

87. "The San Francisco Conference," p. 9.

88. Ibid., p. 10.

89. Ibid.

90. "An International Bill of Rights," p. 12.

91. "San Francisco Wind-up," *Commonweal* 42 (July 6, 1945): 276.

92. "Open Door Policy in World Charter," p. 132.

93. Edgar R. Smothers was born in Rossville, Illinois, on September 26, 1888 to Episcopalian parents. His father was the town's superintendent of schools. At the age of twenty-six, Smothers was converted to Catholicism and in 1914 he entered the Society of Jesus. In the late twenties the young priest was sent to Paris for Early Christian studies at the Sorbonne and at the Institut Catholique to study under Father J. Lebreton. His research on St. Chrysostom's homilies on the *Acts of the Apostles* was recognized internationally. He died on November 18, 1970. (From an unpublished address by the Reverend Francis Gignac, S.J.)

94. Edgar R. Smothers, S.J., "The Charter and Peace," *America* 73 (June 16, 1945):223.

CHAPTER VIII
"Non-Political" Matters

By the beginning of the San Francisco Conference, the State Department's interpretation of the proposed United Nations Charter was highlighting the novelty of the new world organization rather than its continuity with the past. In accord with this strategy, negligible consideration was given to the League of Nations. The League's representation at San Francisco was "unofficial" and was restricted grudgingly to three observers. The US Secretary of State's welcoming address purposely excluded mention of the outmoded confederation "as if even a word of allusion might set the ghost of Woodrow Wilson's failure walking the aisles of the San Francisco Opera House."[1] In the Charter, where convenience would have dictated identical terminology, pains were taken to avoid it: for example, the replacement of "The International Court of Justice" for "The Permanent Court of Justice" and "Trusteeship" for "Mandate."

Yet at Dumbarton Oaks and San Francisco the delegates complimented the League more earnestly than they could have through any conventional recognition: they imitated it. Attention has naturally focused on the difference between the League's Covenant and the Charter, but there is an essential identity shared by the two organizations.[2] Nowhere was this more conspicuous than in the two principal "non-political" branches of the UN: the Economic and Social Council (ECOSOC), which had supervisory power over the International Labor Organization (ILO) and other specialized agencies, and the Trusteeship Council, which was created to administer affairs of colonies, mandates of defeated Axis nations, and other non-self-governing territories. These agencies were seen by many Catholics as the last possible hope for a non-political, non-nationalistic UN, relatively unfettered by the Veto Powers. In this final chapter on the work of the Conference, we shall examine how the UNCIO copied blatantly the League of Nations while it enacted much that was new, if not superior.[3]

The Economic And Social Council

The Charter approved ultimately by the UNCIO would undeniably say much more about economic and social goals than the Covenant. Nonetheless, by 1939 the League's work in that sphere had so escalated that a proposal was put forth that a new League organization, the Central Committee for Economic and Social Questions, should be created to supervise what the organization was doing in that field. The Dumbarton Oaks proposals provided that this committee should be a council but should be a subservient body, operating under the General Assembly with power primarily to make recommendations

> with respect to international economic, social and other humanitarian matters; to receive and consider reports from the economic, social and other organizations or agencies brought into relationship with the Organization, and to coordinate their activities through consultations with and recommendations to, such organizations or agencies. . . ."[4]

The first Catholic response to this action by the conferees at Dumbarton Oaks came in a "for your eyes only" note from Father Conway to Monsignor Howard Carroll and other officials at the NCWC. Conway praised the fact that Chapter IX of the projected Charter placed the ECOSOC under the General Assembly and not under the Security Council. Since this permitted the Economic and Social Council to evade the Big Five veto in the Security Council, Conway hoped "this would make for a considerable amount of local autonomy as well as organized effort." It further appeared to allot to the small nations the role he believed they were best qualified to fulfill—that of developing solutions to the social and human problems of peace, in contrast to the large states, on whom rested the burden of achieving security.[5]

Conway believed that the Dumbarton Oaks suggestions on the ECOSOC were a major improvement over the League of Nations' committee for economic and social matters. The former was much more explicit on the consequences of these factors on both peace and security. This was extremely important for the Catholic Church, since it was in accord with the issues stressed by Pius XII in his Five-Point Peace Program. The proposals offered undoubted possibilities, Conway thought, for creating a pragmatic framework for lasting peace through its establishment of permanent committees and commissions to deal realistically with special problems such as those of colonies and trust territories, labor concerns, and an International Bill of Rights.[6]

In a pointed criticism of much Catholic thought in the United States, and an implicit reproach to the NCWC, Conway said that it was commonplace for Catholics to believe that Church doctrine held the solutions for all the world's problems. This was not true, Conway alleged. Doctrines alone did not solve practical problems. Doctrines put into practice did. No problems would be solved by saying that the Church had all the answers, any more than a sick man could be healed by saying that doctors knew how to make him well. Conway said that many Catholic commentaries had been content to announce that the world was ill and that the Church had the remedy. But the patient would never get better until the Church got the doctor into the sickroom. Besides the easy task of showing what the world would be like if it were wholly converted to Christ, the Church had "the much more difficult and much less pleasant task of grappling with the practical problems of a world full of stupidity and malice."[7]

The Pope had been advocating such an endeavor from the start of hostilities in 1939. Though he failed to call for a better world, Conway stated, he always demonstrated how the present world order was badly in need of reform and how Catholics, and all persons of good will, were to go about changing it. If the Church in the United States wanted to convert anyone to an ethical, Christlike economic and social world order, it must

start with some practical plan. The Dumbarton Oaks proposals—flawed as they were—looked to Conway like a first step
toward such a system. The Pope had been firm in his call for
just such a societal reform; throughout the Dumbarton Conversations, he repeated this message. On September 1, 1944, he
expressed his pleasure that such an attempt was being made
and he hoped that it might achieve the greatest possible success. A Catholic could not think he was following the Pope's
teaching if he did not conscientiously inspect the ECOSOC
proposals and then work for what was best in them.[8]

Along with Conway, Richard Pattee recognized that the
Dumbarton Oaks conferees acknowledged essentially the economic and social underpinnings of an enduring postwar peace.
The fact that an economic and social council was suggested was
testimony to an awareness that it was impossible to conceive
world crises or a recurrence of war as mere matters of political
arrangement between member states. The Charter went far
beyond the League of Nations Covenant in its adjustment to
the reality that war was frequently caused by the prevalence of
ignorance, misery, poverty, and social hopelessness. Answering
Conway's challenge, Pattee urged that Catholics work for the
revision of the Dumbarton Oaks propositions, since he believed that, although fine in principle, they advanced only
equivocal procedures for the execution of true economic and
social justice.[9]

Upon arriving in San Francisco, Pattee was pleasantly surprised to find that many Catholic delegates from Latin America
agreed with him. Father Conway, who also was moving among
the members of these delegations, as well as those from other
"small and middle" nations such as Egypt, discovered that
there was virtual agreement on the necessity of emphasizing
the economic and social order that undergirded the political
organization.[10]

This accentuation of what was being called the "positive
approach to peace" was meant to balance the "negative part"
of the Charter, that is, the powers and provisions entrusted to
the Security Council. The smaller states and their defenders

contended erroneously that for ten or fifteen years after the cessation of hostilities economic and social concerns would far outweigh security problems. They insisted therefore that the powers of the Economic and Social Council, which had been defined only abstractly at Dumbarton Oaks, must be broadened, and the Council be given a position commensurate with the problems that would soon confront it.[11]

By late April Catherine Schaefer was subscribing completely to this estimation of the prospective importance of the Council. In fact, the Catholic consultants and associates were working for a "proper recognition" of the ECOSOC as one of the principal organs of the United Nations. It was the consensus that in all likelihood there would be few opportunities for imposition of economic or military sanctions by the Security Council in the foreseeable future. This theory propounded that none of the states capable of making war on a large scale would have any appetite to do so. They were exhausted by war and craved nothing so much as a peaceful hiatus in which to reestablish their internal harmony and external peace. All the economic, social, humanitarian, cultural, educational, labor, and health problems confronting every member state would be demanding attention and resolution. In these fields, the ECOSOC could have an immediate and unique opportunity to render vital assistance in the "cause of international peace and security by helping to eliminate the underlying causes of war." The Catholic representatives boldly proclaimed, therefore, that such an essential department of the UN should be a coequal counterpart to the Security Council.[12]

In fact, with the Economic and Social Council the Catholic consultants and their allies in San Francisco were to experience their greatest successes at the UNCIO—although ECOSOC equivalency was to prove a chimera. On May 2 Pattee and Mahony lent their support to an Egyptian amendment to the Dumbarton Oaks proposals. This motion stated that, since problems confronting the ECOSOC would be complex, membership should be doubled so that "diversified and intricate tasks set for it may better be accomplished." Far from opposing this, the Big Five, under pressure to appear egalitarian, hastened to give the smaller countries everything they wanted and more. The United States and Great Britain—inspired by a resolution endorsed by most US consultants—actively fostered the Egyptian plan. They also conceded that the Charter need not provide for Big Five seats in the ECOSOC, or veto powers in that UN body, or even the possibility of a Big Five majority, since the ECOSOC would have eighteen elected members.[13]

Hardly believing their luck, the Catholic representatives advised the NCWC to publicly applaud this generous offer. Pattee believed that whatever the motivation—in fact, the Big Five saw no actual threat to their Security Council authority—the permanent members of the UN allowed this branch of the United Nations to come closer to democracy than any other. Pattee hoped that small states might well find in the ECOSOC a leverage denied them in other agencies. For the first time the smaller nations had a real voice in world organization on matters such as higher living standards, full employment, educational cooperation, and the elimination of restrictions on human rights.[14]

Labor And The ECOSOC

For the Catholic consultants at San Francisco the chief means of ameliorating the long-term postwar situation was the theory of "full employment." Pattee and Mahony stressed affirmatively in their communiqués this potential competence of the ECOSOC. Putting aside any fears of imminent wars, Pattee saw the major problem of the peace as "the devastatingly cruel need of feeding the hungry and providing for the millions of unemployed peoples." The Security Council might endeavor to prevent war and to maintain peace, but the Economic and Social Council would be charged with ensuring that the destinies of people under that peace not endanger its maintenance.[15]

To this end the Catholic consultants, in pressing for a delineation of ECOSOC authority in the UN Charter, promoted particularly the Council's projected functions of providing "higher standards of living, full employment and conditions for economic progress and development." Not satisfied merely to recite Pius XII's declarations on labor cooperation and the NCWC's statements on economic opportunities, they threw themselves into the "labor effort" at both the United Nations Conference and another assembly then in progress across San Francisco Bay in Oakland. This meeting, sponsored by the World Federation of Labor Unions (WFLU), addressed among other related topics the future of the League of Nations' International Labor Organization (ILO). In this way it hoped to influence the deliberations of the UNCIO.[16]

The ILO had a fascinating history. This body, which was the only "Geneva creation"—aside from the Opium Board—to keep a continuous association with the League of Nations, established in 1919. With the same membership as the League, it flourished while its parent organization declined. It was, in fact, the one League agency the United States deigned to join, and it was endowed with exceptional leadership by its first director, an American, Albert Thomas. Having attained unique success in its efforts to raise labor standards throughout the world, it survived the twin shocks of the collapse of the League and World War II with its structure intact.[17]

The ILO had two policy-making organs: the General Conference of all members, which held sessions once a year, and the Governing Body of forty, which met quarterly as an executive council. A uniqu tripartite system of representation was used. In the Conference every state had two government representatives and one each for employers and workers; in the Governing Body, twnty participants came from governments, ten from employers, and ten from workers. Voting in the Conference was by a two-thirds majority—plausibly the origin of the UN General Assembly practice.[18]

At the end of the war this organization possessed a strong institutional and international awareness. With its divisions reflecting lines of interest rather than nationality, it had, over the years, gravitated naturally to issues such as hours, wages, and the conditions of laboring people. In 1945 this topical approach to international questions appealed to many who longed to refine the notion of a world organization. Known as "functionalists," these reformers—who included most Catholic representatives at San Francisco—pointed to the ILO as a model for their ideal. It was, they believed, a body that shunned "the minestrewn high road of international politics" and concentrated on the safer levels of universal economic and social need. This was, they theorized, what international cooperation meant.

A network of organizations such as the ILO should be created under the umbrella of the UN Economic and Social Council, which would absorb successive fields of international endeavor. By these means the nations of the world could find themselves one day suitably governed and controlled without having deliberately yielded their abstract rights of sovereignty, points sure to be matters of endless contention in the Security Council and in the General Assembly.[19]

On April 29 a large assembly was held in San Francisco in support of the UNCIO. Under the direction of the American Association for the United Nations and other "crowd-drawing anti-fascists" such as Walter Winchell and Orson Welles; the meeting was by all accounts a smashing success. The gathering drew 10,000 people, many of them delegates from the Conference of the World Federation of Trade Unions.[20] Two of its speakers were prominent Catholic labor leaders, Bob Watt of the AFL and Philip Murray, the head of the CIO. Catherine Schaefer, who attended the rally, spoke glowingly of Murray's "magnificent impression." He lectured on the need for divine guidance and the preeminent role the ECOSOC should play in the forthcoming world organization. Expressing pointedly labor's desire to be a part of that Council, he insisted that no group could better represent the laborer or aid in the development of the Economic and Social Council than the International Labor Organization.[21]

There can be no doubt that in the matter of labor participation in the development of the ECOSOC, no figure at the conference or at the Oakland meeting was as influential as

Schaefer. It was she who first suggested to another Catholic CIO official and consultant, James Carey, that he and the leadership of the rival AFL, as well as consultants from manufacturing interests and other employers, band together in a lobbying effort to "build up the Economic and Social Council" and the ILO's part in it.[22]

Shuttling regularly and frequently across the Bay, Schaefer became the perfect liaison between the two parleys. In San Francisco she was part of a select "core group" that developed a resolution on the part to be played by the ILO in the Economic and Social Council. Made up of Carey, James T. Shotwell, Philip Nash, and consultants from the National Association of Manufacturers, as well as Schaefer, this group was instrumental in coordinating the consultant strategy on this topic.[23]

During the Conference two consultants' meetings were given entirely to the subject of the Council. The essential problem considered was recognition of the principle of tripartite representation in the economic agencies under the ECOSOC. The labor consultants from the CIO, a member of the International Labor Organization, were eager to have the Council adopt this method, which worked so well for the ILO. The AFL, which had not been a member of that League agency and was not participating in the WFTU meeting, needed some reassurance. Schaefer spoke to Bob Watt and coaxed him to a meeting with Carey. Afterward, the AFL official declared that he was heartily in favor of the principle of tripartite representation.[24]

During meetings of the "core group," Schaefer had an opportunity to influence the final development of the International Monetary Fund and the World Bank, which would be placed under the auspices of the ECOSOC. Dr. Shotwell on several occasions expressed to Schaefer his interest in an International Chamber of Commerce and spoke of the possibility of an international "capital" organization as a rival of the ILO. Schaefer advocated convincingly that any body established within the Council should be required to have a tripartite representation on the order of the ILO. Shotwell agreed and a motion was carried that he present his concept to the State

Department. Schaefer was pleased with this outcome; in her opinion chances for serious consideration of her proposal by the American delegation were much improved with Shotwell's advocacy, since he was regarded as "the most influential person among all groups of consultants and with the State Department itself."[25]

At the second consultants' meeting on the Economic and Social Council, Jim Carey, in the name of the alliance of labor, industry, agriculture, and educational interests assembled by Schaefer, submitted a specific proposal to the State Department on the matter of tripartite representation for agencies within the ECOSOC. Secretary of State Stettinius, showing great interest in the proposal, promised to present it to the next session of the American delegation.

This resolution would eventually find its way into the Charter by means of an American amendment upheld by the entire Conference. Along with the structure of the old ILO, it was proposed that the ECOSOC create many new agencies to follow the pattern of that body. Granted a wide berth by the US measure, the ILO would expand its activities. Though still dominated by traditional concerns for wages and working conditions, it would over the years broaden its pursuits to include such objectives as social security, full employment, and economic planning.[26]

Schaefer had every reason to be gratified by the results of her struggle on behalf of the Economic and Social Council. She could also look with pride on the effects of the "hitherto unknown" spirit she engendered among consultants and labor leaders—an atmosphere that encouraged the recognition of the advantage of many of the ILO's operative procedures for the ECOSOC's other member agencies. Moveover, these activities did not go unnoticed by the American Catholic Church. Archbishops Mooney, Stritch, McNicholas, and Amleto Cicognani, the Apostolic Delegate, were all informed of her work and subsequently applauded it.[27]

The Catholic media were likewise pleased with the San Francisco Charter's recognition of the position of the

ECOSOC. *America* quoted approvingly the heartening view-point of Dutch Franciscan Father Didymus, O.F.M. (L.J.C. Beaufort), a member of the delegation of the Netherlands and of the Estates-General, as well as Director of Education of the Catholic Workers' Association of Utrecht. Although he expressed his lack of enthusiasm for Big Power domination of the Security Council, he was reassured by the "distinct advance" that the UNCIO had made beyond the standard obsession with the political aspects of world organization. The wide scope given to the Economic and Social Council was one of the brightest features of the Conference, he maintained. It was "an instrumentality for abolishing the root causes of war, which lie in economic and social evils. . . ."[28]

Commonweal singled out the non-political influence of the ILO as a beneficial influence on the Charter. Just as the International Labor Organization and other such affiliates of the League of Nations accomplished more than its political elements in the period between the wars, so too, this Catholic periodical hoped, the ECOSOC would be able to triumph in spite of the "disappointing rigidity" of so many sections of the Charter. In this area at least, a remnant from the League of Nations was a real boon to the new world-organization.[29]

By the end of June 1945, American Catholics were generally of the opinion that the Economic and Social Council might well be "the greatest long-run achievement of the Conference."[30] If so, the Catholic representatives in San Francisco had much to do with this, especially in economic and labor matters. There were others at the conference who also would pressure for the extension of UN influence into another area of international concern, worldwide educational cooperation. But the position of the Catholic Church on this topic was conspicuous only by its disorientation.

"World Education for World Peace"[31]

The NCWC Administrative Board's November 16, 1944 statement *On International Order* declared that World War II had come from "bad education." It was not caused by the illiterate masses but by theorists who discarded moral principles and asserted the "right of aggression" by subjugating human reason and obliterating awareness of inherent human liberties and obligations in the name of the all-powerful state. The gilded hallucinations of the dictators who dominated these totalitarian systems turned into holocausts and other unspeakable nightmares, which the League of Nations could not prevent because of its woefully inadequate procedures. The only way a just and lasting peace could be achieved, the hierarchy stated, was through

> the creation of a sane realism, which has a clear vision of the moral law, a reverent acknowledgement of God its Author, and a recognition of the oneness of the human race underlying all national distinctions.[32]

The NCWC's distaste for fascist "bad education" was shared by all parties in framing the Charter for the new world organization. At the outset of the UNCIO, Stettinius announced that the sponsoring powers had consented to a proposal offered by China, which stated that the Economic and Social Council should provide specifically for promotion of educational and other forms of cultural cooperation. Because of the vague language in which this resolution was drafted and because the Administrative Board was even less explicit in its pronouncements on this subject, the Catholic consultants at San Francisco sensed correctly that they had few real guidelines by the time precise suggestions for UN educational projects began to appear among the US consultants.[33]

The first volley in a mock-epic battle for the Catholic representatives at San Francisco was fired by the educational consultants under the leadership of the National Education Association (NEA). In a resolution of May 2, addressed to Mr. Stettinius, the authors insisted that the UN Charter should establish a semi-autonomous educational agency within the framework of the ECOSOC. These consultants were at pains to emphasize that they were not advocating that this agency have "authority to intervene in the management, direction, or control of educational methods or policies in any member nation."

Their general resolve was only to promote educational and cultural relations among the signatory states, and to abet systematic study of instructional accomplishments and problems.[34]

The Catholic Conference was immediately thrown off balance by this proposal. Being traditionally geared to oppose the NEA, which favored a US Department of Education but opposed federal aid to Catholic schools and release-time for religious instruction in public schools—positions anathema to the NCWC—it reflexively wanted to know just what the resolution meant by "education."[35] At first Richard Pattee, distrustful of their motives, said he saw "just what they were after." He was heartened by Dean Gildersleeve's aside to him that the resolution had no support in the US delegation and would die a natural death long before it got to any of the commissions.[36]

The two secret qualms that the American Catholic Church had about a worldwide educational agency had to do with its distrust of the liberal, secularist thrust of US education associations and their undoubted influence on the State Department. Monsignor Frederick G. Hochwalt, director of the NCWC Department of Education, once told Catherine Schaefer that he was afraid that the NEA had dreams of establishing a global public-school system that would threaten Catholic schools around the world.[37]

The second misgiving was expressed to Pattee by Monsignor Carroll: the NCWC General Secretary was concerned that no educational arrangement be sanctioned whereby the Soviet Union would gain domination over the education of Europe. The Church authorities thought that after the "sellout" of Eastern Europe by President Roosevelt, the State Department might willingly offer Stalin control over the formation of generations of children on that continent. Furthermore, the NEA and similar organizations, being in a virulently anti-fascist mood, might disregard entirely Soviet influence in this sphere until it was too late to do anything about it.[38]

These trepidations, justified or not, were of little assistance to the Catholic representatives in San Francisco. The proposal made by the NEA consultants and others specified that the office they envisioned should have no control over educational methods or policies but should promote only educational and cultural relations. These assurances gradually won the Catholics in San Francisco, who were forced to put aside their preconceived notions. Schaefer complained not only that the National Conference was not addressing the real content of the NEA resolution but that great pressure was being placed on the Catholic consultants to support this innocuous amendment, since its authors had bent over backwards to alleviate any fears that the Church might still harbor.[39]

Hochwalt told Schaefer that he could certainly appreciate her view that "If we can support what is being done, I think we should." He had been going through the same ordeal in Washington in reference to support for the House and Senate Resolutions calling for an International Education Office—a position he personally did not oppose. "I know that both of us have heard that hopeless edict, 'the Bishops didn't get to it at the last meeting.'" All the groups interested in an International Office of Education had been pestering him for support of the NEA amendment, and he told Schaefer "off the record" that he regretted not being able to give it an official endorsement.[40]

Schaefer was so embarrassed by the Church's position, or lack thereof, that she decided to absent herself from a May 14 educational core-committee meeting because she knew the question of endorsing an international education office would arise again and she did not "feel competent to make a rational decision or argument in the matter." She thought that the "episcopal admonition to steer clear" of the issue, which all Catholics in San Francisco had received, was rendered moot by a CAIP document entitled "A Peace Agenda for the United Nations," which on page twenty-one spoke foursquare in favor of the proposal made by the NEA. She told Father McGowan that it was no longer a matter that could be "steered clear of."[41]

This was indeed the case. At the same May 14 meeting from which Schaefer was truant, a powerful combination of education and economic groups (labor, agriculture, and business)—including such good Catholics as the CIO's James Carey—had persuaded Dr. James T. Shotwell to draft a new chapter for the Economic and Social Council, which would advance a far more extensive international educational agency. One addition to Chapter IX of the UN Charter urged that the Office of International Education be granted a center for research and exchange. Another empowered that ECOSOC agency to "go into a country where inhuman militarist doctrines are being taught (such as Nazi Germany) and make an objective study of the educational system and its content, which would then be given world-wide publicity." Pattee told Monsignor Carroll bluntly that "we are in no position to oppose the thing as it stands nor do I see any real need to."[42]

The true extent of the bishops' untenable position on this issue was made absolutely clear on May 16. In near-panic, Richard Pattee called Carroll at NCWC headquarters to inform him that word had been passed to one of the educational groups by a journalist that the US delegation's "confidential explanation" of its aversion to insertion of the word "education" anywhere in the Charter was "fear of hostility and opposition on the part of the [Catholic] Church." To complicate matters further, for the next day the American delegation had a press conference scheduled and the Catholic consultants "had been especially asked to attend by the State Department." Dreading an ambush at which the Church would be held up as the lone impediment to the reform of international postwar education, Pattee begged for guidance from the Administrative Board.[43]

In a letter to McGowan on May 14 Schaefer predicted that because of the Church's failure to come up with an enlightened policy on this issue its consultants at San Francisco would be forced to assume the role of observers and that therefore the Church would be presented with a *fait accompli* in the matter of education.[44] Such was the case.

During their May 16 telephone conversation Carroll suggested that Pattee call Archbishop Mooney to get immediate advice on the subject. When the NEA resolution of May 14 was presented to Mooney, along with a description of the predicament it caused, the archbishop determined that the Church "could not oppose with reason" any of the proposed amendments. As for their implementation, the Church would have to see that they were not made instruments of secularization in education or of government control of it. Should attempts be made in that direction, Mooney threatened wanly, Catholic sponsorship would remain but there would be objections not only from the NCWC but also from many countries.

A statement to this effect was immediately transmitted to Pattee and he was instructed to present it to the US delegation at 9:00 A.M. on May 17—before the delegation's press conference.[45] On the next day, May 18, *The New York Times* reported that at that meeting most American consultants supported the amendments to Chapter IX of the Charter, which proposed a semi-autonomous international education agency within the Economic and Social Council.[46]

What the *Times* did not report was that the Catholic consultants contributed not a word to the framing of that resolution. And this was not the end. Unbelievably, the NCWC's Department of Education was not able to present its three-page report of rather insightful suggestions on the Draft Constitution for an Educational and Cultural Association of the United Nations until October 1, 1945, months after the Charter of the world organization was ratified by the United States Senate. Furthermore, no Catholic educator would be invited as an American delegate to the London Conference of November 1945, which was to consider creation of the Educational and Cultural Organization. Monsignor Hochwalt's recommendation to the State Department that "all educational interests in the country should be represented" obviously went unheeded.[47]

One cannot but believe that the Catholic Church's inability to join the consultants' discussions of formation of a UN educational policy colored the State Department's view of the quality of the Church's potential contribution to such a process. Catherine Schaefer's prophecy that the Church would be left outside this issue came true with a vengeance, but even she could not foresee that it would extend far beyond the conference to include even the formation of the agency. Culpability for this debacle must be laid at the door of the Administrative

Board, which not only failed to provide a coherent policy on education but in its bewilderment asserted that its representatives at San Francisco "steer clear" of the matter until it was too late to do anything but accept the inevitable.

The Trusteeship Controversy

During the debate in the US Senate over ratification of the United Nations Charter, Senator David I. Walsh, Democrat of Massachusetts and a Roman Catholic, rose to proclaim that while the UNCIO document was a marvelous expression of the hopes and aspirations of the peoples of the world for peace, the United States must always safeguard first its own security. Quoting James M. Forrestal, Secretary of the Navy, Walsh was adamant that the nation maintain an Army and Navy "larger than ever before dreamed of in peacetime," by arranging for retention of military bases in many parts of the world—especially in the Pacific.[48]

In this address the senator mirrored perfectly the mood of the Truman Administration and its Big Power allies, Britain and Russia, who, while thoroughly intent on being proponents of a "peace-keeping" world organization, were just as determined to keep the peace themselves and as much of their military might as possible. For the United States in particular, military policy dictated that bases such as those alluded to by Secretary Forrestal be situated in key strategic areas. For the US Navy in 1945, no locale was seen to fit this description better than the islands and archipelagoes of the Pacific Rim—principally those recently liberated at great price from the Japanese.[49] It was assumed by the Big Three that these territories would certainly revert to their prewar status as colonies or protectorates, called "mandates" under the League of Nations, or be given to them for safeguarding in the name of peace.[50]

A Strategic Policy

A Commission on Permanent Mandates had long been an advisory corporation of the Council of the League, in which ultimate authority for dependent territories had been lodged in Geneva. In the inter-war years the League developed three types of mandated territories: jointly controlled "condominiums" like the Belgium Congo, "trusteeships" exercised by imperial powers on behalf of dependent peoples (Britain in India), and Great Power collectives in "backward" areas such as the Ottoman Empire. During the 1930s there was an increasing demand all over the world for application of the principle of "self-determination" for dependent peoples, and most of the colonial powers had in varying degrees accepted self-government as the ultimate goal for their mandates. On the whole, however, little progress had been made toward the improvement, much less independence, of the peoples under these mandates. Responsibility for this dereliction rested primarily, of course, with the great imperial powers, such as Britain, but also with the smaller colonial nations as well.[51]

The imperialist theory that colonies existed merely for the advantage of the colonizing power had been disparaged by the League, but to little effect. The two greatest Allied Powers during World War II, the Soviet Union and the United States, gave lip-service to this anti-imperialist movement, but there were many skeptics who doubted these protestations of altruism. One certainly would not have noted any anti-imperialist traits while reading the documents from the Big Power conferences that immediately preceded the San Francisco parley.[52]

No reference had been made to the status of dependent or colonial territories in the Dumbarton Oaks proposal or in the official report issued after the Yalta Conference. This ominous silence was interpreted by some NCWC observers, who were concerned about the Church's Asian missions, to mean that the Big Three were prepared to use whatever mandated territories they needed to secure their defense shields. If these Catholics had been privy to some pre-Conference confidential memoranda at the State Department, their worst fears would have been confirmed.[53]

In a confidential, "special guidance" memorandum of March 30, 1945, the Office of War Information (OWI) apprised its department chiefs that territories like Burma, Indo-China, and

Malaya would not be handed over to the new world organization for international supervision. This startlingly candid assessment directed that there should be nothing apologetic in the treatment of the subject when this policy was announced. The OWI did predict that many American would be disappointed by this stance, and therefore officials at the Department of State were free to canvass responsible expression of such points of view, if they so desired. Spokesmen for the United States government must never indicate, however, that the Administration would "advocate freedom for dependent peoples or international supervision of all dependent areas."[54]

Harry Truman was fully informed of the American policy on trusteeships at his first "Top Secret" State Department briefing on the day after he assumed the presidency. On April 13, the date of this meeting, it was still considered an "important open question." Although nothing was released to the world about the Big Three position on territorial trusts after the Crimea Conference, Truman discovered that Churchill, Stalin, and FDR had indeed discussed this issue. The Big Five, it had been agreed, should discuss secretly before San Francisco "the machinery and principles of a trusteeship system" to replace the League's mandate program. It was also agreed that there was to be no discussion before or at the UN Conference of specific territories to be placed under the system; this subject was left to the discretion of the five permanent members of the Security Council.

There were officials, especially at the War Department, who urged strategic status for particular Pacific areas, and in this they had encouragement from the highest levels of the US government. At the time of his death President Roosevelt was scheduled to review on April 19 the situation in the postwar Pacific theatre with the Secretaries of State, War (Henry L. Stimson), and Navy.[55] He had, however, countermanded his edict on silence on the subject, and in the process inadvertently revealed the extensive strategic and military role the United States intended to play in the Pacific. On the day of the Truman briefing, April 13, *The New York Times* related that at his last press conference FDR explicitly stated that "the United States

. . . must accept (i.e., be given) trusteeships over Japanese mandated islands, build new naval and air bases and help the Philippines rebuild," even after the latter had become a self-governing nation.[56] During its last-minute "arrangements for international trusteeship" before the San Francisco Conference, the American delegation received from the State Department the Administration's definitive position on the matter. Beginning felicitously enough, this draft stated that the United States would support three basic objectives at the UNCIO:

(a) To further international peace and security; (b) to promote the political, economic, and social advancement of the trust territories and their inhabitants and their progressive development toward self-government; and (c) to provide for non-discriminatory treatment in trust territories with respect to the economic and other appropriate civil activities of the nationals of all member states.[57]

These three goals, however, were put into proper perspective by three more stipulations placed discreetly down the page. Point Five of the draft set forth the seemingly innocent condition that the trusteeship arrangements in each case should include the terms under which the territory would be administered. Point Six stated that the terms of some trusteeship arrangements might designate certain areas as "strategic" and that this might include part or even all of the territory to which the arrangement applied. Point Seven revealed that the Big Five would insist that "all functions of the Organization relating to strategic areas, including the approval of the trusteeship arrangements and their alteration or amendment," would be discharged by the Security Council. All other trusteeships would fall under the purview of the General Assembly.[58]

By this stratagem the major powers could now exert a nearly total control over their use of strategically mandated territories by deflecting any viable opposition to their plans through the exercise of a Security Council veto. Though all other aspects of the Trusteeship Council would be under the supervision of the General Assembly, a special entitlement was to be extended to those permanent members of the Security Council to whom the world organization had given its protections. This policy implied that defense of world peace was equivalent to defense of the military prerogatives of the Veto Powers; accordingly, little in the way of security for the rights of the populations of strategic territories was granted in this amendment. To that prospect the Catholic Church in America took exception.

A Commission On Dependent Peoples

In the matter of trust territories, American religious groups had taken a completely different tack from that of the State Department; this was evident in the choice of words and even in the concepts used to explain their positions. In November 1944 the Catholic bishops stated that the UN Charter must recognize the "peoples coming of age in the family of nations." In fostering and promoting international cooperation, therefore, the document must guarantee economic opportunities to the weak and the poor nations. The Board's statement likewise stressed that the progress of underdeveloped and colonial peoples must be a goal of the world organization. In this way an end of the exploitation of primitive groups by "enlightened" nations could be achieved. Moreover, the independence of all subject peoples was an obligation of the UN, and a special commission should be established wherein such aims could be realized, both through its advisory and consultative capacities and in its supervision of the existing mandated territories and the new dependent regions taken from enemy states.[59]

The Church in the United States was particularly concerned to safeguard the interests of the Vatican's worldwide missionary effort and especially those missionaries who were laboring in former enemy territories or who were themselves Axis nationals. In his review of the Administrative Board's April statement entitled "Ideological Notes," the Reverend Paul F. Tanner, Assistant General Secretary of the NCWC, put it succinctly: "Freedom of missionary effort—watch it!" Because the NCWC saw the survival of these mission endeavors as inextricable from the progress of the world's many dependent peoples and their religious freedom, it unapologetically crusaded for their survival.[60]

Prior to the UNCIO, Father Conway too cautioned that the Church's missionary interests could be placed in jeopardy by decisions made at the Conference. The Big Three's preoccupation with their own safety was not the only threat. Would UN supervision be a boon or a hindrance to Catholic missionaries? Who would compose the UN commissions? Would Protestants, Jews, or those from other religions countenance Catholic missionary activities? Finally, what would the Charter decide on freedom of religion?[61] Conway suggested that the NCWC begin as soon as possible to campaign in support of the contentions of the Chapultepec Conference and adopt its nonrecognition policy for territorial acquisitions obtained by force, and the principle that all peoples were equally entitled to political independence.[62]

In a speech in Berlin at the end of World War II, President Truman would declare to the victorious American armies that "there is not one piece of territory . . . we want out of this war." This was obviously received with considerable incredulity by many knowledgeable persons, including Catholics who had served as observers or consultants at San Francisco. The matter of Pacific island bases, which everyone at the Conference identified as a major US concern, had been, by American edict, the "hush-hush topic" of the UNCIO.[63]

At their May 16 meeting with Navy Commander Harold Stassen, consultants such as Pattee tried repeatedly to explore the relationship of the trusteeship system to US strategic interests in the Pacific. They were, however, ruled out of order because of the war emergency blackout that enveloped islands that served as air and naval bases, or were answered in ways more confusing than helpful. On no issue at the conference, with the exclusion of the Veto Power, were the consultants less effectual than in the matter of strategic territories; this was simply because the American delegation would not or could not consult anyone on the question. Pattee later stated that he never was consulted on this issue, merely notified.[64]

The fact was that the Army and Navy were naturally on the

job in San Francisco; their goal was to have the Charter so framed that the United States could have any islands it wanted in the Pacific, and on its own terms. Furthermore, because of the impending invasion of Japan, which was scheduled for the fall of 1945, the military and political leaders of the US were not in a position to discuss relinquishing of territories that were then essential to the war effort. Under no circumstances, therefore, did the military want to be under a Charter commitment to place any territory under a General Assembly-supervised trusteeship, or even under the tutelage of its Security Council allies. Harold Stassen played the leading American role in the deliberations on this subject; in this he was ably assisted by Lt. General Stanley D. Embick and Vice-Admiral Russell Willson. These three composed the committee that drew up the "Working Paper" that was to become the basis for Big Power discussions on the question and, with minor alterations, the text for the Trusteeship Chapter of the United Nations Charter.[65]

At the end of the war the Big Three were certainly in a live-and-let live mood when it came to carving out their own spheres of influence; as far as any of them were concerned, the British could maintain the Empire, the Russians would be given nothing less than most of Eastern Europe, and the United States could have any part of the Pacific it fancied. However, as early as May 5 Richard Pattee noticed a modest chink in this wall of *bonhomie*. He reported that even Anthony Eden, the legate of that shameless imperialist Winston Churchill, balked at Stassen's temerity in ignoring a British "working paper" on the subject.

Ostensibly based on various Big Three suggestions, the Britsh draft proposed that all Administrating Powers should be obliged to make reports to the Security Council on the forces, facilities, and various military uses that they were making of their trust territories. This document, however, had been summarily ignored by the United States. Clearly the Navy had no intention of allowing the prying eyes of the United Nations near its bases. By their insistence on this point, the Americans brought the trusteeship discussion to a halt.[66]

By May 14 Pattee could report only that "the trusteeship

business was still bogged down" and that there were rumors that "serious horse-trading" was going on between the United States and the United Kingdom. In these discussions the United States would eventually concede that Britain should not be pressured to liquidate the Empire, and in turn the UK agreed that the Pacific was for all practical purposes a US domain.[67] Senator Connally could therefore report later to the Senate Foreign Relations Committee:

> It was our attitude that if we are in possession of an island which we have acquired from Japan at the cost of blood and treasure we can retain possession of it . . . until we consent that it go under the trusteeship; and when we do agree that it go under trusteeship, we have the right to stipulate the terms upon which it will go there."[68]

This interpretation, it was understood, could not be altered or amended without approval of the Security Council, in which, of course, the United States possessed a veto.

The full meaning of the American concession to the British on the matter of "Empire" soon became clear to Pattee. On May 17, the day after Stassen's evasive meeting with the American consultants, the Commander, as chairman of the Committee on Trusteeships, gave a statement that shocked even the desultory American press. In his comments on the final Big Power amendments to the Charter, he announced that the US would oppose making "a specific promise of independence to colonial peoples."[69] Pattee objected that this statement condemned the Conference to virtual inaction on the true issue facing it, which was not merely UN trusteeships, but rather the destiny of colonial peoples. Now the Charter would be dealing with areas that contained at the most 15,000,000 people, while the colonial territories, most of them within the British Empire, possessed a population in excess of 750,000,000. Pattee believed that the United States, by allying itself with the United Kingdom (and France) in order to acquire the bases it needed in the Pacific, had willingly ignored the fate of the millions who lived as colonials with scant voice in their own affairs.[70]

The Russians and Chinese were urging that "independence" should be advanced as the ultimate goal for dependent peoples and that the "basic purpose" of the UN, referred to above (p. 32), should read "self government or independence." Thomas Mahony wondered why the United States had associated itself with the imperial powers on the principle that "self-governing" did not include "independence." What harm would it have done to include the latter word, which represented the traditional American aspiration? Mahony agreed with his contacts in the smaller nations, who expressed the view that if the phrase stood, no imperial power, old or new, would ever peaceably surrender a colony or mandated territory to trusteeship. Even if it did, such a surrender would still preclude the peoples of that area from achieving independence.[71]

Furthermore, if "strategic areas" were to be trusteed after the war by particular states without the requirement of investigation by the UN, Mahony asserted, then they posed an even greater danger for future peace. Did not this insistence upon secrecy in the fortification of strategic areas hobble UN efforts to maintain the peace and further indicate a collective suspicion within the ranks of the Great Powers? And did not such misgivings augur preparations for other wars?[72]

A natural effect of the alliance of the UK, France, and the US was the inevitable corollary that Molotov would attempt to gain many propaganda points. Predictably, there was much high-flown language from the Soviet delegation about responsibility to the people first, good administration, and decent living conditions. Since the Soviet Union possessed no colonies in the classical sense, it felt free to inject the idea that "independence should be the end of all such administration." China, as the only other Asian power, agreed wholeheartedly. Pattee reported that the "impression was not a happy one." The US now appeared in the eyes of the colonial world as linked with imperialism. The Soviet Union was handed the position of champion of the underdog and accepted it with glee. Eventually, of course, the champion, to get what it wanted in Eastern Europe, would "reluctantly" concede this post in order to prevent a breakup of the conference. In fact, what precipitated this change of heart was Edward Stettinius's note to Molotov that said the US accepted that the Soviet Union was eligible to receive territories for administration under trusteeship.[73]

Accordingly, in the completely new Declaration Regarding Non-Self-Governing Territories advanced by the United States and Great Britain and inserted in Chapter XI of the Charter, the basic object of the system now became first to further international peace and security and only then to promote political, economic, and social advancement of the territories and their inhabitants. The Declaration did not refer, even as an alternative, to the aim of independence. Its careful wording revealed straightway that the imperial powers, old and new, would not admit any genuine UN role in the strategic territories or colonies they prized. The Catholic consultants were unerring in their estimation that the "peace-loving" superpowers were using the League of Nations' platitudes that they once roundly condemned, in order to mask their intentions to subordinate whole regions of the earth.[74]

Disappointment And Shame

In an article in *America* during the first week of the UNCIO, the Reverend Robert A. Graham asked whether the United States "was sacrificing its splendid moral position by stooping to pick up bits of territory here and there," in open contradiction to the Atlantic Charter. In what could have been utilized as a reply to Senator Connally's statement to the Senate Foreign Relations Committee mentioned above, Graham added that the US was putting a very cheap price on American blood if it thought that Iwo Jima and Saipan were the only things the Marines had been fighting for.[75]

This attitude, which was a fair indication of positions taken by American Catholic consultants, was a minority viewpoint in both the national press and popular sentiment. The weight of American opinion was clearly for effective US control of some Pacific islands, on the grounds of either assuring the defense of the United States or of securing Senate approval of the UN

Charter.[76] But the Vatican, in a statement of June 18, 1945, cut through all this purblind nationalism to point out the obvious: within the United Nations a "regime of protection is created over territory of direct domination and a colonial regime is maintained." In other words, the Big Five, with the US leading the way, were given permission by the Charter to be as "imperial" as they wished.[77]

In its May 12 issue *America* speculated how long this compromise could be disguised as anything other than a territorial grab. One urgent question was whether these US bases were for postwar defensive or offensive purposes. Okinawa and Iwo Jima, the editors suspected, could hardly be necessary for the defense of the US mainland. Their obvious military value was as bases for attacks on Japan during the war or to repel future Japanese aggression. If so, should they not be under the surveillance of the Security Council allies, who were assigned to subdue such threats?[78]

Although members of the American delegation and officials of the State Department were guarded in identifying former Japanese islands that were to be retained after the war by the United States, the Truman Administration could not begin to muzzle the enthusiasm of certain high-ranking military officers, who could hardly restrain themselves from claiming specific territories even before the US Senate had an opportunity to ratify the UN Charter. A major controversy arose, therefore, over a loose-lipped statement by the Chief of Army Air Force, General Henry H. (Hap) Arnold. In a speech at Honolulu on July 24 the General cited more than a dozen islands and archipelagoes that were essential to future US security. He declared that after his fact-finding mission to the South Seas he was convinced that America must have a "bridge across the Pacific" and that the US must be given the islands in this chain for its "unrestricted use." "The future peace of the world depends on our doing this," Arnold professed. "Indeed the fate of mankind may depend upon it."[79]

Reacting to this pronouncement, *Commonweal* contended that this was too facile an argument for any nation that occupied enemy territory during the war. To claim such areas outright weakened widespread confidence for peace on any terms except "naked, unilateral force." It would, moreover, provoke similar demands by other Big Powers. The need for adequate defense was undeniable, the editors said, yet the Pacific could not be viewed by the US as a *mare nostrum*. As a member of the United Nations, it had to be "restricted" to some extent "by broader considerations which are as much to our own interest as to that of other nations and dependent peoples." To administer such islands in the name of the UN was a highly preferable means of securing the "fate of mankind."[80]

Commonweal believed that the problem with Chapters XII and XIII of the UN Charter as drafted by the San Francisco Conference was that, although they recognized some excellent principles for administration of dependent peoples, they ignored demands to extend these principles to strategic trusteeships and to colonial peoples. The standards were admirable, but the magazine anticipated intractability, since their being put into effect depended entirely on that questionable commodity, the good will of the major powers.[81]

For most Catholic observers, the truly lamentable fact in the UN Charter's declarations on trusteeship was that they ran contrary to the Atlantic Charter, a supposed antidote to deficiencies of the League and a document that the bishops had frequently called the one indispensable groundwork for true peace in the postwar world.

Anticipating the Administrative Board's future statements, Richard Pattee repeated the major tenets of the September 14, 1941 agreement, signed by Roosevelt and Churchill and later subscribed to, with reservations, by Stalin. The first article of that compact affirmed that the signatory states sought "no aggrandizement, territorial or otherwise"; the second pledged that they coveted no territorial changes that did not correspond to the "freely expressed wishes of the peoples concerned," and the third deferred to the prerogative of all peoples to select the form of government under which they would live. By the end of the conference, Pattee observed, it was evident that these goals of the Atlantic Charter had not been respected; in disposal of territories in the Pacific, in Eastern Europe, and within the British Empire, Soviet reservations would hold sway, as well as some of the worst aspects of the League of Nations.[82]

In the "non-political" matters of economics, social affairs, and the fate of dependent peoples the UNCIO adopted many aspects of the old League of Nations but offered substantial variations, not all of them salutary. As in many other areas of contention, it was impossible to keep Veto-Power domination out of these agencies; more success was achieved in the ECOSOC than in the Trusteeship Council. The American delegates, advisers, and consultants who had debated these and other issues left San Francisco nonetheless with a sense of guarded optimism, tempered, at least in Catholic circles, by a dread that the Big Five would have the same inordinate control over the workings of the United Nations as they had exerted in the drafting of the UN Charter. Therefore the Catholic Church in the United States understood only too well that it had much work to do.

Notes

1. *The United Nations As a Political Institution,* p. 14.
2. Ibid.
3. *The Dictionary of American Diplomatic History,* s.v. "Trusteeship Council (United Nations)."
4. *The United Nations Charter,* p. 15.
5. "Catholics and the Dumbarton Oaks Proposals," p. 9.
6. Ibid.
7. Ibid., p. 2.
8. Ibid.
9. "Some Observations on the San Francisco Conference. . . ," p. 9.
10. ANCWC 11, Pattee to Carroll, [San Francisco], April 30, 1945, p. 2.
11. ANCWC 13c, "Small and Middle Nations Emphasize Importance of Economic, Social Council at San Francisco Parley," Edward A. Conway, S.J., May 5, 1945, p. 2a.
12. Ruth B. Russell, *The United Nations and United States Security Policy* (Washington: The Brookings Institution, 1968) p. 37; AN-

CWC 12, Report to the Post-War World Committee by Catherine Schaefer, [D.C.], July 11, 1945, p. 13.

13. AMU, Series 6, Box 1, U.S. Consultants' Resolution, May 15, 1945, p. 1; "Some Observations on the San Francisco Conference. . . ," p. 10.

14. Ibid.

15. Ibid., p. 11.

16. AMU, Series 6, Box 1, Schaefer to McGowan, [San Francisco], April 30, 1945.

17. *The United Nations As a Political Institution,* p. 138; Anthony Alcock, *The History of the International Labor Organization* (London: Macmillan, 1971), p. 47.

18. *The United Nations As a Political Institution,* p. 138.

19. Ibid., p. 5.

20. The World Federation of Trade Unions Conference, held in Oakland in conjunction with the UNCIO, was a gathering of international trade unions representing 22,000,000 laborers in Europe, Asia, Latin America, and the United States. The CIO, which was the only American trade union present at the conference, declared through its president, Philip Murray, that the WFTU should be allowed to participate in the U.N. in ways other than inclusion of the ILO into the Economic and Social Council. He insisted that the Federation have a consultative capacity in the General Assembly. This proposal was formally rejected by the UNCIO ("Labor Demands Seats in Council," *The New York Times,* May 8, 1945, p. 14).

21. AMU, Series 6, Box 1, Schaefer to McGowan, [San Francisco], April 30, 1945.

22. ANCWC 11, McGowan to Carroll, [D.C.], May 31, 1945.

23. AMU, Series 6, Box 1, Schaefer to McGowan, [San Francisco], May 4, 1945, p. 3.

24. AMU, Series 6, Box 1, Schaefer to McGowan, [San Francisco], May 11, 1945.

25. AMU, Series 6, Box 1, Schaefer to McGowan, [San Francisco], May 4, 1945, p. 2. The International Monetary Fund and the World Bank were already in the development stage at the time of the UNCIO. In July 1944 the Bretton Woods Conference laid the groundwork for these organizations in order to foster global activity in the areas of monetary affairs and development, respectively.

26. *The United Nations As a Political Institution,* p. 138.

27. ANCWC 12, McGowan to Carroll, [D.C.], May 31, 1945.

28. "Judging the UNCIO," *America* 73 (July 28, 1945):326.

29. "San Francisco Wind-up."

30. "Judging the UNCIO."

31. AMU, Series 1, Box 1, Tentative Topic Selection from CAIP Institute, April 2–3, 1945.

32. *On International Order,* p. 57.

33. ANCWC 11, "Russia's Acceptance of Chinese Proposals Outstanding Event of San Francisco Meeting," Edward A. Conway, S.J., April 30, 1945, p. 1.

34. AMU, Series 1, Box 1, Educational Consultants to Stettinius, [San Francisco], May 2, 1945, pp. 1–2, copy.

35. *Pastoral Letters . . . ,* vol. 2, *Statement on Federal Aid to Education,* November 13, 1944, pp. 50–51.

36. ANCWC 11, Pattee to Carroll, [San Francisco], May 3, 1945, p. 1.

37. AMU, Series 6, Box 1, Hochwalt to Schaefer, [D.C.], May 19, 1945, copy.

38. ANCWC 11, Carroll to Pattee, [D.C.], May 7, 1945.

39. AMU, Series 6, Box 1, Schaefer to McGowan, [San Francisco], May 16, 1945.

40. Hochwalt to Schaefer, [D.C.], May 19, 1945.

41. Schaefer to McGowan, [San Francisco], May 14, 1945.

42. Ibid., p. 3; U.S. Consultants' Resolution on ECOSOC, May 15, 1945; ANCWC 15, Pattee to Carroll, [San Francisco], May 16, 1945, p. 2.

43. AMU, Series 6, Box 1, Schaefer to McGowan, [San Francisco], May 16, 1945, copy; ANCWC 15, Pattee to Carroll, [San Francisco], May 16, 1945, copy.

44. Schaefer to McGowan, [San Francisco], May 14, 1945.

45. ANCWC 15, Carroll to Pattee, [San Francisco], May 16, 1945, copy.

46. Along with sensible proposals such as "full exchange of information about educational activities," more immoderate suggestions were heard. Chancellor Ben Cherrington of the University of Denver proposed that postwar fleets of "education airplanes" constantly fly back and forth for conferences, carrying educators for weekends to Rio de Janeiro and Moscow, etc. ("Educators Push Post-War Program," *The New York Times,* May 18, 1945, p. 12).

47. R.G. 59a 2232, Folder 6, Hochwalt to Francis H. Russell, [San Francisco], October 1, 1945, p. 1.

48. U.S. Senate, Senator David I. Walsh speaking in behalf of Senate Ratification of United Nations Charter, 79th Cong., 1st sess., July 28, 1945, *Congressional Record* 91:7434.

49. In this discussion on trusteeships, it must be remembered that during the Dumbarton Oaks Conversations, the Yalta Conference, and the UNCIO, the United States and its allies were still engaged in a tremendous conflict in the Pacific. At a staggering human price the United Nations allies had already recaptured many key islands in their advance toward Japan, but the Department of War estimated that a full-scale invasion of the Japanese mainland would take at least another year and maybe more. The reclaimed Pacific islands were to play an essential part in that attack. No one could guess in the first half of

234 AMERICAN CATHOLICS AND THE UNITED NATIONS

1945 that V-J Day, August 15, 1945, would come as soon as it did.

50. *The Semblance of Peace,* p. 422.

51. Harriet Eager Davis, ed., *Pioneers in World Order: An American Appraisal of the League of Nations* (New York: Columbia University Press, 1944), "Dependent Peoples and Mandates," by Huntington Gilchrist, p. 125.

52. *The United Nations As A Political Institution,* pp. 17, 28–29.

53. *Yearbook of the United Nations,* "Yalta Agreements" and "Dumbarton Oaks Conversations."

54. RG 59i, Box 1, Folder 1, "Special Guidance on Trusteeships for Dependent Areas," March 30, 1945.

55. RG 59a 1991, Folder 3, "United Nations Conference on International Organization at San Francisco," Edward R. Stettinius, April 13, 1945, pp. 2–3.

56. "Victory in Sight When Death Came," *The New York Times,* April 13, 1945, p. 9.

57. RG 59i, Box 2, Folder 1, "Arrangements for International Trusteeship," April 24, 1945. p. 1.

58. Ibid., p. 2.

59. "Your Role in San Francisco," p. 2.

60. "Ideological Notes," p. 2.

61. "Catholic Interests Involved in the San Francisco Conference," "Dependent Peoples."

62. ANCWC 15, "On World Security Organization," [London], April 19, 1945. p. 3, copy.

63. "What the Navy Did at U.N.C.I.O.," *America,* 73 (August 4, 1945):352.

64. RG 59a 2001, Folder 4, Minutes of U.S. Consultants' Meeting, May 16, 1945, 8:15 P.M., p. A-7.

65. "What the Navy Did at U.N.C.I.O.," p. 352.

66. ANCWC 11, Pattee to Carroll, [San Francisco], May 5, 1945; At Yalta, Churchill had likewise been unreceptive to US proposals on international trusteeships. When American negotiators raised the matter, Churchill rejected it outright and FDR backed down, and agreed to further discussions (Warren F. Kimball, ed., *Churchill and Roosevelt: The Complete Correspondence,* 3 vols. [Princeton: Princeton University Press, 1984], vol. 3: *Alliance Declining: February 1944–April 1945,* p. 528).

67. Pattee to Carroll, [San Francisco], May 14, 1945, p. 1.

68. U.S. Senate, Senator Connally speaking in behalf of the United Nations Organization, 79th Cong., 1st sess., October 2, 1945, *Congressional Record* 91:10249.

69. "US Avoids Pledge to Free Colonies," *The New York Times,* May 18, 1945, p. 1.

70. "Some Observations on the San Francisco Conference. . . ," p. 15.

71. AMU, Series 6, Box 1, "Observations Upon the Conference IX," Thomas H. Mahony, May 28, 1945, p. 1.

72. Ibid., p. 2.

73. *America, Britain and Russia,* p. 16; *The Semblance of Peace,* p. 422.

74. *The United Nations As a Political Institution,* p. 30.

75. "Shall We Keep the Atolls?" *America* 73 (May 5, 1945):91.

76. RG 59f, Box 22, The United Nations Conference as Reported by U.S. Press and Radio Comment, July 1945, p. 4.

77. "Article in Vatican Paper Says World Organization Plan Contains Perplexities," p. 4.

78. "Trusteeship Moves On," *America* 73 (May 12, 1945):106.

79. "Those Pacific Bases," *Commonweal* 42 (July 6, 1945):276.

80. Ibid.

81. "What Was Done At San Francisco," p. 323.

82. "Some Observations on the San Francisco Conference. . . ," p. 14.

CHAPTER IX

Uncharted Territory

On November 28, 1945, a curious scene was enacted in the halls of the Vatican's Secretariat of State. An incredulous American priest, Monsignor Walter Carroll, who was attached to the Congregation for the Propagation of the Faith, was unexpectedly called to the office of Monsignor Giovanni Battista Montini, pro-secretary for the Internal Affairs of the Church, who was directly responsible to Pope Pius XII. Montini, the future Pope Paul VI, summoned Carroll especially to tell him how delighted he was with the recent US bishops' statement of November 18, a document with which Carroll had no connection whatsoever.

That same day the American wrote to his brother, Monsignor Howard J. Carroll at the NCWC, that Montini went out of his way to congratulate him ("I don't know why me") and the American hierarchy for a job well done.

> He [Montini] added that it was a source of profound joy and satisfaction to him to know that a group of bishops in the world today could issue a statement on that high plane of understanding, intelligence and diplomacy. I don't know that I have ever seen him more pleased about anything and I am confident that his views reflect those of his superiors and collaborators.[1]

In his interview with Carroll, Montini repeated often that the priest must convey his sentiments to Archbishops Mooney and Stritch, who he knew were expressly responsible for the framing of the document.

Montini's reaction was not an isolated one in the Vatican. The entire text of the Administrative Board's declaration was printed on page one of *Osservatore Romano,* and Carroll reported that the reaction everywhere in ecclesiastical Rome was superb. "Incredibly so."[2]

Grounds for this Roman elation were to be found in the 1945 Annual Statement issued by the NCWC Administrative Board. Entitled *Between War and Peace,* it was an unlikely object of praise by Vatican officials, since it roundly condemned the thwarting of the peace by all the Great Powers, including the United States. The Vatican had cultivated good diplomatic relations with the US since the early days of the Roosevelt Administration and had been reticent to criticize such a powerful friend.[3]

The bishops contended that from the Big Three meeting at Moscow in 1943 to the UNCIO and the Potsdam Conference the US, UK, and USSR had set out to do nothing less than impose their will on the nations of the world. This brought about neither peace nor a proper peace plan, since these powers did little to sustain the principles they had acknowledged in the Atlantic Charter. After resisting one totalitarian dictatorship, fascism, which refused to recognize innate human freedoms, the United States and Great Britain were tolerating Soviet Communism, which spouted disingenuous democratic slogans while it subjugated a sizable part of Eastern Europe.[4]

The San Francisco Conference was a singular disappointment, the bishops said, since it failed to produce a genuine "world organization of nations." The UN Charter was better than the Dumbarton Oaks proposals, but it did not lay a foundation for a sound international community. The only resolute conviction that could be discerned in the document, the Administrative Board contended, was its odious support of an alliance of the Veto Powers in the Security Council: a compact "above the law" that undermined the core of the international association.[5]

Unfortunately it was too late to do anything about the Conference, but it was unthinkable that democratic America would fail to join the United Nations, since world chaos would result. Americans who believed in democratic principles owed it to the future of civilization to fight for free institutions within the new world body, not only for their country's interests but also for the foundation of liberty and justice for all peoples. On the other hand, Americans who were prepared to excuse any atrocity by the Russians were to be opposed resolutely, the bishops affirmed. "We may well pity those who in their half-veiled sympathy for totalitarianism are playing with the thought that perhaps in this great emergency its day is at hand." The document concluded by stating the belief that the United Nations should become the chosen battlefield for a confrontation with the new tyranny: Sovietism.[6]

At the Potsdam Conference, held between July 17 and August 2, there were signs that the era of wartime cooperation between the United States and the Soviet Union might be ending. This encouraged the bishops in the hope that the United States and Great Britain might once again promote the democratic compact they pledged themselves to defend in the Atlantic Charter. This became possible through creation of the UN and through the power these two democracies had in the Security Council, the General Assembly, and the Economic and Social Council. In these branches of the world organization there was a prospect that the defects of Yalta and of the Dumbarton Oaks Conversations could be eliminated and the recognition of the rights and duties of international society preserved.[7]

In the main, the Catholic consultants at San Francisco informed the NCWC that the efforts of the conference left much to be desired, but reforms could be accomplished if the Church made a commitment to begin such work at the start of UN activities. This chapter will be devoted to a survey of the initiatives taken by the Catholic Church in the United States to sustain its influence in international affairs after the San Francisco Conference, efforts that would culminate, after a year of experimentation, in the establishment of an on-site NCWC office to monitor the United Nations in New York.

Departing San Francisco

Even as the American delegates, advisers, reporters, and consultants were packing after the UNCIO closing ceremonies of June 26, their views on the parley and its Charter diverged significantly. This reflected popular opinion in the United States, which was anything but univocal on the topic. Although the media covered the conference with hundreds of journalists and correspondents, and public opinion consistently registered general approval of the principle of a United Nations, this nebulous faith in its prospects was only an expression of vague hopes and promises. This was so because, in reality, the public never had a chance to focus undivided attention on the issues and ramifications of world organization.[8]

Throughout the two months of the UNCIO, reports on its activities had to vie with a blizzard of sensational headlines: the discovery of Buchenwald and Dachau (April 28–29), the execution of Benito Mussolini (April 28), the suicide of Adolf Hitler (April 30), the surrender of Nazi Germany (May 7), the liberation of Okinawa (June 21), and the continuing war in the Pacific, to name only a few. The story at San Francisco could not begin to compete with these accounts for newsprint space or time on the radio. Therefore the shaping of mass opinion on the UN Charter had not solidified. This was as true for Catholics as for the rest of the population. During the Conference, even the Catholic consultants and observers could not absorb all the implications of events at San Francisco and the almost daily milestones that were occurring as the war drew to a close.[9]

Once the conference concluded, the former Catholic observers took the opportunity to discuss whether the UNCIO could be considered an overall success. Officials at the NCWC and at the Catholic Association for International Peace were soon receiving both optimistic and pessimistic estimations. Three days after the closing ceremonies, however, the NCWC News Service chose to publish Father Conway's extensive and positive two-part analysis of the Charter and of the alleged contribution by the Catholic Church in the United States. It was the first official Catholic word on postwar international organization following the Conference, and reflected the NCWC's uncertain and undeveloped stance on the subject.

From the beginning of his introductory article, Conway

stated that it was difficult to apportion responsibility for the "hundreds of liberalizing changes" that "transformed" the Dumbarton Oaks proposals. The Charter resulted from the fusion of many streams of thought, including the Catholic tradition. He maintained, however, that a tally would show that nine of the ten major points made by the American bishops on international organization, points that faithfully reflected the thought of Pius XII, were incorporated into the UN Charter. For Conway the authentic contribution of the American hierarchy was its adaptation of the peace principles articulated by the pope to the Dumbarton Oaks proposals. This procedure served to prepare US policy makers and the American people for the constitutional convention in San Francisco. As a result of this ecclesiastical endeavor, on the matters of "need of organization, membership, international law, General Assembly powers, peaceful change, economic cooperation, the trusteeship system, human rights, and the world court," the Charter met or approached the recommendations of the bishops." Only on the question of the veto power had the delegates at San Francisco failed to adopt suggestions put forth by the American bishops.[10]

Conway went on to show how Catholic thinking had been brought to bear promptly on the problem of instituting the peace. This was catalyzed by the American bishops' publications *On International Order* in response to Dumbarton Oaks and, directly before the UNCIO, with *On Organizing World Peace*. In the first document the hierachy commented only indirectly on the proposals, but by late spring they reaffirmed and further clarified the rationale of the November pronouncement, applied it specifically to Dumbarton Oaks, and made definite recommendations for its improvement. Conway claimed that nationwide circulation of these two statements in a leaflet entitled *The Bishops Speak Out On World Peace* convincingly influenced the delegates and their advisers at the conference.[11]

Conway supported these far-reaching assertions by arguing that Pius XII's six Christmas allocutions from 1939 to 1944 and other papal messages constituted a "blueprint for the future."

Commonly referred to as the "Pope's Peace Plan," these Catholic concepts stimulated popular thought on the nature of a juridical world-order. In the United States the pope's program, the "most complete and far reaching of any proposed for the guidance of modern men in search of a world at peace," was augmented by a "nation-wide educational campaign" conducted by the Bishops' Committee on the Pope's Peace Plan. Through this effort, Conway declared, these principles had become familiar to millions. In his opinion, general tenets such as

> (a) the present necessity of an international organization to guarantee the loyal fulfillment of the peace conditions, and in the case of recognized need to revise them; (b) endowment of this organization with power sufficient to smother in its very beginning any threat of isolated or collective aggression; (c) making use, if necessary, of economic sanctions and even armed intervention.

were now commonplace references for educated American citizens.[12]

Though all this must have seemed very reassuring to the average Catholic reader, it came as quite a shock to anyone familiar with the tumult that surrounded the San Francisco Conference and the drafting of the proposed UN Charter. This was especially true of Catholic pundits who attended the Conference and of members of the Bishops' Peace Committee. Even a perfunctory examination of the two Administrative Board documents to which Conway referred, and of the hierarchy's subsequent pronouncement of November 18, 1945, would have disclosed that, although the US Catholic Church did not advocate rejection of the UNCIO's work, it did advise from the outset a drastic Charter review. Only the Economic and Social Council and the projected International Bill of Rights won praise from the American hierarchy, and even with these there were still qualms.[13]

To say the least, there were many points on which the bishops disagreed with the UNCIO Charter. For example, in the statement of November 18 the hierarchy expressed hope that an ongoing revision of the Charter would be instituted immediately to make the UN an institution based on law rather than the Big-Power alliance it had become. For this it was necessary that the Big Three contribute to an armed UN enforcement agency and divest themselves of their military forces. These were, however, not proposed at San Francisco.

On the matter of UN membership, to cite another instance, the statement of November 16, 1944 would have committed the UN to a universalist policy of automatic membership and constrained all signatories to respect "basic equality of rights" for all nations and all populations within those nations. The Charter should have offered thereafter neither the right to withdraw for member states nor for itself the power of expulsion. These points, in the bishops' view, had likewise not been addressed properly at the Conference.[14]

In his article analyzing the San Francisco Conference, however, Father Conway clearly ignored or brushed aside these differences between the UN Charter and the stipulations of the American hierarchy on disarmament, international law, membership, and other issues.[15]

On the matter of the Security Council Conway had to concede that the bishops' warning about an "inequitable and dangerous" Big-Power veto was an ever-present threat hanging over the world body. He disregarded, however, the essential fact that the General Assembly was given no genuine authority to make laws for prevention of war, a verity that the April 15, 1945 statement had condemned. Conway could report only that dozens of amendments designed to rectify these inequities had been adopted. Though these amendments were not figments, they did not go to the heart of the issues.

On matters judicial the Administrative Board insisted in November of 1944 that the UN should institute a *bona fide* World Court, one with power to refer its decisions to the UN for enforcement. In his analysis, however, Conway merely listed this category as one of ten successes for Catholic influence at San Francisco even as he explained that the Big Powers rendered the Court nothing but an advisory bench, which the member-states could ignore at will, and whose decisions the Security Council need not implement. By placing this section next to the one on the veto power he hoped evidently that no one would notice that the NCWC's efforts in behalf of a sound World Court had been, in reality, one of the worst failures for the Catholic Church during the UNCIO.[16]

The two final Charter topics, which had likewise not turned out as the bishops recommended, were the questions of "peaceful change" and of trusteeships. The Vandenberg Amendment had been revised beyond recognition by the conference, and the definition of the word "situations," which replaced the word "treaties," no longer fitted the conditions set down by the NCWC in its November 1944 communiqué. In that paper, the bishops specified that the Charter must "provide for the revision of treaties in the interest of justice and the common good of the international community." With the word "situations," any nation could legally exempt its previous treaties from UN modification. In fact, the Soviet Union had exempted its European pacts from this obligation.

With regard to the UN Trusteeship System, Conway contented himself with the thought that the Trusteeship Council fulfilled the bishops' demand of November 1944 for "the recognition of a people's coming of age in the family of nations." Without once mentioning the embarrassment of strategic trusteeships exempt from General Assembly protection and even Security Council purview, and the total abandonment by the world organization of the 750,000,000 colonials in Asia, Africa, and the Pacific region, Conway professed, by some tortured logic, that the UN Charter gave promise for adequate consideration of unnamed "objectives."[17]

This cheerful picture of the San Francisco Charter could well have been written by a State Department publicist. In fact, it mirrored much of the propaganda produced by the Truman Administration at the end of the conference. At this time, as was documented in Chapter III of this study, State Department officials were saluting Conway's propaganda efforts in behalf of the Charter and professing their willingness to extend any assistance for his task in behalf of ratification of the document. Father Conway's views, however, do not appear to have unduly influenced the judgments of his Catholic colleagues at the UNCIO.[18]

Diverse Opinions

For Richard Pattee the keynote of the UN parley was a negative one: "security." In his view the hundreds of delegates assembled in the San Francisco Opera House spent their days between April 25 and June 26 scrambling in search of mechanisms not to uphold justice but to secure a defense against a dead past and an unknown future.

In the post-Conference period Pattee, though he did not ignore specific lapses of the UN Charter, occupied himself with a general appraisal of the gathering. He focused on the central predicament that he feared would undermine the world organization: that the wartime coalition of the United States, the Soviet Union, and the United Kingdom, which resulted in victory over the Nazi Reich, must be maintained after the war as an indispensable prerequisite for building a durable peace.

In practical terms, Pattee explained, "unanimity" among the Great Powers meant simply that action could be taken to settle international disputes that might otherwise lead to war only if there was agreement among the five permanent members of the Security Council—the enforcement agent of the United Nations. Pattee had been told often by its proponents that this unanimity rule, or loosely named "veto power," conformed to the reality of the international situation. Therefore it best safeguarded the peace and sovereignty of the smaller nations. According to current wisdom, the Great Powers possessed the military, industrial, and moral resources to prevent aggression. While they remained united there was no possibility of a conflict's getting out of hand, but if they were to divide, war was inescapable.[19]

From this viewpoint, the peace of the world, and therefore the success of the United Nations, was the work of the Great Powers with all their mighty resources. Unfortunately, Pattee argued, therein lay the gravest defect of the San Francisco Conference. Its Charter was too much the result of a "realistic" estimate of the international situation, and there was in consequence "an astounding absence of appeal to reason and justice regardless of the situation, as the only permanent and sound basis for world organization." Paraphrasing an article of Bishop Paul Yu-Pin of China, Pattee agreed that the Charter had developed into little more than a technique for whitewashing the Great Powers before they began their work of manipulating the UN for their own purposes. It was "a sort of absolution before the sin was committed."[20]

Grasping the logical consequences of this situation, Pattee was confident that the complex machinery created by the Charter would be effective only if a smaller nation not allied to a Great Power were involved in a conflict. It was perfectly clear to him that the strongest powers could under no condition be indicted for any act categorized as belligerent. Their "impeccability" was established from the start as a principle of world organization. One of the curious contradictions in all this, Pattee mused, was that these nations that now heralded themselves as unstintingly "peace-loving" were unwilling during the conference to allow many opportunities for criticism by others or even for debate of acts in which they might be engaged. One of the obstacles to genuine world peace at San Francisco, Pattee theorized, was a state of mind satisfied with the belief that peoples everywhere should feel grateful for the Great Powers' determination to protect them, rather than themselves cooperate in development of security through a truly democratic world-system of justice under law.[21]

The former consultant was particularly distressed by much of the deliberation he witnessed at the conference. It smacked of nothing so much as of the centuries-old subservience to the perpetuation of power politics, the state of mind that spawned both World Wars. Perhaps the greatest adverse impression Pattee received at San Francisco was that of statesmen demonstrating little sign that they were thinking unconventionally as a result of the trials and horrors of those conflicts. The intellectual perspective, the spiritual standpoint, and the sense of ethical responsibility were not perceptibly different from those of debates at the Versailles Conference in 1919.

Pattee claimed that the spirit pervading the conference was that of "rampant nationalism." This was displayed in the indignant feeling of national integrty of the French, in the bland assumption of imperial destiny of the British, and in the constant expression of reluctance on the part of all nations that had colonies to allow any change in the UN structure that might affect their peculiar interests. To say the least, willingness to give up national sovereignty was muffled. Some progress was unquestionably made, but Pattee could not say that the San Francisco Conference was an edifying experience.

Though it was true that many of those present at the UNCIO insisted on the term "interdependence" as the key word of the "new age," this was rarely extended beyond the realm of gesture. When an issue arose that demanded a demonstration of this new spirit, "nationalism tended to creep in and assert itself as emphatically and vigorously as in the past." Pattee had seen no sign of Conway's much-vaunted Catholic influence in such situations. Unfortunately, he reported, the Pope's blueprint for world order, which had condemned the notions that utility was the foundation and aim of law and that might equaled right, had not been frequently utilized at the Conference.[22]

Picking these papal themes as the basis for his evaluation of the UNCIO, Thomas Mahony was not pessimistic about the future of the UN. He did not manifest, for example, Pattee's horror of the United Nations Organization as an alliance of the Great Powers. The undeniable redistribution of power among the Big Five, and especially in the US and the USSR, only underscored for him the necessity of maintaining friendly relations between these two states and between them and the United Kingdom. If these powers preserved their wartime amicable attachments, then international peace was "pretty certain to be assured." Anything that improved relations among these states would conserve the peace, and anything that interfered with such relations, such as questioning of each other's regional arrangements, would increase the danger of another world war.

In spite of this rather significant difference of opinion on a fundamental principle of world organization, Pattee and Mahony agreed on the reasons for the conference's specific successes and failures and on the need for a major renovation of its Charter. Like Pattee, Mahony believed that the Conference was limited precisely by the fear that any attempt to increase the power of the UN by limiting national sovereignty would probably meet with a refusal of ratification by the Great Powers. For this reason glaring defects and obvious shortcomings had to be noted by the American Catholic Church before it could determine how it would deal with the new world organization.

Father Conway notwithstanding, Mahony singled out seven facets of the UN Charter in need of major revision, as well as some solutions that he and others envisioned. Most significantly, the Charter contained no specific reference to the sovereignty of the moral law and therefore did not provide recognition of the principle that the moral law was supreme and controlled the relations of states as it did the relations of persons. Since the document did protest ostentatiously its regard for law, justice, and human rights, Mahony thought that this could be the basis for an amendment that concretely recognized that no state was absolute or unqualifiedly sovereign under the moral law.[23]

Related to the above imperfection in the Charter was the absence of any stipulation that the exercise of national sovereignty by any state must not intrude on the exercise of the same right by other states, and that this autonomy must be exercised with due regard for the rights of the international community. Furthermore, the Charter did not provide any restriction of national supremacy in favor of the international community of states. Once again, however, Mahony found some solace in the fact that it did provide ample opportunity for General Assembly deliberation on situations involving this principle. He proposed, therefore, as an extension of this prerogative, an amendment to commission the General Assembly to act as a genuine legislative branch of the UN, with power to legislate on most phases of global relations.

Mahony noted that the delegates at San Francisco had not set up any organ with power to legislate on international relations, rights, or obligations, but had given the General Assembly the means of recommending such action and developing a code of law. It had declned to set up a judicial tribunal with compulsory jurisdiction and power to compel obedience to its orders. It had refused, furthermore, to provide any executive or police power to effect the decisions of the International Court of Justice. Mahony's solution for these three deficiencies in the Charter was straightforward: he proposed an amendment to establish compulsory jurisdiction for the Court and a prerequisite of implementation of its decisions by some agency for that function.[24]

Forced to return inescapably to the one great failing of San Francisco, Mahony concluded his post-Conference analysis by stressing that the Charter retained an absolute veto in favor of the five Great Powers. In order to make the UN less an alliance of the Great Powers and more a democratic organization, the amendment procedure of the Charter must be liberalized. An amendment limiting the veto power of the permanent members of the Security Council was fundamental. By this means the Great Powers would surrender part of their unequivocal hegemony over reform and would estabish a more equitable basis for voting.[25]

With their suggestions for emendation of the United Nations Charter specified for the Administrative Board to study, Pattee and Mahony then turned to another pertinent question: who among the Great Powers could be prodded to right all the transgressions and omissions of San Francisco and thereby could qualify to lead the United Nations into the postwar era?

Sweet Land Of Liberty

Though not included in his seven "Shortcomings of the Conference," a clarification of the relation of regional organizations to the United Nations was one of Thomas Mahony's most important goals for the international association. This, one of the most serious disputes at the Conference, had not been settled because of "political issues" in the European region, especially the acute problem of Poland's national boundaries, continental Europe's relation to Britain and Russia, and the affiliation with Germany to the rest of Europe. This dispute was neglected also because of the vested interests of the two great superpowers, the United States and the Soviet Union. During the war the world witnessed a tremendous concentration of political, economic, and military power in these two nations, and the issue of "blocs" in Latin America and Eastern Europe was inextricably tied to their rise to power.[26]

Although Mahony was more willing than Pattee to acquiesce in a Big-Power UN, he was not blind to the fact that the five permanent members were acting unilaterally to assure their national security in the event that the international organization did not work. It was necessary, he believed, to persuade these states to give up such unrestrained actions and to convince them that, with their unselfish cooperation, the United Nations could furnish effective national and collective security. Accomplishing this praiseworthy end, Mahony argued, required a "fair, just but firm attitude" on the part of an altruistic United States with reference to Russia, Britain, France, China, and other member states. It meant, furthermore, that the US must lead the way in establishing a high standard of global probity to which every state would be expected to conform. It would require forbearance in an attempt to minimize dissensions and to nurture reciprocal trust in the fairness and good faith of member states, and "above all, the constant exercise of the virtues of justice and charity."[27]

Richard Pattee certainly concurred that the United States should make the principal bid to pilot the new international organization into just and peaceful waters, but he wondered if the Truman administration was adequate to the challenge. America stood, at the end of the war, as the virtual chief of the absolute conquerors of the earth. But victory, no matter how brilliant, was not peace, Pattee reminded his readers. It was merely preliminary to a potential era of tranquility and well-being, which could be achieved only after "more painstaking effort, more sacrifice, and more wisdom" than was required in the triumph of arms.

In the first flush of exhilaration at the conclusion of hostilities, however, there was a tendency in the United States to emphasize security as the mainstay of the nation's international designs. It could not be emphasized too strongly, Pattee went on, that if the US continued to insist upon an impregnable defense as the best means of preventing a recurrence of bloodshed, then it could not coax any member of the United Nations toward a just peace. If justice was absent in the organization of peace, there might be a temporary avoidance of war and a reasonable period of successful fortification against assault, but this would not endure and it would not be a valuable contribution to the creation of an abiding world-order based on peace. Only an honorable peace, based on the principles of justice and charity sanctioned by all, was guarantee of lasting surety.[28]

During World War II the United States had committed itself to collaborate in a new world-order and had assumed the responsibility, with others, of sharing the task of constructing an organization that would respond to the needs of a society of nations. Pattee believed that most Americans realized that there was no road back to the complacency of an isolationist past, which many citizens, including many Catholic leaders, had cherished. That die was cast. But would America use its genius for democratic organization, which had made it the oldest continuous democracy in the world, to facilitate the UN's transformation into an institution based on human rights and moral responsibility? At Yalta and San Francisco and minor meetings of the Allies at the end of the war, this egalitarian tendency exposed a disparity of outlook within the Big Three.[29]

At these parleys the United States and the United Kingdom, whose political ideas were predicated in principle on common conceptions of freedom, integrity of the individual, and limits on the state, were torn between yielding to or clashing with the representatives of the Soviet Union. The latter intended to secure the welfare of its citizens, Pattee claimed, through "sheer might and mind of the civil authority." Therefore at Dumbarton Oaks and San Francisco the US and the UK sought to draft a Charter that would provide a working organism capable of life and growth; they understood that "life and growth depended not only on the words of the Charter, but on the way the very different Member-States met the responsibilities and exercised their rights and privileges under it." An honest recognition of discrepancies did not render a plan of interaction unthinkable: in fact it might be expeditious. Pattee was firm in stating, however, that America could never acquiesce in the neglect of basic human rights "for the sake of a false and apparent cooperation."[30]

By accepting the challenge of world influence, the United States placed its hopes in the international security organization. Because of its special mission within that association, Pattee lectured, it must adhere securely to the principles that the Founding Fathers had bequeathed to it, define them explicitly, and integrate them, whenever possible, into the structure of the UN. Persisting in a policy of expediency and temporization in the name of false realism—a *modus operandi,* he contended, that the American delegation resorted to excessively at San Francisco—would only undermine the moral strength of the nation at a time when a debilitated world needed it most. He ended with an eloquent and chilling admonition, which conveyed the full weight of his argument in one verbal stroke. "Our treason to principle," he said, "would produce the bitterest disillusionment and nullify the courageous efforts to bring the rule of justice and charity out of the barbarism and degradation that war had produced."[31]

The bishops of the Administrative Board would resolutely opt for the postwar vision tendered by Richard Pattee, their consultant at San Francisco. Disdaining both Conway's overly optimistic clarification of many articles of the UN Charter and Thomas Mahony's somewhat benign interpretation of Big Three unanimity, they judged that although the war had ended, peace had not yet come. And certainly it had not arrived in the form of the Great Power alliance devised at Dumbarton Oaks and at San Francisco. At once defiant and humble, the bishops refused to renounce the ideal of peace that "had sustained us through the war," and urged America to ask God to help it be the "vigorous champion of democratic freedom and the generous friend of the needy and oppressed throughout the world." To help it along in these prayers and good works, the NCWC hoped to offer the US government a program of its own.[32]

The Post-Conference Predicament

In a November 1945 statement, *Between War and Peace,* the members of the American hierarchy admonished the Truman administration on the State Department's want of an intelligible strategy for negotiating in time of peace. Although this was an accurate assessment, the Administrative Board should have aimed a similar criticism at itself. In its program for a US policy with regard to the United Nations, the NCWC had clearly enunciated general principles in terms of all the definite questions at issue, supported the notion of frank, encouraging discussions, and advocated further collaboration with the Allies in the making of a good peace. What it had not determined, however, was the particular role the Catholic Church in the United States was to play in influencing the international postwar situation now that the San Francisco Conference had ended.[33]

To some extent this was understandable. Circumstances had moved at an accelerated pace since the closing session of the UNCIO. In a bewildering series of events, the evolving shape of the postwar world came into clearer and, in the opinion of the Catholic leaders, more complex and disturbing focus, in the late summer of 1945.

The NCWC was increasingly alarmed in the interim between the conclusion of the San Francisco Conference and the Big Three meeting at Potsdam, since that period ripened into "a fruitful one for the extension of Soviet influence." First of all, in the Mediterranean, the Soviet Union was granted status by the Allies as one of the participants in the administration of the international zone of Tangier. The USSR was also pressuring Turkey for a reconsideration of the status of the Dardanelles and was undermining the British government in Greece. In Eastern Europe, meanwhile, in a bilateral arrangement, Czechoslovakia ceded Ruthenia to the Soviet Union and thus placed the Communists over the Carpathian people without regard for the principle of self-determination. Moreover, Soviet control over the Tito regime in Yugoslavia and the formation of puppet governments in Rumania, Hungary, Bulgaria, and Albania firmly attached to the Soviet Motherland a western arc of security. Finally, simultaneous visits to Moscow of the Chinese Premier T.V. Soong and the Mongolian Premier, along with Russia's publicly stated interest in Manchuria and its declaration of war on Japan at the behest of the United States, opened the way for the spread of Soviet influence in the Far East.[34]

Pattee was dumfounded by this last move by the United States, since it seemed much wiser to refrain from pressuring the USSR in order to avoid the creation of a situation in which that power would now have a right to be heard during the Pacific settlements. This move, with the other occurrences mentioned above, further strengthened the hand of the Soviet negotiators as they arrived in Germany for the Potsdam Conference.[35]

From July 17 to August 2 these Big Three deliberations were held in Potsdam, near Berlin. President Harry Truman, Marshall Joseph Stalin, and Prime Minister Winston Churchill were there to forge an Allied position on the defeated Third Reich. This conference was never fully satisfactory. The mood of instability was further aggravated on July 28, when Churchill was replaced unexpectedly by a new British Prime Minister, Clement R. Attlee, leader of the Labour party, who defeated Mr. Churchill's Conservatives in a general election.[36]

At this conference the world leaders agreed that Germany be disarmed and demilitarized, that her National Socialist institutions be dissolved, that her Nazi leaders be tried as war criminals, and that democratic ideals, such as local self-government and freedom of speech, press, and religion, be encouraged by the occupying powers. Furthermore, the manufacture of war materials was to be prohibited. The three leaders drafted an ultimatum demanding an unconditional surrender of the Empire of Japan. Potsdam is best remembered, however, as the summit meeting where animosity between the Soviet Union on one side and the US and Great Britain on the other finally broke out into the open.[37]

State Department officials realized that the United States lacked the power to directly influence events in places such as Rumania and Bulgaria. They had supposed, however, that the US could gain some leverage in that region by privately informing Stalin that the United States would withhold diplomatic recognition of such governments and refuse to make peace with them until Russia abided by its Yalta promises to hold free elections in the former German satellites. Truman informed Stalin of the successful atomic bomb test at Alamogordo and of the American intention of using the bomb, if necessary, against Japan. All these ploys went for naught.[38]

Pattee quoted approvingly James Reston's comment in *The New York Times* that the US entered negotiations at Potsdam armed only with the bomb and "a vast collection of notes," but that "a sheaf of notes does not constitute a policy." At the conference, Pattee asserted, the United States had only the vaguest outline of what it conceived to be the future of Europe, and an even more rudimentary idea of what to do with Germany and Austria. The Soviet Union, on the other hand, came prepared to battle for its own "*cordon sanitaire* in reverse," and did so through an unapologetic use of power politics and various rationalizations for expansionism. When Stalin pressed his excessive claims over certain Polish boundaries, the US and the UK, without a concerted policy to guide them, simply postponed any decisions on these matters until the next meeting of the Council of Foreign Ministers. This was done in order to keep the facade of Allied unity intact while the war was still raging in the Pacific.[39]

If the State Department anticipated that dropping atomic bombs on Hiroshima (August 6) and Nagasaki (August 9) and the resulting appeal for peace by Japan on August 10 would serve as a substitute for a coherent foreign policy with which to overwhelm the Russians, it was disabused of such idle hopes at the initial meeting of the Big Five Foreign Ministers. At these sessions, which began in London on September 11, 1945, statesmen from the US, the USSR, the UK, China, and France met to draw up peace treaties for Finland, Hungary, Rumania, and Bulgaria—all former German satellites. Sticking to the American resolve at Potsdam, Secretary of States Byrnes informed Molotov that when these territories were put on a basis whereby the West could have free access to them, "then the United States would recognize their governments but no sooner."[40]

The Russians, however, were even less compliant in London than at Potsdam, and a new postwar reality emerged at this conference that made abundantly clear that the Soviet Union had no intention of continuing its wartime cooperation with its former allies. Molotov pressed immediately for Stalin's bid for control of former Italian colonies in Africa, accused the Americans of supporting anti-Soviet activists in Eastern Europe, and avowed that the regimes in Rumania and Bulgaria were more representative than the British-sponsored administration in Greece. Trying to reason with the Soviet Foreign Minister, Byrnes notified Molotov secretly that although the United States did not wish to impose inimical governments along Russia's borders, the US Senate would unquestionably rebuff any treaty he signed with Bucharest and Sofia, since the West had no way of knowing first hand at if these regimes were violating the Yalta Declaration on liberated Europe. Could not coalitions be formed, he pleaded, which would be friendly to the Russians and at the same time representative?[41]

Molotov was not swayed by such sweet reasoning. In fact, he quickly parried with a series of his own demands. On September 22 he called for the exclusion of France and China from further discussions of peace treaties with the erstwhile German satellites, since their presence there was a violation of the Potsdam agreement. Two days later he demanded establishment of an Allied Control council for Japan, composed of the US, USSR, Great Britain, and China, to supervise the policies of General Douglas MacArthur and the American occupational forces. On October 1 Byrnes refused to concede either of these points and the next day the conference disbanded without even a joint communiqué.[42]

Pattee observed, in his general summary of both the Potsdam Conference and the Foreign Ministers' meeting, that their sum total was negative. Mutual recriminations tainted the atmosphere immensely. If nothing else, these gatherings showed that to placate the Soviets and prevent their exiting parleys "in a huff, there is nothing short of complete surrender of position." He concluded that there was little basic difference between these experiences and the tactics of Hitler at Munich. Commenting on a current publication by the historian Nathaniel Peffer, which presented four options for America's place in the world, Pattee asserted that the Catholic Church could only continue to counsel the way of "prevention through full participation" in the UN. Any other course would be seen as a revival of isolationism, and tantamount to capitulation to the new bully on the block.[43]

In spite of unsatisfactory encounters at Potsdam and London, international cooperation remained the Administration's announced intent. It elected, therefore, to proceed with its UN activities even if it had to withhold some information from Congress. Although the members of the Senate Foreign Relations Committee applauded Secretary of State Byrnes on October 8 when he told them, following the Foreign Ministers' Conference, that America would never compromise with the "insufferable" Russians in these matters, he confided to Joseph Davies that if the Senate learned how the Soviets behaved at London, the situation would become "very much worse." For this reason it was fortunate for the State Department that the United Nations Charter had sailed briskly through the US Senate during the summer of enthusiasm following the UNCIO. On July 28, 1945, the Charter had received the consent of the Senate by a vote of eighty-nine to two.[44]

Indeed, so swiftly was the process moved through that chamber by Senator Tom Connally that the NCWC was not afforded an opportunity to testify before the Foreign Relations Committee. The fault for this oversight, however, was that of the sluggish Administrative Board.

On July 2 Monsignor Carroll, in a letter to Archbishop Mooney, noted that he had read in the paper that hearings on the question of ratification of the UN Charter would begin on July 9. Without hesitation, he recommended a concerted Catholic approach to Charter ratification. On the assumption that the NCWC was likely to be invited, "if not urged, to offer some expression of opinion at the Hearings," the General Secretary suggested a three-pronged attack: a letter from the Administrative Board chairman, statements on behalf of the Bishops' Peace Committee and CAIP to be inserted into the Senate record, and testimony by Father Conway, "who will no doubt be asked to say something as an NCWC representative."[45] Carroll heard nothing from Mooney for almost ten days.

On the evening of July 9, the date of the opening of the Committee hearings, Archbishops Stritch and Mooney held a telephone conference and determined that, at the very least, the NCWC should testify before the Senate. But by the time that Carroll received Stritch's letter to this effect on July 11 the instruction was already irrelevant. The Foreign Relations Committee decided to conclude its business on July 13, and Conway informed the General Secretary that the Catholic Conference could no longer be given time to present its case since the panel's docket was filled.[46]

According to Stritch's instruction to Carroll, one of the points that the Bishops' Peace Committee would have underscored, had it been able to testify, was that although there seemed to be "a hindrance to the working of the international organization in the attitude of a certain great power," this should not prevent the US from "doing our utmost in these times for every hope for the organization of the world community."[47]

The Catholic press echoed these sentiments. *America* noted that within the span of several weeks the United States Senate had reversed the century-old foreign policy of US isolationism. In rapid succession it had ratified the Bretton Woods Agreements establishing the International Monetary Fund, increased the lending power of the Export-Import Bank in the hope of stabilizing world currencies and expanding international trade, approved membership in the United Nations Food and Agricultural Organization, and ratified the UN Charter. This "dawning internationalism" was sincere, the journal believed, and something Americans were getting into "with our eyes wide open."[48]

Commonweal remarked that only a few weeks before the Charter vote in the Senate, fear was widespread that a two-thirds majority for treaty ratification was beyond reach. After the practically unanimous tally, however, it was necessary to ask why no real opposition materialized within the Congress or around the nation. Its editors concluded that

> the American people, having realized that attempted isolation had failed to keep them out of war, now vaguely turned to international cooperation. We have been forced to see that henceforth the tenor of our lives is strictly dependent upon what takes place in other lands. The big danger is that we shall be satisfied with merely having joined the club.[49]

Obviously concurring, the Truman administration kept a hectic foreign-policy pace after the UNCIO. From August 16 through October 27 the United States had taken part fully in the fourteen-member Executive Committee of the United Nations Preparatory Commission in London. The commission convened in London on November 20 to approve the Executive Committee's recommendations for the time and place of the first meetings of the General Assembly, the Security Council, the ECOSOC, and the Trusteeship Council. The most intense speculation naturally focused on the General Assembly, since the Preparatory Commission sanctioned its initial meeting for January 10, 1946, as the earliest major branch of the world organization to convene.[50]

On December 18 Congress gave its final approval to enabling legislation that made the United States an active force in the United Nations. On that same day President Truman nominated American delegates and alternates to this General Assembly session. They were Secretary of State Byrnes as ex-officio senior representative, former Secretary of State Stettinius as designated principal representative, Senators Connally and Vandenberg, and Mrs. Eleanor Roosevelt. An exalted group to be sure, but once again the administration failed to nominate a Catholic delegate to an important international gathering.[51]

Toward A Permanent Office In New York

The NCWC was disconcerted that no Catholics were put forward as American delegates to the UN General Assembly. On December 20 Archbishop Stritch, recently elected chairman of the Administrative Board, was notified, however, that a "friend at the State Department," Mr. Robert Lynch, had been asked by Byrnes's office to submit a list of "Catholics from the West Coast" from which one would be chosen as an alternate in London. Nevertheless, before Lynch was able to act on this directive, former Postmaster General Frank Walker, an old Democratic crony and cabinet member in the Roosevelt administration, was selected by the president.[52] Lynch expressed his regret and that of Edward Stettinius, who "was not having any 'say' about the composition of the delegation," that the selections were manifestly determined by the White House on political and regional grounds. Both Lynch and Carroll surmised correctly that Walker, who had no foreign policy experience, would carry little weight in the delegation and was chosen merely to assuage Catholic feelings.[53]

Expecting such reactions from organizations that would discern that their interests were not be be represented at the General Assembly meeting, the State Department excluded requests for special positions in London before announcement of the make-up of the American delegation. Accordingly Carroll received notice from Francis H. Russell, Chief of the State Department's Division of Public Liaison, that barred any possibility that representatives of national organizations would be permitted to appoint consultants to the delegation at the General Assembly. As a salve to their pride, the Department planned to assist designated organizations, such as the NCWC, by providing their on-the-scene representatives in London with liaison facilities such as admission tickets, conference documents, and opportunities for meeting with American delegates, advisors, and technical experts. This was all the Catholic Conference needed to know. It immediately extended an invitation to Father Conway to serve in that capacity.[54]

On December 21, however, Conway was informed by his Jesuit Provincial that a London trip would not be possible. After a long and fruitless search for another observer at the General Assembly and other UN branches that would be meeting in the British capital, Carroll was given Stritch's sanction to ask the Reverend Robert A. Graham, S.J., to act unofficially for the NCWC. Graham was in London as an accredited correspondent for *America.* With John Eppstein, Catholic editor of *The British Survey,* he had been recognized formally by the UN as a representative of the Catholic Association for International Peace.[55]

During the three months when he covered the General Assembly and the Security Council, which met and organized immediately after election by the Assembly of its first six nonpermanent members, Graham sent back a series of very informative reports and analyses of the initial activities of the United Nations. Through these he helped to mold the NCWC attitudes that were the basis of a permanent Catholic office at the United Nations.

Graham was particularly concerned lest Catholic officials in the United States be excessively influenced by NCWC News dispatches from London that contained excerpts from the four British Catholic weekly newspapers.[56] The tone of these articles, Graham believed, was uniformly "critical, cynical and pessimistic." Having been much closer to the UN scene than any of his English counterparts, he was at a loss to discover where they found such clear evidence of "frailty, ineptitude or downright wickedness of the London Assembly." Most of their harsh judgments, he suspected, were based on a tendency to read too much into incidentals that were not indicative of the tenor of the UN.

> For example, we would all like to see every international gathering opened with prayer. But to assert as many have

asserted that this omission involved a studied insult to Almighty God is far-fetched and can only do harm in the long run to the cause of religion. The days of the French Freemasonry is [sic] over. Their customs may remain but why blame the modern politicians for following established practice?[57]

Graham fostered in his bulletins a policy of subscribing to the best in the United Nations, while reserving the right to criticize what he thought was defective in its operations. This "constructive, encouraging, and participating" point of view was the only logical course "if we [the Catholic Church in the United States] have chosen not to play a minor role" in the international organization. An attitude of non-participating criticism would be disastrous for Christianity, he contended, not only in America but even more so in Europe.

One journalist was not identified with the negative "British Viewpoint." Graham found that the opinions of John Eppstein were not identical with those of the correspondents from the four Catholic newspapers. For Eppstein, the UN was simply too important, whatever its drawbacks, for Catholics to abstain from it merely on the grounds that it did not measure up to Catholic ethical standards. On this point Eppstein profoundly influenced Graham. Both men now declared that the American hierarchy should examine how it might exercise a positive role in the UN. In Eppstein's words, it should practice the *"politique de présence,"* or "getting into the game." The opposite course, *"politique de bouderie,"* or "strategy of grumbling," was not worthy of the Catholic Church of such a great country as the United States.[58]

In fact, the Administrative Board had already taken at least one tentative step in this direction when it warmly approved Richard Pattee's selection by the State Department as a "Technical Expert" to a United States delegation at the conference on the creation of a UN Educational, Social and Cultural Organization (UNESCO) held in London during November of 1945.[59] Graham's reports from Britain several months later strengthened the Board's resolve to move quickly whenever possible to place Catholic experts at strategically important UN locations. The next such opportunity arose in the early spring of 1946, when the Security Council inaugurated its sessions at Hunter College in New York on March 25.[60]

Once it was known that the Security Council would relocate in the United States, the National Catholic Welfare Conference and its affiliated organization, the Catholic Association for International Peace, determined concurrently to send temporary observers to its meetings. The Peace Association selected Dr. Elizabeth Lynskey, a professor of history at Hunter College, who would become deeply involved with Catholic participation in the writing of an International Bill of Rights. The Catholic representative who most profoundly influenced the Administrative Board on the matter of Catholic representation at the UN, however, was the NCWC observer, Dr. Ross J. S. Hoffman. Hoffman, chairman of the History Department at Fordham University, was a reluctant enlistee. He agreed to accept the position only as a favor to the Administrative Board, since his obligations at the university were quite extensive and attendance at the sessions were a great sacrifice for him.[61]

The historian's accounts from the Security Council were superb and garnered much praise from members of the Bishops' Peace Committee. But from the very start, even though Carroll continually assured him of the fact that "our principal interest is to know what is really going on," Hoffman insisted that the NCWC appreciate that there were two types of "observers" at the Security Council sessions: "simple observers" and "observers who are at the same time 'representatives' of organizations." The latter had many more responsibilities than the former and were expected to join other agents in formulating policies and approaches to international issues that came before the Council. He frankly apprised Carroll that the NCWC needed a representative in New York; there were too many important UN matters, such as the Soviet withdrawal from Iran, Poland's indictment of Franco Spain, and the drafting of recommendations for an International Bill of Rights, which required the thorough attention of a permanent observer.

But the Catholic Conference was not yet ready to make such a move and Carroll pleaded with Hoffman to remain.[62]

When the Economic and Social Council began to organize its commissions at the end of April, Hoffman was faced with the impossible task of attending even more meetings. Although as a "historian and political scientist" and not a "sociologist or welfare worker," he had neither expertise nor inclination to attend the sessions, he did understand that the NCWC ought to be well informed about these UN activities. Nothing less than a full-time observer could possibly fulfill that obligation, with all the others that were piling up every day. Hoffman let it be known that he would be delighted to make way for such a person. Carroll, however, gained some time for the NCWC by persuading the Fordham professor to stay on "until further notice." This sleight-of-hand was accomplished by apprising him that Father Conway and Dr. Lynskey would cover the sessions of various commissions and agencies of the ECOSOC that he could not attend. But Hoffman would not be put off forever, and even the high art of procrastination at the Administrative Board could no longer postpone a final decision on the matter of a permanent UN observer for the NCWC.[63]

Father Conway had plainly been more impressed with Hoffman's arguments than the Catholic officials in Washington. He had concluded not only that a permanent UN observer was essential, but also that he was the obvious choice for the post. On May 30, 1946, he had a conversation with Monsignor Carroll during which the topic arose. Such a full-time observer, Conway noted, would serve in the dual capacity of "rapporteur to the NCWC and as liaison between the NCWC and the US delegation." According to the Jesuit, what seemed to be needed was someone who would follow developments in the various agencies, prepare summaries thereon, and make sure that the Catholic viewpoint was advanced whenever critical issues were being deliberated and opinions requested.

Conway had discussed this matter ahead of time with Chester Williams, public liaison officer with the American delegation, and Williams had indicated that he would be "eager" to have one person from the NCWC with whom he could keep in contact. Eventually, he reported, the State Department intended to build an elite group of such observers representing the major interests of the country.[64] For the time being, according to Conway, Williams was content to hope that the Catholic Conference would write him a letter requesting authorization for the Jesuit to "act as observer for the NCWC at UN, to cover the meetings of the various Councils and Committees and . . . Security Council as might be necessary." Carroll was assured that this would in no way disturb Hoffman's status as observer for the Security Council.[65]

Cardinal Stritch would approve Conway's accreditation as a temporary NCWC observer to assist Hoffman wherever needed, but Conway's angling for the position of permanent observer did not produce the same results.[66] From previous episodes, the Catholic Conference instinctively distrusted any Conway assessment. This case proved no exception, since Conway frankly admitted that one of his incentives for wanting such a "definite position" was the potential danger of being banished to his Jesuit Province in Wisconsin to teach.[67]

With this in mind, the Administrative Board dispatched Catherine Schaefer to New York to make inquiries, in the name of the CAIP, on "the advisability or practicability of establishing an office . . . near the seat of the United Nations." To everyone's surprise, she found that Chester Williams and others attached to the US delegation were as interested as Father Conway had claimed in having a permanent observer on the scene to represent concerned American Catholic organizations. Her explicit recommendation was, therefore, that a Catholic UN office should be established whether or not consultative status was granted to Catholic organizations by United Nations branches such as the ECOSOC. She was reassured, nevertheless, that some form of consultation privileges would be granted to American national organizations by the US delegation. She contended that there would be a pressing need for getting complete information and securing its collation in the interests of the four Catholic organizations concerned with international affairs, the NCWC, the CAIP, the National

Council of Catholic Women, and the National Catholic Educational Association—as well as Catholics throughout the world.[68]

Father Raymond McGowan, Schaefer's superior, fully endorsed her analysis on the establishment of "some kind of observing and reporting office" at United Nations headquarters. He extended the concept to embrace the principle of a "center . . . to bring together the Catholic representatives to the UN and the Catholics of the US, first, for social purposes and then for purposes of policy." These emendations as well as a synopsis of Schaefer's memorandum were then presented to the July 2, 1946 meeting of the Administrative Board. Approving the proposal, the Board authorized a committee to study the matter and draw $10,000 *per annum* on the treasury of the NCWC to finance it.[69]

The committee, which consisted of Cardinal Stritch, Cardinal Spellman of New York, and Mosignor Carroll, met at Spellman's residence at 452 Madison Avenue on August 7. At that gathering it was decided that a Catholic Conference office be set up "for the purpose of obtaining and disseminating more regularly and efficiently information about the activities of the United Nations, as a basis for the determination by the Administrative Board of the policies of the NCWC with respect to such matters." It was agreed that Cardinal Spellman would provide temporary office space at 17 East Fifty-first Street until a permanent location could be found. As the office would be located within this archdiocese, Spellman's coadjutor, Archbishop James Francis McIntyre, would act as the ecclesiastical delegate of the chairman of the Administrative Board.[70]

None of this was unexpected. A surprise came, however, with the designation of Catherine Schaefer to head the new office under the title of Assistant to the General Secretary of the NCWC for United Nations Affairs. She was handed her letter of appointment on September 11 and assumed her duties on October 1, 1946. Father Conway meanwhile was to continue his attendance as temporary observer for the NCWC whenever his services were required.[71]

In her letter of August 21 to Monsignor Carroll, in which she expressed her general understanding of the position she had been offered, Schaefer noted that details of the appointment should not be construed rigidly at the beginning, "since the field was somewhat a *terre inconnue.*" Acknowledging that the list of duties by which the Administrative Board defined her position was substantial, she nonetheless requested an opportunity to discuss her selection with him before she accepted it. In commenting on the responsibilities of her office she noted that any Assistant for UN Affairs would have one duty above all. If that officeholder was intent on assisting the Administrative Board in its formulation of an international policy, he or she would have to "establish relationships with persons and organizations concerned, both within and without the United Nations."[72]

In the fall of 1946 this shrewd insight reassured the Catholic Conference that it had chosen well. Schaefer would remain in her post until the office was abolished in 1972.[73]

Notes

1. AAC 2967C, "Excerpt from a letter of Monsignor Walter Carroll" (to Howard Carroll), [Vatican City], November 28, 1945, copy.

2. Ibid.

3. *The Vatican and the American Hierarchy,* pp. 248–51.

4. *Between War and peace,* p. 62.

5. David E. T. Luard, *Conflict and Peace in the Modern International System* (New York: Little, Brown, 1960), p. 284.

6. *Between War and Peace,* pp. 63, 64.

7. Ibid.

8. Lincoln P. Bloomfield, *The United Nations and U.S. Foreign Policy* (Boston: Little, Brown, 1960), p. 3.

9. RG 59e, Box 23, Folder I, Daily Summary of Opinion Developments, June 20, 1945, p. 1.

10. "U.S. Bishops' Recommendations Seen as Substantially Reflected in Charter of United Nations," p. 1.

11. Ibid., p. 2.

12. Ibid.

13. *A Statement on International Order,* p. 56; *Between War and Peace,* p. 62; *On Organizing World Peace,* p. 1.

14. AAC 2825S, Clark-Sohn Proposals, 1954, p. 2.

15. ANCWC 11, "Nine Out of Ten Points Made by Hierarchy Wholly or Partly Covered—Appraisal of Extent to Which Catholic

Influence Contributed Towards Liberalizing Dumbarton Oaks Proposals Declared Difficult," E. A. Conway, S.J., July 2, 1945, p. 2.

16. Ibid., p. 2b.

17. *The United Nations as a Political Institution,* pp. 132–37.

18. This topic was discussed in Chapter III, pp. 12–14.

19. "Some Observations on the San Francisco Conference. . . ," p. 3.

20. ANCWC 13b, "Time For Fine Words Past," Bishop Paul Yu-Pin, May 14, 1945, p. 2.

21. "Some Observations on the San Francisco Conference. . . ," p. 4.

22. Ibid., p. 5; Harold E. Stassen, *Man Was Meant to Be Free: Selected Statements by Harold E. Stassen: 1940–1951,* ed. Amos J. Peaslee (Garden City: Doubleday, 1951), pp. 62–63.

23. "The United Nations Conference," p. 17.

24. Ibid., p. 20.

25. Ibid., p. 21.

26. *The United Nations Charter,* p. 21.

27. Ibid., p. 23.

28. ANCWC 11, Pattee to Carroll, [D.C.], October 23, 1945, p. 2.

29. *The Semblance of Peace,* p. 215.

30. Benjamin V. Cohen, *The United Nations* (Cambridge, Mass.: Harvard University Press, 1961), p. 30; Pattee to Carroll, [D.C.], October 23, 1945, p. 6.

31. Ibid., p. 8.

32. *Between War and Peace,* p. 64.

33. Ibid., p. 36.

34. David E. T. Luard, ed., *The Cold War: A Reappraisal* (New York: Frederick A. Praeger, 1964), "The Partition of Europe," by Wilfrid Knapp, pp. 50–53.

35. "Some Observations on the San Francisco Conference. . . ," p. 31.

36. Winston S. Churchill, *Memoirs of the Second World War* (Boston: Houghton Mifflin, 1948), p. 995.

37. U.S. Department of State, *Foreign Relations of the United States: Diplomatic Papers, 1945,* vol. 2, *The Conference of Berlin (Potsdam),* Department of State Pubn. No. 7163 (1960), pp. 175–77.

38. *The United States and the Origins of the Cold War,* p. 37.

39. Ibid., p. 38.

40. James F. Byrnes, *All in One Lifetime* (New York: Harper, 1958), p. 288; on July 3, 1945, three days before his departure for Potsdam, Truman named James F. Byrnes to replace Edward Stettinius as Secretary of State. Byrnes had attended the Yalta Conference at Roosevelt's request, but otherwise had little diplomatic experience. He did have an impressive domestic record, however, having served in both houses of Congress, on the Supreme Court, and as director of the

Office of War Mobilization and Reconversion. The new Secretary of State looked forward to applying the negotiating techniques he had found useful in these jobs to the problems of foreign affairs. (*The United States and the Origins of the Cold War*, p. 238).

41. *The United States and the United Nations*, p. 7.

42. RG 59j, FR:1945, II: 194–202, 243–47. *Bohlen Minutes,* Byrnes-Molotov conversations, September 16 and 19, 1945.

43. "Some Observations on the San Francisco Conference. . . ," p. 39; Nathaniel Peffer, *Basis for Peace in the Far East* (New York: Harper & Brothers, 1942), pp. 245–46. The four options were "relaxation," isolation, U.N. participation, or imperialism.

44. RG 59j, Davies MSS, Box 22, October 9, 1945, Davies notes of conversation with Byrnes.

45. ANCWC 15, Carroll to Mooney, [D.C.], July 2, 1945, p. 1, copy.

46. ANCWC 15, Stritch to Carroll, [Chicago], July 10, 1945 (Additional notes by Carroll).

47. Ibid.

48. "Toward World Order," *America* 73 (August 4, 1945):354.

49. "No Opposition to the Charter," *Commonweal,* 42 (August 10, 1945):396.

50. RG 59, United Nations Preparatory Commission, Background Information, p. 1.

51. "UNO Bill Passed," *The New York Times,* December 20, 1945, p. 1.

52. Frank Comerford Walker was born in Plymouth, Pennsylvania, on May 30, 1986. His family moved to Montana when he was three and he grew up in Butte. He attended Gonzaga University and Notre Dame Law School. After he moved to New York City in 1924 he became a successful businessman and Democratic activist and contributor. He supported Franklin D. Roosevelt in his gubernatorial and presidential campaigns. Once in the White House, FDR would rely on him heavily for political advice. Among many positions he held were Chairman of the Democratic National Committee (1943–1944) and U.S. Postmaster General (1940–1945). He died on September 13, 1959 (*Dictionary of American Catholic Biography,* "Walker, Frank Comerford").

53. ANCWC 10, Carroll to Stritch, [D.C.], December 20, 1945, pp. 1–2, copy.

54. ANCWC 10, Francis H. Russell to Carroll, [D.C.], December 13, 1945.

55. ANCWC 10, Stritch to Carroll, [Chicago], January 30, 1946; Graham to Carroll, [London], March 11, 1946, p. 1.

56. *The Tablet* (founded in 1840), *The Catholic Times* (1859), *The Universe* (1860), and *The London Catholic Herald* (1894).

57. Graham to Carroll, March 11, 1946, p. 2.

58. Ibid., p. 5.

59. In August of 1946 the NCWC would apply for "consultative status" with the Economic and Social Council under the terms of Article seventy-one of the UN Charter, but would be refused this position because it was not "international in its structure." (ANCWC 19, Henri Laugier to "Mr. Carrtoll," August 5, 1946); McGowan to Carroll, August 12, 1946; "Revised Report of the Committee on Arrangements for Consultation with Non-Governmental Organizations," June 19, 1946, p. 2.

60. RG 59a 2232, Folder 1, William M. Benton to Pattee, October 20, 1945, copy; ANCWC 16, Francis H. Russell to Carroll, March 14, 1946, p. 1.

61. ANCWC 16, Carroll to Hoffman, [D.C.], March 25, 1946.

62. ANCWC 16, Hoffman to Carroll, [New York], April 30, 1946.

63. ANCWC 16, Hoffman to Carroll, [New York], April 1, 1946; Hoffman to Carroll, [New York], April 30, 1946; Memorandum from Caroll, [D.C.], May 22, 1946, copy.

64. AMU, Series 11, Box 1, Conway to Carroll, [New York], May 31, 1946, pp. 1–3, copy; Carroll to Chester Williams, [D.C.], June 1, 1946, copy.

65. "My F.B.I. contact just left. They have two men on [J. Robert] Oppenheimer always. Eighteen members of the House are Commies. Just a few of his tid-bits. My Atomic Information Fund Campaign hit 30,000 today" (AMU, Series 11, Box 1, Conway to Carroll, [D.C.], June 24, 1946).

66. Stritch, with Archbishops Francis Spellman of New York, Edward Mooney of Detroit, and John Glennon of St. Louis, was elevated to the College of Cardinals by Pius XII on February 18, 1946. It was the Vatican's first postwar consistory (Robert Leckie, *American and Catholic* [Garden City: Doubleday, 1970], p. 325).

67. AMU, Series 11, Box 1, Conway to Caroll, [New York], May 31, 1946.

68. AMU, Series 11, Box 1, "Report on Trip to New York, June 13–18," Catherine Schaefer, pp. 1–4.

69. ANCWC 8, McGowan to Carroll, [D.C.], June 22, 1946, p. 2; ANCWC 21, MAB 684, July 2, 1946.

70. ANCWC 8, Stritch to Schaefer, [Chicago], August 19, 1946.

71. ANCWC 8, Schaefer to Carroll, [D.C.], August 21, 1946, pp. 1–4; "Order Establishing Office of the N.C.W.C. for U.N. Affairs," August 26, 1946; Schaefer to J. Francis McIntyre, [New York], September 17, 1946.

72. ANCWC 8, Schaefer to Carroll, [D.C.], August 21, 1946, p. 2: "Uncharted territory."

73. Except for a brief mention by the NCWC News Service of the establishment of the UN Office, this landmark action by the Administrative Board was overlooked by the Catholic press as well as by the secular media.

CHAPTER X

Twenty Months

In the period framed by this study, the Catholic Church in the United States, with scant firsthand direction from the Vatican, made a concerted effort to play a central role in world affairs through participation in the creation of the new postwar international order exemplified by the United Nations Organization.[1] During these twenty months, the National Catholic Welfare Conference, the administrative agency of the American bishops, presumed to take a greater role in foreign affairs than ever before. From January 1945 until August 1946, the NCWC Administrative Board did nothing less than attempt to reinvent American Catholic global policy. This change signaled the NCWC's recognition that the epoch of World War II, a period of unprecedented Big Power cooperation in which the Church had reluctantly acquiesced, had ended, and that a new era of Great Power stalemate and Soviet "containment," the Cold War, emerged. This transformation, it should be noted, was not a turn of events unwelcome to contemporary American Catholic leaders.

By surveying the interval between the announcement of the UNCIO at San Francisco and the decision to establish the National Catholic Welfare Conference's Office of United Nations Affairs in New York, I have discovered four pivotal facets of the Catholic Conference's international policy-making agenda that were its hallmarks during the 1940s.

1. Consultant Influence

The perception that the Catholic Conference was exclusively an episcopal or at least clerical entity, a notion that is generally presumed when discussing the NCWC prior to the

Second Vatican Council, is put into question by the mechanism whereby the leadership of the American Church garnered its information about the United Nations Conference. Dependent largely on lay experts, the Administrative Board relied principally on these professionals for the information and advice necessary for its own high-level decision-making. These procedures occurred primarily either 3,000 miles from San Francisco in the nation's capital or in Detroit and Chicago, the archdioceses of Edward Mooney, chairman of the Administrative Board, and of Samuel Stritch.

Even before the State Department invited the National Catholic Welfare Conference and the Catholic Association for International Peace to the UNCIO, the leadership of the Church in America had decided to send informants to San Francisco to observe and report events. The first of these was Edward A. Conway, S.J. An ambitious and knowledgeable NCWC staffer who bylined for the News Service, Conway was slated initially to be an observer for the Social Action Department as well as a representative for the News Service. Once the US State Department permitted the selection of consultants, however, the NCWC, fearing correctly that Conway would mix promotion for his own peace objectives with his journalistic duties, dispatched a professional newsman, Burke Walsh, as its designated correspondent. The Jesuit would still serve as something of a NCWC *primus inter pares,* with at least as much influence and authority as Walsh.[2]

Conway can rightly be credited with breaking "ecumenical" ground through a 1943 pamphlet, *Pattern for Peace,* which became an interdenominational model for what was regarded by most American religious leaders as an ethical approach to world organization. By April of 1945 he was again collaborating with Protestant and Jewish leaders on the publication *Goals for San Francisco,* an interfaith compendium intended to influence the writing of the UN Charter. In a decidedly non-ecumenical age, Conway shrewdly garnered the blessing of the naturally-reluctant Administrative Board. He was encouraged in his activities by certain figures at the State Department such as

Archibald MacLeish, who hoped that such pro-United Nations literature would aid their already extensive propaganda campaign. The NCWC seemed to tolerate Conway's dual role in the expectation that it could not hurt to have an "insider" close to the Administration. In retrospect it is obvious that Conway's first allegiance was to the Catholic Church and that he rarely allowed his dalliance with key politicians and diplomats to interfere with his judgment.[3]

As the opening of the UNCIO drew near, the Church attempted to delineate better its approach to international issues so that its observers at San Francisco could introduce clear and authoritative Catholic positions in the Conference debates. In a NCWC memorandum Conway divided such topics into "Ideological Issues" such as "The Great Powers and World Security" and "Practical Issues" such as the question of religious freedom. On this latter point, the Administrative Board asked assistance from John Courtney Murray, a Jesuit theologian and expert on the subject. He provided theoretical and practical counsel which they used in their private discussions and public statements. Unfortunately they solicited this seminal study not from a forward-looking approach, but to forestall predicted American Protestant allegations at the UN Conference that the Church in South America was barring non-Catholic missionary activities. Although Murray did not attend the conference, his influence on the bishops resulted in their patronage of a UN Bill of Rights.[4]

As the Conference began, consultants from the two Catholic organizations soon discovered that they were allotted more responsibilities than they anticipated. Promised frequent access to the US delegation through meetings and intelligence sessions, they sensed that they might play a real part in the UN deliberations through their ability to recommend proposals to the American delegates. From the outset, however, they were confronted with opposition to some of the Church's positions from consultants and from the press corps. Their varied responses to this criticism were telling.

Richard Pattee, the NCWC consultant, retreated into parochialism. He adopted a highly individualistic approach to the conference; this limited his intercourse with non-Catholic consultants and envoys and thereby his effectiveness as a spokesman for the church within these circles. At the same time he maintained great authority and moral suasion among delegations from South and Central America. On several key issues his leverage was obvious.

In spite of any opposition, the CAIP consultants, Thomas Mahony and Catherine Schaefer, who like Conway were disposed to work with a wide variety of groups and opinions over the years, plunged into the thick of American delegation activities. Accordingly, they collaborated with, and did not merely lobby, the other consultants. In this way they effected some of the most significant "Catholic" changes in the UN Charter.

Though it can be said that Mahony exerted little sway in debates on important topics such as the "veto power" and the "Vandenberg Amendment," he more than made up for this with his groundbreaking efforts on behalf of the reform of international jurisprudence. Believing that the Big Three—more attentive to their own security needs than to justice—had prohibited at Dumbarton Oaks a consideration of moral principles and a codification of international ordinances, he served at San Francisco as the principal mentor to an *ad hoc* committee of lawyer-consultants whose ambition it was to amend the UN Charter. Toward this goal he proposed that the General Assembly be given direct power to establish a commission to codify international law and to convoke a constitutional convention after five years. Only partially successful in this, he and his allies could nevertheless claim much progress. Through his efforts the Assembly was granted deliberative faculties and could offer non-binding recommendations on international law as well as mandate a commission to formulate a codification of legal principles for the consent of the members. Because of the General Assembly's merely quasi-legislative powers, however, Mahony deemed that the Charter had yet to exhibit enough regard for law as the basis of world order. He therefore urged that the Catholic Conference, through the auspices of the CAIP, continue to work for juridical reform of the world organization once it initiated operations. His advice was duly heeded by the NCWC Administrative Board.[5]

Following their admittedly limited achievements in the sphere of international law, the Catholic representatives determined that the best avenue for change was through a new quasi-independent agency, the Economic and Social Council (ECOSOC). Mandated to deal with the many practical problems faced by a majority of the world's population and therefore not concerned *per se* with nationalistic interests, the ECOSOC was regarded by smaller nations and by the US Catholic Church, as "non-political." In other words, it was one of the last UN bastions against Great Power politics and a potential focal point for maintaining the best that the League of Nations had offered.[6]

In a December 1944 memorandum Father Conway had endorsed a Dumbarton Oaks proposal to place the ECOSOC under the General Assembly. This, he asserted, would permit its agencies to avoid a Security Council veto and give them freer rein over the economic and social issues that would largely determine the quality and duration of the postwar peace. Because praxis and not doctrine alone, not even Catholic doctrine, solved practical problems, he and Richard Pattee encouraged all Catholic delegates in San Francisco to uphold the ECOSOC articles. With allied delegates and other consultants, they successfully lobbied for American sponsorship of an amendment to grant proper recognition to an Economic and Social Council. Labelled a "positive approach to peace," it extended real control over fiscal and humanitarian issues to the General Assembly. But Catherine Schaefer's dream that the Economic Council would become a coequal branch with the Security Council never materialized.[7]

By stressing economic progress, higher standards of living, and full employment for all laborers of the world, Catholic "functionalists" such as Schaefer attempted to incorporate the League's International Labor Organization into the new world-body. With the blessing of Pattee and Mahony, who were tied to other conference matters, Schaefer shuttled between a World Federation of Labor Unions meeting in Oakland, and the UN-CIO. Through these efforts she helped arrange an alliance between American labor leaders and sympathetic delegates and consultants. This group pressed effectively for inclusion of the ILO into the United Nations and persuaded the delegates to accept the association's "tri-partite formula" for representation in all ECOSOC agencies. Schaefer must, accordingly, be duly recognized as the key person in several matters relating to labor issues at the conference, and Thomas Mahony declared that she was so credited at San Francisco.[8]

It can, therefore, be said that a few Catholic consultants at San Francisco and elsewhere played an influential part in formulating the thinking of the bishops of the Administrative Board and the delegates, advisors, and consultants at the conference. In matters such as pre-Conference ecumenical cooperation for peace, Western Hemispheric solidarity, universal human rights, codification of international law, the Economic and Social Council, and worldwide labor dialogue, contributions of the representatives of the NCWC and the CAIP are well documented. Although the next section of this summary catalogues the deficiencies and shortcomings of the Catholic consultant enterprise at the incorporation of the United Nations, one can make a case that the effective Catholic presence at San Francisco was typified more by Mahony, Pattee, Conway, and Schaefer than by the signatures of Mooney and Stritch that graced numerous admittedly useful telegrams and dispatches.[9]

2. Catholic Dichotomies And Their Consequences

Although the American hierarchy, or at least the bishops of the NCWC Administrative Board, willing launched a campaign to lobby on behalf of the relevancy of Catholic principles in the postwar world, it is confirmed in this investigation that the Catholic Church in the United States was frequently divided over solutions to many of the global problems facing the victorious Allies in their bid to displace the League of Nations. Nowhere is this illustrated better than in the procedural and ideological dichotomies that separated the NCWC and the CAIP, especially in their fundamental divergence on whether the United Nations as conceived by the Dumbarton Oaks agreements was potentially a viable institution.

In January of 1945, owing to its size and international makeup, the Catholic Church in the United States, represented by the NCWC, posed the most significant sectarian threat to the Dumbarton proposals. Speaking for the church as chairman of the Committee to Implement the Pope's Peace Plan, Samuel Stritch, archbishop of Chicago, denounced the Dumbarton Oaks peace plan as a transparent attempt to set up "a Big Three Powers world control" which did not provide for a just and peaceful settlement of disputes among member states of the United Nations. The only hope for justice, Stritch believed, was for the United States to work for a "good peace."[10]

But the NCWC was not alone among Catholic groups preoccupied with obstacles besetting the establishment of an alliance for peace. The Catholic Association for International Peace, though ostensibly under the "guidance" of the bishops' organization, expressed a surprisingly divergent opinion on the matter. To the exasperation of some key members of the Administrative Board, the CAIP's autonomous stance thwarted the Board's attempt to present a united front on international matters.

In fact, a serious internal controversy raged within the joint offices of these two Catholic organizations over whether the new world organization had already been so morally tainted by Dumbarton Oaks that it deserved the Church's condemnation. This position was held by Stritch and by many NCWC officials. Father Conway spoke for many in the CAIP, however, when he stated that the proposed United Nations Organization, although flawed, was still a viable institution that needed unequivocal Catholic encouragement and participation. Within

Catholic circles this confrontation would become the overarching pre-Conference debate. In this instance the NCWC Administrative Board would finally be persuaded by the CAIP's cogent arguments.[11]

Once they agreed that reform of the Dumbarton Oaks proposals was the essential goal for Catholic participants in the UNCIO, the NCWC and the CAIP instigated a passionate, if only partly successful, crusade to arouse both the delegates at San Francisco and the American public to accept their perception of authentic world peace and security. Some of the ensuing failures were a result of certain Catholic organizational defects and shortcomings, but others were a consequence of disagreements among consultants at San Francisco.

Soon after the conference began, strains developed from the necessity of coast-to-coast communications between Washington and San Francisco. There was virtually total dependence by NCWC and CAIP consultants and correspondents on a few key bishops for the "final word" on all subjects. This inability of the non-episcopal consultants to share equally in the final stages of the decision-making process occasioned predicaments in which the church was unable to cope adequately with fluid situations as they were developing.

As has been shown in Chapter VII, this phenomenon was most dramatically illustrated in the debate over a United Nations Education Office. Although the NCWC would eventually accede to the position of the consultants on the scene, it would do so only after the greatest pressure from these highly respected and seasoned professionals. Unfortunately, on the education issue this capitulation came too late.

During the conference the split between the NCWC and Catholic consultants on UN educational policy was allowed to fester back in Washington. Although the NCWC theorized that World War II resulted from bad education, it was suspicious both of the goals of US educational groups such as the National Education Association (NEA) and perceived Communist designs on European pedagogy. Therefore it balked at the NEA's

Charter amendments, which encouraged substantial UN oversight of cultural and educational standards under the direction of an International Office of Education. After NEA assurances that these alterations were meant merely to promote global cooperation on these affairs, Richard Pattee and Catherine Schaefer were soon convinced that the revisions were not inimical to Catholic interests. Belatedly challenging the NCWC, they ultimately induced the Administrative Board to reverse its position and to lend its support to these reforms. Schaefer's prophecy, however, that the church's original intransigence and its failure to develop a concrete policy on this matter would damage its reputation, was verified. It is likely that in the absence of Catholic leadership on the education issue at San Francisco, the State Department downgraded the Catholic presence at the UN's Educational Conference held in London in October of 1945.[12]

Another division within Catholic circles, this time at the conference, probably delayed the NCWC's recognition of the implications of the aggressive posture that the Soviet delegation was assuming at San Francisco. Though most other American consultants regarded the question of the conference presidency as a minor crisis, a disagreement soon arose among some Catholic observers over its significance. Conway, disagreeing with his sources at the US State Department, sided with the majority opinion mentioned above, but Pattee supported the Latin American contention, which viewed this procedural matter as a hemispheric struggle between the democratic spirit of American continentalism and old-world nationalistic imperialism. Rather than capitulate to the Soviets and thus advance their totalitarian world plans, he advised that the conferees should accept the Act of Chapultepec, the compact of the Inter-American states signed on March 8, 1945. With this agreement as a guide, they could incorporate republican neighborliness, the principles of universal and equal representation, and the "Anglo-Latin" tradition of Christian liberty, justice, and truth into the UN Charter. Faced, however, with such an evident division of opinion on the matter, the

Catholic Conference never launched a lobbying effort in behalf of the South American recommendation.

The issue of the conference presidency, which was to be resolved during the plenary sessions of the UNCIO, was of little concern to most delegates except those of the United States and its hemispheric allies. As Thomas Mahony noted insightfully, however, the really troubling question was not how the Pan-American Union somewhat ambiguously viewed world peace but whether that organization, composed of all the nations of the Western Hemisphere except Canada, should continue to exist.[13]

Far from taking Latin American advice, many delegates at the UNCIO—as well as public opinion in the United States—challenged the very concept of hemispheric association. Although the State Department desperately tried to present the Pan-American Conference as a harmless regional grouping, it was generally perceived as undermining UN solidarity. Under intense pressure from its non-American partners and dreading a serious loss of prestige at the conference, the US, in Pattee's view, was constraining the Western Hemisphere to repudiate tacitly its right to self-defense except as formally sanctioned by the Security Council. At the same time, Pattee believed that the United States had accorded just such a privilege to Soviet bilateral agreements.

The initial Latin American reaction to this turn of events was one of shock and outrage. Agreeing with this point of view, Pattee, Conway, and others successfully strove to convince the US delegation that it had bowed unwisely to outside pressures and endangered hemispheric security. Mahony did not disagree with this estimation, but since he was not as unalterably opposed to "sensible" Big Power control in the Security Council as Pattee, he stressed the importance of placing superior power in the hands of the Council so that it could prevent the exercise of force by regional arrangements until all other means were exhausted. Nevertheless, both Pattee and Mahony were dissatisfied with the final US-Soviet compromise because it adopted paradoxical principles of autonomy and of subservience to the UN for regional arrangements. Once again, however, NCWC and CAIP officials in Washington received mixed signals from their experts in San Francisco, and this prevented any concerted Catholic effort in the matter.[14]

The most prescient Catholic commentary on this came not from the Administrative Board but from *Commonweal.* Through this settlement the Big Powers sanctioned continuation of their regional arrangements, and thereby hobbled overall UN effectiveness. Furthermore, *Commonweal* claimed, the phenomenon of an American "bloc" in the Western Hemisphere would induce the Soviets to retain real authority in the Security Council so that their veto could restrain any unfriendly actions from that bloc. Would that the Administrative Board had been able to contribute such a lucid analysis of the situation during the UN Conference debates.[15]

A final division of opinion, this time over the importance of certain general principles to be included in the UN Charter, probably resulted in a diminution of respect for the American hierarchy within foreign-policy circles. Fortunately, the fact that the Administrative Board took wrong advice on a matter concerning an International Bill of Rights did not result in any permanent injury to that noble endeavor.

Although the Dumbarton Oaks proposals spurned specific reference to the sovereignty of moral law, the Church still yearned to bend the UN toward a greater juridical and moral awareness and away from its obsession with security. To achieve this end, the NCWC was advised by its consultants and representatives in San Francisco, most imperatively by Conway, to champion an International Bill of Rights that would serve as a criterion for membership in the UN. The consultants were unanimous in support of Marshal Smuts's Preamble to the Charter, which eloquently professed respect for fundamental human rights and for the sanctity of the human person. They were divided, however, on whether a commission to draft a separate Bill of Rights should be part of the UNCIO deliberations or instituted after establishment of the Economic and

Social Council, which was slated to have supervision in such affairs.

Father Conway, having won the Administrative Board to his view, called emphatically for adoption of the former position, but Pattee and Mahony more astutely counseled that a Bill of Rights would fare better in an ECOSOC commission, away from the tumult of conference business. A consultants' Commission on Human Rights eventually put aside the urgent pleas of Conway and the NCWC and proposed instead a stipulation within the Charter that would mandate a rights panel as a constituted agency of the ECOSOC. Inauguration of this commission, however, was delayed until after the Conference. The two principal Catholic pundits at San Francisco played no part in this consultant endeavor, partly because of their disagreement with the Administrative Board on timing.[16]

3. Disharmony With The US Government

One paradox of the Catholic experience at the San Francisco Conference was that the NCWC/CAIP consultants found themselves recurrently in opposition to the Truman Administration and to a majority of the American delegation. Since the consultants were guided by the Administrative Board's recent statements on international order, it was all but predetermined that they would eventually oppose many of the recommendations that emerged from Dumbarton Oaks. The Board had publicly asserted, after all, that these proposals were concocted not only to insure postwar peace, but also to preserve Big Three hegemony after cessation of hostilities.

Even before the UN Conference, the Catholic Church in the United States had taken a forceful stand on universal UN membership, and so its representatives at San Francisco were virtually united in their efforts on this question. Unlike the Yalta conferees, they favored eventual admission of neutrals and even of former enemies into the world organization. Also, through its agents in San Francisco, the Church lobbied futilely for admission of the Catholic-dominated Polish government-in-exile, then located in London, a proposition the US delegation eventually rejected.[17]

The bishops did support the dubious but successful US drive for Catholic Argentina's participation in the conference, although at least one Catholic journal, *Commonweal*, held that this was a move counter to Christian ethics. Because of controversy over this "fascist" state's admission to the UNCIO, a majority of delegates opposed Franco's bid for UN membership for Falangist Spain, one of the NCWC's preeminent goals.[18]

The Catholic Church, which had long defended this Roman Catholic country, once more came to its aid, as Pattee and Conway spent long hours in lobbying the American delegation. This attempt to paint Spain as a "peace-loving" nation was ineffective, however, and all American Protestant consultants worked against the Catholic effort. Even Thomas Mahony, for reasons unknown, failed to rally to this cause. Under a provision upheld by a sizable majority at San Francisco, the Franco regime was barred from the security organization because allegedly it had been established with the aid of the Axis. The Catholic consultants were unable to prevent even the United States from opposing Spain's bid for membership.[19]

In the two most controversial debates at the UNCIO, examination of the "veto power" in the Security Council and the altercation over what came to be called the "Vandenberg Amendment," the Catholic experts at San Francisco allied themselves with those who strove to make these tactics implements of international justice. In this, therefore, they found themselves in a head-on confrontation with their government.

The Yalta Formula, which required the permanent members of the Security Council to carry the burden for UN peace-keeping efforts, stipulated also that their delegations be given "veto power" over all investigations of and military responses to global security problems. The Soviet Union interpreted this agreement as encompassing even discussion of such issues, but its associates in the Big Five disagreed. Aligning themselves with the "Little 45," they affirmed that deliberation in such matters was essential to UN aspirations for a germane world organization. Sensing a chance to draw some Soviet diplomatic blood, Pattee and Mahony encouraged this American effort in behalf of smaller nations. To add impetus to their endeavors, the chairman of the NCWC Administrative Board, at the behest of Conway, sent a telegram to President Truman asking him to reject all Soviet maneuvers to remove "freedom of speech" from the Security Council. Ultimately the other Great Powers "forced" Stalin to back down, but not before he received concessions from the non-permanent members that ensured that on all other security questions the Big Power veto was still in place. On this latter point, an odious arrangement in the estimation of the NCWC, the State Department had fully concurred.[20]

Pattee and Mahony were likewise dissatisfied with the "unanimity principle" that emerged from Yalta. They protested vehemently that the other permanent members must share the blame with Russia for rendering the ideal of the Atlantic Charter an illusion and for substituting a "Great Power alliance." Conway alone asserted that, in spite of his reservations on the outcome of the veto debate, satisfactory progress was being made in the evolution of world organization.

In conclusion, therefore, most Catholic observers favored majority rule in the Council or, at least, complete rejection of the "veto power." The United States, however, despite all pleas to the contrary, would see to it that, in general, the principle of the veto was a sacrosanct topic, above the insignificant consideration of the ordinary delegate or consultant at UNCIO.[21]

In the General Assembly the outstanding controversy swirled around the pacific settlement of disputes. At issue was of course the "Vandenberg Amendment." Senator Vandenberg proposed initially that, as a matter of justice, the Assembly should investigate and recommend revision of previously contracted treaties that were a threat to world peace. The NCWC and the Catholic Association for International Peace supported this motion; Conway stated that it represented the views of Pius XII and the American bishops.[22]

In adopting this proposal the American delegation replaced the word "treaties" with "situations" and limited the scope of General Assembly action to mere recommendation rather than investigation of settlements. In the controversy that arose over definition of the term "situations," the United States, while publicly claiming that the term still embraced treaty arrangements, privately supported the Soviets and most South Americans, who wanted a restricted definition of the word. By this time even Senator Vandenberg elected to reject the original intent of his measure, and Conway, who came into his own during this controversy, opined glibly, and in bad taste, that the amendment now looked like "a survivor from a Nazi torture camp."[23]

The Jesuit discovered that several powerful blocs had conspired to undo this amendment. By limiting its scope the South Americans hoped to avoid reopening border conflicts on their continent that might result from a general reappraisal of past treaties. The Soviets, on the other hand, allied with the French, were afraid that the amendment would be used to lighten the restrictions placed upon Germany after the war. Moreover, France accused the Vatican, American big business, and the Republicans in the American delegation of exploiting US religious support for "peaceful change" in the expectation of trade with Germany once sanctions were lifted. Although the NCWC distanced itself from John Foster Dulles, the preeminent Republican advisor at San Francisco, who may or may not have tried to co-opt the Church for his own purposes, the Catholic Conference decided to launch a month-long drive for ratification of the amendment. This was done, as Conway noted aptly, although the Church had been put in an impossible situation.[24]

In this bid the officially designated Catholic consultants played little part. Mahony was silent during the discussions with the American delegates and other consultants, and Pattee, who was working closely with many of the Latin Americans, made only one proposal, albeit a significant one. Attempting to bridge the chasm between the views of the NCWC and of his Latin American associates, he proposed a fundamental principle that would allow revision of treaties and other agreements only when such action was required by justice and world security.[25]

The final compromises on "veto power" and "peaceful change" reflected a few NCWC tenets, but the overwhelming opinion of Catholic consultants and observers in San Francisco was that the Big Five, with the United States collaborating in order to maintain Great Power unity, had conserved the preponderance of the Yalta concessions.[26]

The paramount juridical crisis at San Francisco involved redesigning the system of international tribunals. Sandwiched between the Big Powers, who favored a weak judiciary with optional jurisdiction on the order of the League of Nations' Permanent Court, and the smaller nations, which preferred a compulsory bench, the UNCIO was constrained to agree with the former. Both the NCWC and the CAIP objected that because of Big Power control of the Security Council, the permanent members of the Council would constitute *de facto* their own appeals bench for International Court rulings.[27]

Catholic representatives vehemently resisted this outcome. Pattee termed it "serious and possibly dangerous"; Mahony fumed that the US delegates were admitting off the record that compulsory jurisdiction was a sound principle but that political pressures militated against it. Conway protested that the Security Council would be the real supreme court of the United Nations, since it alone would have wide discretionary prerogatives in enforcement of the Court's decisions.[28]

Thomas Mahony found inordinate solace in the Charter's meager attempts to support the Court in principle, which as CAIP consultant he elected to interpret as altruism on the part of the Security Council's permanent members. This excessive enthusiasm was understandable in light of his earnest efforts at the UNCIO in behalf of a legitimate international juridical system. Such references in the Charter "implying" an underlying worldwide judicial order gave little comfort to *Common-*

weal. Its editors doubted that sentiments in the document would survive. The next few years were to prove their pessimistic deduction correct.

Therefore, although US Catholics had gone into the Conference intent on opposing their own government by working to raise the new world organization upon a solid basis in law and by rejecting the League's "optional jurisdiction" for the Court, they were only partially successful in preventing the Big Power bloc, in this case led by the US State Department, from thwarting these goals.[29]

On the matter of trusteeships and colonial territories, the Big Three at Yalta, and later the Big Five at San Francisco, would ostracize all other member states and UN observers from decisions related to strategic areas or to colonial territories. At first China and the Soviet Union criticized the US, Britain, and France for failing to recognize the independence of such territories, but ultimately they too acquiesced in this policy. Stalin, for example, was guaranteed his own "trusteeships," if he would collaborate in this subterfuge.

Though it promised economic advancement, self-government, and non-discriminatory treatment to all populations within the General Assembly trusteeships, the US refused adamantly to allow even Security Council supervision of its own strategic territories. Richard Pattee challenged this course and stressed the need of progress for underdeveloped and colonial peoples; yet he received little more than a civil hearing from Commander Stassen and the other American delegates, who were under strict injunction from the State Department to avoid any substantial discussion of the issue. Although Pattee objected that such conduct condemned the conference to virtual inaction on a matter that concerned more than 750,000,000 persons, he was helpless to effect any change in Administration policy.

Nothing could better express the general Catholic feeling on the US role as a "Great Power" leader at the conference than Thomas Mahony's chagrin at America's behavior during the trusteeship controversy. He was dumbfounded by American solidarity with the imperialistic goals of Great Britain and France and insistence on absolute control of American strategic areas without so much as cursory surveillance by the Security Council.[30] Accordingly, the Catholic representatives were understandably anxious about the fate of the missions in the former Japanese-held islands in the Pacific and about the fortunes of the hundreds of millions who were not to be represented directly by the United Nations. They expressed a thoughtful apprehension for the postwar peace that the world organization, in the firm grip of the Great Powers, professed to protect.

4. A Cold-War Policy

On April 15 the NCWC Administrative Board issued *On Organizing World Peace,* a pronouncement expressly aimed at the upcoming UN deliberations in San Francisco. This document praised the Atlantic Charter of 1941 but purported to detect an unremitting backslide from that Charter's spirit in the Dumbarton Oaks proposals and in the Yalta agreements. It castigated such measures as the voting procedures proposed for the Security Council and the refusal of the Great Powers to submit to world authority. The bishops pronounced the Polish situation discouraging, an International Bill of Rights essential, and Marxism and democracy incompatible.[31] Although this seemed a victory for the "hardliners," externals proved to be deceptive. The State Department accepted the document at face value and was genuinely disturbed by this release because it intimated that the Church believed a real peace was virtually impossible.

In hindsight, public statements notwithstanding, it is obvious that even throughout the many internal Catholic debates during the formation of the United Nations Organization, the leadership of the American Church never seriously considered any other policy but benign sufferance for the world organization. This patronage was perceived as essential to strengthen the United States's evolving and much-hoped-for position of intransigence toward the hostile and acquisitive policies of the burgeoning Soviet bloc. Thus the NCWC contributed to an East-West dischotomy, which would permeate world relations for four decades.[32]

In surveying the carnage after skirmishes over UN membership in the early stages of the UNCIO, the agents of the Catholic Church in San Francisco were not pleased with the progress of their crusade for a sympathetic security conference. Their only clear victory, Argentina, was a propaganda defeat that directly resulted in Spain's failure to gain admittance into the United Nations. The Soviets had obtained admission of two communist governments and would eventually succeed in obtaining membership for a third, the Polish Lublin Committee. Moreover, by its resistance to "fascist" membership in the world body, this great enemy of Catholicism had portrayed itself as the champion of "peace-loving" peoples everywhere.

Just before the opening session of the UNCIO, the Catholic bishops in the United States had stated that Marxism and democracy were irreconcilable. As if to emphasize the point, the National Catholic Welfare Conference commissioned a study by John F. Cronin, S.S., to examine the extent of Communist inroads into American institutions. Even from this perspective, the hierarchy realized sensibly that an up-to-date assessment of the Soviet Union was called for in light of the apparently predetermined postwar situation. A fresh appraisal became more urgent following the debates over Argentina's qualifications for UN membership and Franco's application to the UNCIO, controversies for which the Catholic observers at San Francisco were sorely unprepared.[33]

The Catholic exegesis of Soviet motives was a mixed bag indeed. Obstructionism, a desire for favorable concessions, diplomatic ineptitude, sheer propaganda, and a sincere desire for peace were some of the motives that Pattee suggested. Father Conway proposed that Soviet bloc-building and fear of being beset by democratic states went far in deciphering Soviet behavior. Finally, Thomas Mahony concluded that Soviet misconduct could be ascribed to a national inferiority complex and to unfavorable experiences at previous international conferences. Catholic observers concurred unanimously that despite these factors, the USSR could and should be dealt with at the Conference and in the United Nations.[34]

In tandem with this Catholic analysis of Soviet motives, Russia's wartime allies, including the US, conducted an informal assessment. Since Yalta the other great powers had grown weary of Russian diplomatic tricks and less needful of her support in the war. At first the United States sought to appease the Kremlin, but by the opening session of the parley Thomas Mahony detected a "hardening" of US attitudes toward the Soviets. This became evident, for example, during the "Presidency crisis," the introductory question at San Francisco. The Russians "won" that round, and a pattern of superpower discord was thereby solidified, at least for the first half of the UNCIO. Although there would be a thaw during the latter part of the conference, the bitter initial experiences would not be forgotten.[35]

By the end of the conference it could be seen that, in "nonpolitical" matters of economic redevelopment, social affairs, and the fate of dependent peoples, the UNCIO had adopted many aspects of the old League of Nations, while it offered some substantial variations, not all of them, in Catholic opinion, salutary. As in other areas of contention, it was impossible to keep veto power domination out of these agencies; more success was achieved in the ECOSOC than in the Trusteeship Council. Departing San Francisco on June 26, the American Catholic consultants and observers who had weighed these and other issues retained a guarded optimism. This was further tempered by dread that the Big Five would have the same unwarranted control over everyday UN operations that they wielded during the Conference. Hence the Catholic Church in the United States was faced with some important decisions.

Catholic observers at San Francisco and the American Church's leadership were divided on the achievements of the conference and on the efficacy of its Charter as a means to bring peace in the postwar world. Conway, who was permitted to release the first Catholic evaluation of the conference, was unduly confident that most articles in the Charter were sufficient to effect an ethical global order. This optimism accorded with his long-held, if erroneous, theory that the key to the future of world peace lay primarily in establishment of the machinery for international organization, however flawed. He believed that the Charter's imperfections could be corrected, that with the assistance of the Church and Pius XII's Five Point Peace Program, the United Nations had an excellent chance to succeed.[36]

But Richard Pattee and Thomas Mahony and the NCWC Administrative Board believed that a prompt, meaningful emendation of the Charter was indispensable if peace with justice was to be secured under UN auspices. Pattee's negative judgment on the "ethical irresponsibility" of the Great Powers at San Francisco clashed somewhat with Mahony's appraisal. The CAIP consultant still had hope for the promise of Big Three unanimity. This hope, however, was based on the tenuous assumption that the US, USSR, and UK would keep intact their friendly wartime collaboration and would relinquish their unrestricted hegemony over the international scene.

Yet there was no disagreement within American Catholicism on the necessity of the United States' remaining in the UN to promote establishment of an international system in which free institutions could be sustained.[37]

In order for the US to lead such a worldwide reform, however, the Catholic consultants declared, it was crucial for the State Department to renounce its blatantly self-serving methods as well as its dreams of a US-Soviet postwar alliance. Intent on steering the administration in this direction, the NCWC Board would opt eventually for Pattee's solemn UN-CIO analysis as the basis for its uncompromising November 1945 statement. All that remained now was the search for a viable plan by which to affect the thinking of the United States and of the UN.[38]

After the conferences at Potsdam and London in the summer of 1946, the NCWC sensed for the first time that the Truman administration understood that its quixotic scheme for extensive collaboration with the USSR now lay in ruins. The Administrative Board determined, therefore, on a course of maximum UN participation as the primary vehicle for a policy to forestall the spread of Soviet totalitarianism. Given this assumption, the task of assisting the US in its "international obligations" through an infusion of Christian principles became a fundamental aspiration of the Catholic Conference. Over the first eight months of 1946 the Board came to realize that a permanent office at the United Nations was integral to attainment of this goal. The establishment of the NCWC Office for UN Affairs would help to usher in a new phase in the history of the Catholic Church in the United States.[39]

Notes

1. After a thorough review of documents in the NCWC archives and the eleven (really twelve because Vol. 3 is in two parts) volumes of the *Actes et Documents du Saint Siège Relatifs à la Seconde Guerre Mondiale* (Libreria Editrice Vaticana, 1965–1981), I have uncovered no direct instructions by the Vatican to the American hierarchy pertaining to its participation in or activities regarding the UNCIO or the United Nations Organization. Nevertheless the NCWC Administrative Board was naturally guided in all such undertakings by Pius XII's many statements on postwar international organization.

2. ANCWC 12, Carroll to Mitty, [D.C.], March 13, 1945; ANCWC 15, Hall to Carroll, [D.C.], April 4, 1945.

3. AAC 2967M, Conway to Mooney, [D.C.], March 7, 1945, copy.

4. ANCWC 15, Conway to Carroll, [D.C.], April 11, 1945.

5. AMU, Series 6, Box 1, Schaefer to Carroll, [San Francisco], May 4, 1945, p. 3; "Observations on the San Francisco Conference," May 7, 1945, p. 1; ANCWC 12, McGowan to Carroll, [San Francisco], May 25, 1945; "The San Francisco Conference," p. 8.

6. *The Dictionary of American Diplomatic History,* "Trusteeship Council (United Nations)."

7. "Catholics and the Dumbarton Oaks Proposals," p. 9; "Some Observations on the San Francisco Conference. . . ," p. 9; ANCWC 15, Pattee to Carroll, [San Francisco], April 30, 1945, p. 2; ANCWC 13c, "Small and Middle Nations Emphasize Importance of Economic Social Council at San Francisco Parley," Edward Conway, S.J., May 5, 1945, p. 2a; ANCWC 12, Report to the Post-War World Committee,

Catherine Schaefer, July 11, 1945, p. 13.

8. *The United Nations as a Political Institution,* p. 138; ANCWC 12, McGowan to Carroll, [San Francisco], May 31, 1945; AMU, Series 6, Box 1, Schaefer to McGowan, [San Francisco], May 4, 1945, p. 3.

9. It should be noted that these documents, more often than not, contained thoughts and opinions of these four experts.

10. ANCWC 21, MAB 29–31, November 16, 1944.

11. AAC 2964C, Stritch to Carroll, [Chicago], March 10, 1945; ANCWC 4, McGowan to Carroll, [D.C.], March 23, 1945; Conway to Carroll, [D.C.], December 1, 1944.

12. *On International Order,* p. 57; AMU, Series 1, Box 1, Educational Consultants to Stettinius, May 2, 1945, p. 2; Hochwalt to Schaefer, [D.C.], May 9, 1945; Schaefer to McGowan, [San Francisco], May 16, 1945; ANCWC 15, Pattee to Carroll, [San Francisco], May 16, 1945, p. 2.

13. ANCWC 13a, "Thoughts on a Momentous Occasion," E.A. Conway, S.J., April 30, 1945, p. 1; RG 59f, Box 22, The United Nations Conference as Reported by US Press and Radio, July 1945, p. 3; "Observations Upon the Conference VIII," p. 1.

14. ANCWC 11, "What is the Alternative?" Richard Pattee, June 11, 1945, p. 1; *The United Nations Charter,* pp. 6–7.

15. ANCWC 13c, "Latin Americans See Threat to Chapultepec," Richard Pattee, May 14, 1945, p. 2a; "Observations Upon the Conference VIII," p. 2; ANCWC 11, "Report on the United Nations Conference. . . ," p. 13; "America's Bloc," *Commonweal,* May 25, 1945, p. 131.

16. "The San Francisco Conference," p. 3; ANCWC 15, Conway to Carroll, [D.C.], March 27, 1945, p. 4; "That All Important Preamble," p. 1; ANCWC 11, John A. Donovan to Carroll, [San Francisco], May 5, 1945; "Observations on the San Francisco Conference," May 3, 1945, p. 1.

17. "La Grande Argentina," p. 325.

18. Ibid.

19. ANCWC 11, Pattee to Carroll, [San Francisco], May 11, 1945; "Observations on the International Conference VI," p. 1.

20. "Report on the United Nations Conference. . . ," p. 15; "Observations Upon the Conference VIII," p. 2; Report of Interview with Senator Vandenberg and John Foster Dulles, June 5, 1945.

21. "Report on United Nations Conference. . . ," p. 15; "Satisfactory Progress Seen in Proposed Charter Toward *Goals For San Francisco,*" p. 8; ANCWC 15, "Memorandum on Some Aspects of a World Security Organization. . . ," April 19, 1945, p. 4; "Some Observations on the San Francisco Conference. . . ," p. 18.

22. "Those Big Four Amendments," p. 1.

23. ANCWC 11, Conway to Carroll, [San Francisco], May 13, 1945, p. 1.

24. ANCWC 11, Conway to Clarence Enzler, [San Francisco], May 19, 1945, p. 3; AAC 2966M, Stritch to Mooney, [Chicago] May 15, 1945, p. 1; AAC 2967C, Conway to Carroll, [San Francisco], May 19, 1945.

25. "Some Observations on the San Francisco Conference. . . ," p. 19.

26. "Peaceful Change Clause of Charter Remains Open to Varying Interpretations," p. 20.

27. "Implementing the World Court"; *On International Order,* p. 2.

28. "Some Observations on the San Francisco Conference. . . ," p. 8; "U.S. Bishops' Recommendations Seen Substantially Reflected in Charter of United Nations," p. 2b.

29. "The San Francisco Conference," p. 9; "The San Francisco Wind-up," p. 276.

30. ANCWC 15, Conway to Carroll, [D.C.], March 27, 1945, p. 5; RG 59a 2001, Folder 4, Minutes U.S. Consultants' Meeting, May 16, 1945, 8:15 P.M., p. A-7; "Some Observations on the San Francisco Conference. . . ," p. 15; AMU, Series 6, Box 1, "Observations Upon the Conference IX," Thomas Mahony, May 28, 1945, p. 1.

31. *On Organizing World Peace,* pp. 1–2.

32. RG 591, Box 2, Folder 1, MacLeish to Stettinius, [D.C.], April 20, 1945; "Ideological Notes."

33. ANCWC 2a, Cronin to Ready, [Baltimore], November 17, 1944; ANCWC 21, MAB 29, November 16, 1944.

34. ANCWC 13c, "Molotov's Motives Analyzed," Richard Pattee, May 3, 1945, p. 4; "Russia Remains a Riddle," Edward A. Conway, S.J., May 3, 1945, p. 3; "Observations on the San Francisco Conference," May 3, 1945, p. 1.

35. "Observations Upon the Conference III," pp. 1–2; RG 59a 1996, Folder 4, Memorandum of Conversation, April 24, 1945.

36. "U.S. Bishops' Recommendations Seen as Substantially Reflected in Charter of United Nations," pp. 1–2.

37. "Memorandum on 'Peace Through Disarmament and Charter Revision,'" p. 2; "Some Observations on the San Francisco Conference. . . ," p. 3; "The United Nations Conference," p. 17.

38. *The United Nations Charter,* p. 21; "Some Observations on the San Francisco Conference. . . ," p. 2; *Between War and Peace,* p. 64.

39. "Some Observations on the San Francisco Conference. . . ," p. 39; ANCWC 10, Graham to Carroll, [London], March 11, 1946, p. 2; ANCWC 16, Hoffman to Carroll, [New York], April 30, 1946; AMU, Series 11, Box 1, "Report on Trip to New York—June 13–18," Catherine Schaefer, pp. 1–4; ANCWC 21, MAB 684, July 2, 1946; "Order Establishing Office of the NCWC for UN Affairs."

Essay on the Sources

At present four archives in the United States are rich sources of information on the American Catholic Church's participation in the formation of the United Nations. These repositories are the Archives of the Archdiocese of Chicago, the Marquette University Archives, the State Department Papers at the National Archives, and most notably the Archives of the National Catholic Welfare Conference at the United States Catholic Conference.

At the Archives and Records Center of the Archdiocese of Chicago one can examine materials from the episcopacy of Samuel Cardinal Stritch, who during the 1940s was Chairman of the Bishops' Peace Committee and the hierarchy's foremost expert on international affairs. These papers consist of two collections: the Chancery Correspondence Files and the Stritch Personal Papers. The Chancery Correspondence Files are arranged in yearly alphabetical files containing correspondence generated at the Chancery. Although they consist chiefly of day-to-day business of the archdiocese, correspondence regarding matters outside the archdiocese is included.

The Stritch Personal Papers consist of three series: personal correspondence, NCWC items, and "Ephemera." In January of 1988 these papers were virtually unprocessed and remained in the order and condition in which they were transferred to the Archives. Although the problem this presents is one of access—only box-level descriptions are available, for example—the archivists at Chicago are most helpful and do everything possible to assist scholarly researchers.

The Records and Papers of the Catholic Association for International Peace are housed in the Department of Special Collections, Memorial Library Archives, Marquette University. These documents are processed and are organized according to a specific schedule of twelve series, which are further subdivided into boxes and folders. The series encompass such topics as annual conferences, executive affairs, correspondence, peace statements and other publications, histories of the association, news releases, projects, relations with the American hierarchy, and "Human Rights in the era of the UN Charter discussion, 1945–1950" (Series 6).

The policy of the Memorial Library Archives is one of access to its special collections within the bounds of Marquette University regulations. These controls are not onerous. The CAIP Collection is very well organized and is an invaluable record of American Catholic efforts in the field of international understanding and peaceful global relations from the late 1920s through the early 1960s.

The International Affairs Files of the Archives of the National Catholic Welfare Conference are located at the headquarters of the National Conference of Catholic Bishops/United States Catholic Conference in Washington, D.C. Although the NCCB/USCC offices were located at 1312 Massachusetts Avenue for many years, they have been transferred to a new headquarters, 3211 Fourth Street, adjacent to the campus of the Catholic University of America. The archives too are located there.

All principal extant documents, correspondence, and memoranda relating to the NCWC's blueprint for peace, pronouncements, and activities during World War II, its participation in the San Francisco Conference and other related parleys, and its subsequent affiliation with the United Nations Organization through its UN Office in New York have been processed and are to be found in this incomparable archive. Thousands of minor entries are located in the USCC storage facility located in a Washington suburb. Access to these files is granted through the Conference archivist. Many CAIP records are to be found at the USCC. For an investigation of the NCWC's United Nations operations, these NCCB-CAIP files should be consulted, since there was a significant overlap in the personnel and undertakings of the two organizations.

The Department of State Archives (RG 59) are located in the National Archives on the Federal Mall in Washington, D.C.

There one can obtain a Research Identification Card, which permits access to the various State Department collections. Most materials relating to the Dumbarton Oaks Conference, the Yalta Conference, and the UNCIO are to be found in the Decimal Files. These records are subdivided into boxes and folders.

There are, however, other State Department collections that touch on Catholic participation in the San Francisco Conference. The UNCIO File of Alger Hiss and the Records of the Assistant Secretary of State for Public Affairs and Cultural Relations (Archibald MacLeish) yield much information about the process whereby Catholics and other representatives of concerned citizens' groups were chosen to be "consultants" to the American delegation at the UN Conference. The Records of Harley A. Notter, 1939–45, moreover, contain the minutes of meetings at which various members of the US delegation addressed the assembled consultants and entertained questions from them.

Finally, the John K. Mullen of Denver Library at the Catholic University of America in Washington maintains a microfilm file of NCWC News Service dispatches.

Archival Abbreviations

AAC   Archives of the Archdiocese of Chicago (boxes used were 2825, 2826, 2964, 2965, 2966, 2967, 2968, 2969, 2971, 2973, 2974, 2975; each box is divided by two or more letters of the alphabet and those letters are used in the citations: for example, AAC 2825)

AMU   Catholic Association for International Peace Collection, Department of Special Collections and University Archives, Marquette University (Series 1, Box 1; Series 6, Box 1; Series 8, Box 2; Series 10, Box 8; Series 11, Boxes 1 and 6)

ANCWC 1   Archives of the National Catholic Welfare Conference (General Secretary Files) United States Catholic Conference/National Conference of Catholic Bishops: Church and State: Envoy to the Vatican: 1913–1950

ANCWC 2a ANCWC: Communism: General: 1944

ANCWC 2b ANCWC: Communism: General: 1945

ANCWC 3a ANCWC: Communism: Cronin, John F., Report: 1945a

ANCWC 3b ANCWC: Communism: Cronin, John F., Report: 1945b

ANCWC 4   ANCWC: International Affairs: Dumbarton Oaks Conference: 1944–1945

ANCWC 5   ANCWC: International Affairs: General: 1952–1955

ANCWC 6   ANCWC: International Affairs: General Secretary: 1944–1949

ANCWC 7a ANCWC: International Affairs: Spain: 1932–1936

ANCWC 7b ANCWC: International Affairs: Spain: January–October 1937

ANCWC 7c   ANCWC: International Affairs: Spain: November 1937–January 1938

ANCWC 7d   ANCWC: International Affairs: Spain: February–April 1938

ANCWC 8   ANCWC: International Affairs: United Nations: Catherine Schaefer Correspondence

ANCWC 9   ANCWC: International Affairs: United Nations: Human Rights: January 1946–June 1947

ANCWC 10   ANCWC: International Affairs: United Nations: London General Assembly: 1945–1946

ANCWC 11   ANCWC: International Affairs: United Nations: San Francisco Conference: NCWC Coverage: Conway, Pattee, Walsh: 1945

ANCWC 12   ANCWC: International Affairs: United Nations: San Francisco Conference: NCWC Coverage: May–October 1945

ANCWC 13a   ANCWC: International Affairs: United Nations: San Francisco Conference: NCWC News Service Coverage: 1945: Days of Decision

ANCWC 13b   ANCWC: International Affairs: United Nations: San Francisco Conference: NCWC News Service Coverage: 1945: Catholic Spotlights

ANCWC 13c   ANCWC: International Affairs: United Nations: San Francisco Conference: NCWC News Service Coverage: 1945: General Articles

ANCWC 14   ANCWC: International Affairs: United Nations: San Francisco Conference: Non-NCWC News Coverage: 1945

ANCWC 15   ANCWC: International Affairs: United Nations: San Francisco Conference: 1945

ANCWC 16   ANCWC: International Affairs: United Nations: Security Council: 1946–1947

ANCWC 17a   ANCWC: International Affairs: United Nations: 1946–1947

ANCWC 17b   ANCWC: International Affairs: United
            Nations: 1955
ANCWC 18   ANCWC: International Affairs: United
            Nations Office: Foundation: Catherine
            Schaefer Papers
ANCWC 19   ANCWC: International Affairs: United
            Nations Organizations: 1945–1946
ANCWC 20   ANCWC: International Affairs: 1944–1949
ANCWC 21   MAB ANCWC: Minutes of the Administrative
            Board (These are bound with continuous
            pagination; thus a reference to this will be
            with page, followed by date, for example:
            ANCWC, MAB, November 9, 1941)
ANCWC 22   MGM ANCWC: Minutes of the General
            Meetings of the Hierarchy (these are bound
            with separate pagination for each annual
            meeting; thus a reference to this will be with
            the number of the annual meeting, followed by
            the page, followed by the date, example:
            ANCWC MGM 25: 9, November 10, 1943
            [Minutes of the 25th annual meeting, page 9,
            the first day of the General Meeting,
            November 10])
ANCWC 23   ANCWC: National Catholic Welfare
            Conference (NCWC): International Affairs:
            1919–1950
ANCWC 24a   ANCWC: NCWC: Administrative Board:
            Statements: 1941–1943
ANCWC 24b   ANCWC: NCWC: Administrative Board:
            Statements: 1944–1948
ANCWC 25   ANCWC: NCWC: Bishops' General
            Meetings: Committees: Bishops' Peace
            Committee: 1941–1943
ANCWC 26a   ANCWC: NCWC: Bishops' General
            Meetings: Committees: Bishops' Peace
            Committee: January–June 1944
ANCWC 26b   ANCWC: NCWC: Bishops' General
            Meetings: Committee: Bishops' Peace
            Committee: July 1944–1945

ANCWC 27	ANCWC: NCWC: United States Government: State: 1941–1944
ANCWC 28	ANCWC: Organizations, Lay: 1944–1948
ANCWC 29	ANCWC: Social Action: Catholic Association for International Peace: Atomic Bomb Statements
ANCWC 30	ANCWC: Social Action: Catholic Association for International Peace: 1939–1955
NCWCAR	National Catholic Welfare Conference Annual Reports located in the John K. Mullen of Denver Memorial Library at the Catholic University of America
RG 59a	National Archives. State Department Papers. Record Group 59: General Records of the Department of State: Decimal Files 1945–1949 (boxes used were 1977, 1980, 1982, 1991, 1994, 1996, 2001, 2006, 2016, 2232; each box is divided by folders and they will be indicated in the citations: thus, for example, RG 59: 1977: Folder 1)
RG 59b	RG 59: General Records of the Department of State: Harley A. Notter Papers: 1939–1945: United States Delegation: UNCIO: Box 191
RG 59c	RG 59: General Records of the Department of State: International Conferences Division: Records of the United Nations Conference on International Organization (UNCIO): 1945
RG 59d	RG 59: General Records of the Department of State: Office of Public Opinion Studies: 1943–1965: Dumbarton Oaks Conference: December 1944–April 1945
RG 59e	RG 59: General Records of the Department of State: Office of Public Opinion Studies: 1943–1965: On Functions and Organization of the United Nations: San Francisco Conference: 1945
RG 59f	RG 59: General Records of the Department of State: Office of Public Opinion Studies: 1943–

1965: On Functions and Organization of the United Nations: UN Reports: January 1944–September 1945

RG 59g RG 59: General Records of the Department of State: Office of Public Opinion Studies: 1943–1965: Opinions and Activities of American Private Organizations and Groups: 1945–1948

RG 59h RG 59: General Records of the Department of State: Papers of Alger Hiss, Director, Office of Special Political Affairs: 1940–1946: UNCIO Subject Files: 1945: Unofficial Organizations

RG 59i RG 59: General Records of the Department of State: Records of the Assistant Secretary of State for Public Affairs and Cultural Relations (Archibald MacLeish) 1945: Chronological File: 1944–April 13, 1945: Lot 52–249

Bibliography

Alcock, Anthony. *The History of the International Labor Organization.* London: Macmillan, 1971.

America, April 21, 1945–September 29, 1945.

Angell, Sir Ralph Norman. *The Great Illusion: A Study of the Relation of Military Power to National Advantage.* 4th ed. London: G.P. Putnam's Sons, 1913.

Armstrong, James David. *The Rise of the International Organization: A Short History.* New York: St. Martin's Press, 1982.

Barros, James, ed. *The United Nations: Past, Present and, Future.* New York: The Free Press, 1972.

Bennett, Sir John Wheeler, and Nicholls, Anthony. *The Semblance of Peace: The Political Settlement After the Second World War.* New York: St. Martin's Press, 1972.

Bidault, George. *D'une Résistance à l'Autre.* Paris: Les Presses du Siècle, 1965.

The Bishops Speak Out on World Peace: Two Statements by Catholic Bishops of the United States. Washington, D.C.: National Catholic Welfare Conference, 1945. *On Organizing World Peace,* April 15, 1945.

Blet, Pierre, Robert A. Graham, et al., gen. eds. *Actes et Documents du Saint Siège Relatifs à la Seconde Guerre Mondiale.* 10 vols. Cittè del Vaticano: Libreria Editrice Vaticana, 1965–1980.

Bloomfield, Lincoln P. *The United Nations and U.S. Foreign Policy.* Boston: Little, Brown, 1960.

Boyea, Earl. "The National Catholic Welfare Conference: An Experience in Episcopal Leadership, 1935–1945." PhD dissertation, The Catholic University of America, 1987.

Broderick, Robert C., ed. *The Catholic Encyclopedia.* Nashville: Thomas Nelson, 1976. S.v. "Pope."

Buehrle, Marie Cecilia. *The Cardinal Stritch Story.* Milwaukee: Bruce, 1959.

Byrnes, James F. *All in One Lifetime.* New York: Harper, 1959.

Carlen, Claudia. *The Papal Encyclicals.* 5 vols. Wilmington, North Carolina: McGrath, 1981.

Campbell, Thomas M. *Masquerade Peace: America's U.N. Policy, 1944–1945.* Tallahasee: Florida State University Press, 1973.

———, and Herring, George C. *The Diaries of Edward R. Stettinius, Jr., 1943–1946.* New York: New Viewpoints, 1975.

Cerny, Karl H. "Monsignor John A. Ryan and the Social Action

Department: An Analysis of a Leading School of American Catholic Social Thought." PhD dissertation, Yale University, 1954.

Cohen, Benjamin V. *The United Nations.* Cambridge, Mass.: Harvard University Press, 1961.

Cole, Wayne S. *Roosevelt and the Isolationists, 1932–1945.* Lincoln: University of Nebraska Press, 1983.

Commonweal, April 27, 1945–August 10, 1945.

Conway, Edward A., S.J. *Goals for San Francisco.* Washington, D.C.: National Catholic Welfare Conference, 1945.

———. *Pattern for Peace.* Washington, D.C.: National Catholic Welfare Conference, 1944.

Conway, John S. "Myron C. Taylor's Mission to the Vatican, 1940–1950." *Church History* 44 (1975): 85–99.

Crosby, Donald F. *God, Church, and Flag.* Chapel Hill: N.C.: The University of North Carolina Press, 1978.

Dallek, Robert. *Franklin D. Roosevelt and American Foreign Policy, 1932–1945.* New York: Oxford University Press, 1979.

Davies, Norman. *God's Playground: A History of Poland.* 2 vols. New York: Columbia University Press, 1982.

———. *The Heart of Europe: A Short History of Poland.* Oxford: Oxford University Press, 1987.

Davis, Harriet Eager, ed. *Pioneers in World Order: An American Appraisal of the League of Nations.* New York: Columbia University Press, 1944. "Dependent Peoples and Mandates," by Huntington Gilchrist.

Delaney, John J. *The Dictionary of American Catholic Biography.* Garden City, New York: Doubleday, 1984. S.v. "Doyle, Michael Francis," "LaFarge, John," "Mitty, John Joseph," "Murray, John Courtney," "Walker, Frank Comerford."

Divine, Robert A. *Second Chance: The Triumph of Internationalism in America During World War II.* New York: Atheneum, 1967.

Doering, Bernard E. *Jacques Maritain and the French Catholic Intellectuals.* Notre Dame, Indiana: University of Notre Dame Press, 1983.

Dolan, Jay P. *The American Catholic Experience: A History from Colonial Times to the Present.* Garden City, New York: Doubleday, 1985.

Donovan, Robert J. *Conflict and Crisis: The Presidency of Harry S. Truman, 1945–1948.* New York: W.W. Norton, 1977.

Douglas, Roy. *From War to Cold War, 1942–1949.* New York: St. Martin's Press, 1981.

Ebersole, Luke. *Church Lobbying in the Nation's Capital.* New York: Macmillan, 1951.

Ellis, John Tracy. *American Catholicism.* Chicago: The University of Chicago Press, 1956; Second edition, revised, 1969.

————. *The Life of James Cardinal Gibbons*. 2 vols. Milwaukee: Bruce, 1952.

Ferrell, Robert H., gen. ed., *The American Secretaries of State and Their Diplomacy*. 17 vols. New York: Cooper Square Publishers, 1965. *E.R. Stettinius, Jr.*, by Richard L. Walker.

Findling, John E., ed. *The Dictionary of American Diplomatic History*. Westport, Conn.: Greenwood Press, 1980. S.v. "Archibald MacLeish," "Trusteeship Council (United Nations)."

Fine, Sidney. *Frank Murphy*. 3 vols. Ann Arbor: University of Michigan Press, 1975–1984.

Freidel, Frank. *Franklin D. Roosevelt*. 4 vols. Boston: Little, Brown, 1952–1973.

Flynn, George Q. *Roosevelt and Romanism: Catholics and American Diplomacy, 1937–1945*. Westport, Conn.: Greenwood Press, 1976.

Fogarty, Gerald P., S.J. *The Vatican and the American Hierarchy From 1870 to 1965*. Wilmington, Delaware: Michael Glazier, 1985.

Gaddis, John Lewis. *The United States and the Origins of the Cold War: 1941–1947*. New York: Columbia University Press, 1972.

Gaffey, James P. *Francis Clement Kelley and the American Catholic Dream*. 2 Vols., Bensenville, Illinois: Heritage Foundation, 1980.

Gignac, Francis T. "Edgar R. Smothers." Detroit, January 10, 1971. (Typewritten).

Gildersleeve, Virginia C. *Many a Good Crusade*. New York: Columbia University Press, 1954.

Gill, George J. "The Myron C. Taylor Mission, the Holy See and 'Parallel Endeavor for Peace,' 1939–1945." *The Records of the American Catholic Historical Society of Philadelphia* 98 (March–December, 1987):29.

Gleeson, Philip. "In Search of Unity: American Catholic Thought, 1920–1960." *Catholic Historical Review* 65 (April 1979):185–205.

Gonella, Guido. *Digest of A World to Reconstruct*. Chicago: Cuneo Press, 1945.

————. *A World to Reconstruct: Pius XII on Peace and Reconstruction*. Trans. T. Lincoln Bouscaren, S.J. Milwaukee: Bruce, 1944.

Graebner, Norman A., ed. *An Uncertain Tradition: American Secretaries of State in the Twentieth Century*. New York: McGraw-Hill, 1961. "Edward R. Stettinius, Jr.," by Walter Johnson.

Graham, Robert A., S.J. *Vatican Diplomacy: A Study of Church and State on the International Plane*. Princeton, New Jersey: Princeton University Press, 1959.

Greer, Thomas H. *What Roosevelt Thought: The Political and Social Ideas of Franklin D. Roosevelt*. East Lansing, Michigan: Michigan State University Press, 1965.

Gross, Franz B., gen. ed. *The United States and the United Nations*. Norman, Oklahoma: University of Oklahoma Press, 1964. "Introduction," by Robert Strausz-Hupe.

Haberlach, Kay Esther. "An Investigation and Analysis of the International Activities of the National Catholic Welfare Conference." MA thesis, American University, 1962.

Halsey, William M. *The Survival of American Innocence: Catholicism in an Era of Disillusionment, 1920–1940.* Notre Dame, Indiana: University of Notre Dame Press, 1980.

Hamer, Jerome. "Les Conférences Episcopales, Exercice de la Collégialité." *Revue Théologique* 85 (1963):966–69.

Harriman, W. Averell, and Elie Abel. *Special Envoy to Churchill and Stalin, 1941–1946.* New York: Random House, 1975.

Hazzard, Shirley. *The Defeat of an Ideal.* Boston: Little, Brown, 1973.

Heath, Jim F. "Domestic America During World War II: Research Opportunities for Historians." *Journal of American History* 58 (September 1971):384–414.

Hennesey, James, S.J. *American Catholics: A History of the Roman Catholic Community in the United States.* New York: Oxford University Press, 1983.

Herring, George C., Jr. *Aid to Russia, 1941–1946: Strategy, Diplomacy, the Origins of the Cold War.* New York: Columbia University Press, 1973.

Holmes, J. Derek. *More Roman Than Rome.* London: Burns and Oates, 1978.

Hoopes, Townsend. *The Devil and John Foster Dulles.* Boston: Little, Brown, 1973.

Huber, Raphael M., ed. *Our Bishops Speak.* Milwaukee: Bruce, 1952.

Jedin, Hubert; Konrad Repgen; and John Dolan, gen. eds. *The History of the Church.* 10 vols. New York: Crossroad, 1965–1985.

Kauffman, Christopher J., gen. ed. *The Bicentennial History of the Catholic Church in America Authorized by the National Conference of Catholic Bishops.* 6 vols. New York: Macmillan, 1989. Vol. 5: *Public Catholicism,* by David O'Brien.

Kelley, Francis Clement. *The Bishop Jots It Down.* New York: Harper and Brothers, 1939.

Kimball, Warren F., ed. *Churchill and Roosevelt: The Complete Correspondence.* 3 vols. Princeton, New Jersey: Princeton University Press, 1984. Vol. 3: *Alliance Declining: February 1944–April 1945.*

Koenig, Harry Corcoran, ed. *Principles for Peace: Selections from Papal Documents: Leo XIII to Pius XII.* Washington, D.C.: National Catholic Welfare Conference, 1943.

Kutner, Raymond W. "The Development, Structure, and Competence of the Episcopal Conference." JCD dissertation, The Catholic University of America, 1972.

LaFarge, John, S.J. *Judging the Dumbarton Oaks Proposals.* Washington, D.C.: Catholic Association for International Peace, 1945.

Leckie, Robert. *American and Catholic.* Garden City, New York: Doubleday, 1970.

Liddell-Hart, Basil H. *History of the Second World War.* New York: G. P. Putnam's Sons, 1970.

Luard, David Evan T. *Conflict and Peace in the Modern International System.* New York: Little, Brown, 1960.

————. ed. *The Cold War: A Reappraisal.* New York: Frederick A. Praeger, 1964. "The Partition of Europe," by Wilfrid Knapp.

————. *A History of the United Nations.* Vol. 1: *The Years of Western Domination, 1945–1955.* New York: St. Martin's Press, 1982.

Lukas, Richard C. *The Strange Allies: The United States and Poland, 1941–1945.* Knoxville: The University of Tennessee Press, 1978.

McGrath, J. "F.A. Hall, First Director of the N.C.W.C. News Service." *Catholic Press Annual* 3 (1962):38–41.

McKeown, Elizabeth. "The National Bishops Conference: An Analysis of Its Origins." *Catholic Historical Review* 66 (October 1980):565–83.

McNeal, Patricia. *The American Catholic Peace Movement 1928–1972.* New York: Arno Press, 1978.

McNeill, William H. *America, Britain, and Russia: Their Cooperation and Conflict, 1941–1946.* London: Survey of International Affairs, 1953; reprint ed. New York: Johnson Reprint Corporation, 1970.

Mahony, Thomas H. *The United Nations Charter.* Washington, D.C.: The Catholic Association for International Peace, 1945.

————. *The United Nations Conference.* Washington, D.C.: The Catholic Association for International Peace, 1945.

Martel, Gordon, ed. *"The Origins of the Second World War" Reconsidered: The A.J.P. Taylor Debate after Twenty-Five Years.* Boston: Allen & Unwin, 1986.

Marty, Martin E. *Religion and Republic: The American Circumstance.* Boston: Beacon Press, 1987.

Mews, Stuart. "The Sword of the Spirit: A Catholic Cultural Crusade of 1940." In *The Church: Papers Read at the Twenty-First Summer Meeting of the Ecclesiastical History Society,* pp. 409–30. Edited by W. J. Sheils. [London]: Blackwell, 1983.

Middleton, Neil, ed. *The I.F. Stone Weekly Reader.* New York: Vintage Books, 1973.

Miller, James Edward. *The United States and Italy, 1940–1950: The Politics and Diplomacy of Stabilization.* Chapel Hill: University of North Carolina Press, 1986.

Miller, Mark A. "The Contribution of the Reverend Raymond A. McGowan to American Catholic Social Thought and Action, 1930–1939." MA thesis, The Catholic University of America, 1979.

Moloney, Thomas. *Westminster, Whitehall and the Vatican: The Role of Cardinal Hinsley, 1935–43.* London: Burns & Oates, 1985.

Montavon, William F. "The National Catholic Welfare Conference." In *The American Apostolate,* pp. 241–77. Edited by Leo R. Ward. Westminster, Maryland: Newman Press, 1952.

Morgan, Ted. *FDR: A Biography.* New York: Simon and Schuster, 1985.

National Catholic Welfare Conference Annual Reports: (1935–1945).

National Catholic Welfare Conference: Its Organization, Departments, and Functions. Washington, D.C. National Catholic Welfare Conference, 1935.

National Catholic Welfare Conference: Its Organization, Departments, and Functions. Washington, D.C. National Catholic Welfare Conference, 1942.

Neumann, William L. *After Victory: Churchill, Roosevelt, Stalin and the Making of the Peace.* New York: Harper & Row, 1967.

The New Catholic Encyclopedia. 1967 ed. S.v. "National Catholic Welfare Conference," by Francis T. Hurley.

The New York Times, February 5, 1945–October 12, 1945.

Nicholas, H.G. *The United Nations as a Political Institution.* London: Oxford University Press, 1959.

Nolan, Hugh J., ed. *The Pastoral Letters of the United States Bishops.* 3 vols. Washington, D.C.: United States Catholic Conference, 1984. Vol. 2: *1941–1961. Between War and Peace.* November 18, 1945.

———. *The Essentials of a Good Peace.* November 11, 1943.

———. *A Statement on Federal Aid to Education.* November 13, 1944.

———. *A Statement on International Order.* November 16, 1944.

Norman, Edward. *The English Catholic Church in the Nineteenth Century.* Oxford: Clarendon Press, 1984.

Nuesse, Joseph C. "The National Catholic Welfare Conference." In *The Catholic Church, U.S.A.,* Ed. Louis J. Putz. Chicago: Fides Publishing Association, 1956.

O'Brien, John A. *The Pope's Way to Peace.* Huntington, Indiana: Our Sunday Visitor Press, 1944.

O'Connor, Raymond G. *Diplomacy for Victory: FDR and Unconditional Surrender.* New York: W.W. Norton, 1971.

Osmanczyk, Edmund Jan. *The Encyclopedia of the United Nations and International Agreements.* Philadelphia: Taylor and Francis, 1985.

Overberg, Kenneth R. *An Inconsistent Ethic? Teachings of the American Catholic Bishops.* Lanham, Maryland: University Press of America, 1980.

Page, Joseph A. *Perón: A Biography.* New York: Random House, 1983.

Parsons, Wilfrid, S.J. *American Peace Aims.* Washington, D.C.: Catholic Association for International Peace, 1942. Appendix C. "An International Bill of Rights."

Paterson, Thomas G. *On Every Front: The Making of the Cold War.* New York: W.W. Norton, 1979.

Pattee, Richard F. "Scope of Catholic Participation in San Francisco

Conference Analyzed by NCWC Observer." National Catholic Welfare Conference, Washington, DC, April 1945.

———. "Some Observations on the San Francisco Conference of the United Nations and the International Situation Since that Date." National Catholic Welfare Conference, Washington, DC, 1945.

———. "Report on United Nations Conference on International Organization Convened at San Francisco on April 25, 1945." National Catholic Welfare Conference, Washington, DC, June 1945.

Peffer, Nathaniel. *Basis for Peace in the Far East*. New York: Harper & Brothers, 1942.

Pelotte, Donald E., S.S.S. *John Courtney Murray: Theologian in Conflict*. New York: Paulist Press, 1976.

Perrett, Geoffrey. *Days of Sadness, Years of Triumph: The American People, 1939–1945*. Madison: The University of Wisconsin Press, 1973; reprint ed., 1979.

Peters, Walter H. *The Life of Benedict XV*. Milwaukee: Bruce Publishing Company, 1959.

Pius XII, Pope. *The Pope Speaks Out: The Words of Pius XII*. Edited by Edwin S. O'Hara: *Christmas Message, 1939*. New York: Harcourt, Brace, 1940.

———. *Pius XII and Peace: 1939–1944*. Ed. Catherine Schaefer: *Christmas Message, 1940*. Washington, D.C.: National Catholic Welfare Conference, 1944.

———. *Pius XII and Peace: 1939–1940. To Those in Power and to Their Peoples*. Washington, D.C.: National Catholic Welfare Conference, 1940.

Ramsey, Paul. *The Just War: Force and Political Responsibility*. New York: Charles Scribner's Sons, 1968.

Rhodes, Anthony. *The Vatican in the Age of the Dictators, 1922–1945*. New York: Holt, Rinehart and Winston, 1974.

Roy, Ralph Lord. *Communism & the Churches*. New York: Harcourt, Brace, 1960.

Russell, Ruth B. *The United Nations and United States Security Policy*. Washington, D.C.: The Brookings Institution, 1968.

The [San Francisco] Monitor, April 20, 1945–April 29, 1945.

Sheen, Fulton J. *Treasure in Clay*. Garden City, New York: Doubleday, 1980.

Sherry, Michael. *Preparing for the Next War: American Plans for Postwar Defense, 1941–1945*. New Haven: Yale University Press, 1977.

Shotwell, James T., gen. ed. *The Economics and History of the World War,* 150 vols. Washington, D.C.: Carnegie Endowment for International Peace, 1924. Vol. 3: *The Effects of War Upon America,* by John Maurice Clark. New Haven: Yale University Press, 1931.

Stassen, Harold E. *Man Was Meant to Be Free: Selected Statements* by Harold E. Stassen: 1940–1951. Ed. Amos J. Peaslee. Garden City, New York: Doubleday, 1951.

Taylor, A.J.P. *The Origins of the Second World War.* 2nd ed. Greenwich, Connecticut: Fawcett, 1966.

———., ed. *Churchill Revisited: A Critical Assessment.* New York: Dial Press, 1969. "The Politician," by Robert Rhodes James.

Toulouse, Mark G. *The Transformation of John Foster Dulles.* Macon, Georgia: Mercer University Press, 1985.

Truman, Harry S. *The Truman Memoirs.* Vol. 1: *Years of Decision.* Garden City, New York: Doubleday, 1955.

Trythall, J.W.D. *Franco: A Biography.* London: Rupert Hart-Davis, 1970.

U.N. *The Charter of the United Nations, 1945.* Lake Success, New York: Department of Public Information, United Nations, 1946.

———. *Documents of the United Nations Conference on International Organization, San Francisco, 1945,* 16 Vols. New York, 1946.

———. *Yearbook of the United Nations, 1946–1947.* Lake Success, New York: Department of Public Information, United Nations, 1947. "Dumbarton Oaks Conversations," "Yalta Agreements."

U.S. Congress. Senate. 79th Cong., 1st sess., March 15–October 2, 1945. *Congressional Record,* vol. 91.

U.S. Department of State. *Foreign Relations of the United States: Diplomatic Papers, 1945.* Washington D.C.: U.S. Government Printing Office, 1955. *The Conferences at Malta and Yalta.*

U.S. Department of State. *Foreign Relations of the United States: Diplomatic Papers, 1945.* Washington, D.C.: U.S. Government Printing Office, 1960. *The Conference of Berlin (Potsdam).*

U.S. Department of State. *Foreign Relations of the United States: Diplomatic Papers, 1945.* Washington, D.C.: U.S. Government Printing Office, 1967. Vol. 1. *General: The United Nations.*

Valaik, J. David. "Catholics, Neutrality, and the Spanish Embargo, 1937–1939." *Journal of American History* 54 (June 1967):73–85.

Vandenberg, Arthur H., ed. *The Private Papers of Senator Vandenberg.* Boston: Houghton Mifflin, 1952.

Walsh, Burke. "The National Catholic Welfare Conference Press Department." *American Ecclesiastical Review* 148 (April 1963):236–49.

Wayman, Dorothy Godfrey. *David I. Walsh: Citizen Patriot.* Milwaukee: Bruce, 1952.

Weinstein, Allen. *Perjury: The Hiss-Chambers Case.* New York: Alfred A. Knopf, 1978.

Welles, Sumner. *Seven Decisions That Shaped History.* New York: Harper and Brothers, 1950.

Willkie, Wendell L. *One World.* New York: Simon and Schuster, 1943.

Index